COMMUNISM AND THE
POLITICS OF DEVELOPMENT

Moscow and the Communist Party of India: A Study in the Postwar Evolution of International Communist Strategy, 1956

Political Change in Underdeveloped Countries: Nationalism and Communism, 1962

Communism and the Politics of Development

PERSISTENT MYTHS AND CHANGING BEHAVIOR

John H. Kautsky

WASHINGTON UNIVERSITY
ST. LOUIS

JOHN WILEY AND SONS, INC.
NEW YORK | LONDON | SYDNEY

To my mother

Contents

Introduction

Communism is a phenomenon of underdevelopment. Only exception-ally have Communist parties attained significant strength in advanced areas, as in the industrialized sections of France and Italy, where they appear as the representatives of an alienated working class—heirs of anarcho-syndicalism—in a generally relatively backward environment. And only exceptionally, and as a result of foreign pressure, have Commu-nist parties come to power in industrially advanced areas, as in East Germany and the Czech portions of Czechoslovakia. On the other hand, Communist parties have indigenously developed considerable strength and influence in such major underdeveloped countries as India and Indo-nesia as well as Brazil, Argentina, and Chile. They have come to control some small underdeveloped countries from Yugoslavia and Albania to North Vietnam to Cuba. Above all, they came to power in two of the three largest underdeveloped countries in the world, Russia and China.

In spite of the fairly obvious link between underdevelopment and Communism, the vast literature on these two subjects has remained oddly distinct. Writers on the politics of development, whose work has contributed so much to a new flowering of the field of comparative politics in recent years, have tended to shy away from the subject of Communism. Major works on the politics of the developing areas barely touch on China or the Soviet Union, as if these were not developing areas, or on Communist movements in non-Communist underdeveloped countries, as if these were not modernizing movements.[1]

The failure of so many students of comparative politics to analyze Communism has implied that Communism is somehow not comparable

[1] At the 1966 meeting of the American Political Science Association panels in com-parative politics, presumably reflecting the state of the discipline, were divided into three categories: "Developed Systems," "Developing Systems," and "Communist Systems"—evidently on the assumption that when a country comes under Communist control it is, oddly, neither "developed" nor "developing." I remarked on this in the course of more extensive comments on the same subject in my "Communism and the Comparative Study of Development," *Slavic Review*, XXVI, No. 1 (March 1967), 13–17.

to other political movements and ideologies (which would merely indicate the lack of a conceptual framework permitting comparison, for any two things are comparable given such a framework). The avoidance of the subject of Communism in the literature on the politics of developing areas has also suggested that Communism in underdeveloped countries cannot be explained in terms of the politics of development and has thus tended to support the notion that it is everywhere an alien movement imported from abroad. This notion understandably underlies much popular thought in this country, where Communism has virtually no indigenous base. It is nevertheless manifestly absurd, since Communism must have originated somewhere and does gain the support of the natives of many countries. It must hence be explicable in terms of the politics of some countries.

If comparative politics specialists have tended to neglect Communism, experts on Communism have tended to neglect the study of comparative politics. The ever-growing scholarly literature on Communism has largely been produced by people who specialize in the subject of Communism. They are naturally inclined to assume that Communism is distinct from all other political phenomena and may well develop a stake in keeping its study a distinct branch of political science.[2] Whether they are or began as Soviet experts or not and whether they deal with Communist parties in underdeveloped countries or not, Communist experts tend to emphasize one or both of two elements in Communism—the ideological component of Marxism-Leninism and the international nature of Communism, particularly the links between individual Communist parties and Moscow. These, however, are the very elements that are unique in Communism, virtually by definition, for a Communist party may be defined as one that officially considers itself Marxist-Leninist and/or (at least until very recently) as one that looks to Moscow for leadership. Emphasis on these elements, then, makes Communism seem quite different from other movements and ideologies with which it shares many other characteristics.

Thus both the failure of experts in the politics of developing societies to deal with Communism and the way in which Communist experts have dealt with it have tended to leave or take the study of Communism

---

[2] Scholars in this field have their own organization, the Conference of Soviet and Communist Studies, and tend to publish in their own journals, such as *Problems of Communism* (Washington, D.C.) and *Survey* (London), in addition to area journals devoted to the Soviet Union, Eastern Europe, and China.

out of the study of comparative politics—to the detriment of both. Students of non-Communist political systems have been deprived of the opportunity of drawing comparisons with Communist movements, ideologies, and institutions. Students of Communism have been unable to explain Communism by placing it in the context of the processes of political change.

I, too, began my academic career with an interest in Marxism and the relationship of Marxism to Leninism,[3] and I, too, became subsequently concerned with the nature of the relationship between a Communist party and Moscow[4]. However, my interest in Marxism, both as an early attempt at a social scientific explanation of the impact of industrialization on politics and as itself an ideological reflection of that impact also led me to study the role of industrialization in the process of politics, and hence particularly the politics of underdeveloped countries. As I sought to pursue my interest in Communism in this context, I became increasingly aware of and impatient with the gap between the literatures on development and on Communism and I have, in my own work, groped for ways of closing this gap.

I hope that in a number of articles and papers, written over a period of more than a decade, I may have helped to place Communism in the context of the politics of development and thereby have evolved an interpretation of the subject that, running counter to more generally accepted ones, may throw some light on the nature of Communism, and therefore also of international relations in the present world. It is this hope that encourages me to publish a collection of some of these articles and papers in this book. Although the early ones are inevitably out of date in some respects, they may all jointly serve the function of relating Communism and Soviet policy to political change in the process of development.

Even though, particularly after the first two articles, the focus of my interest widened from one on Communism to one on the politics of development, the changing policies of Communist parties remain my central concern in the articles reprinted here. However, I came to look upon Communist movements, beginning with the one in Russia, as mod-

[3] See my unpublished doctoral dissertation, *The Political Thought of Karl Kautsky,* Harvard University, 1951.
[4] See my *Moscow and the Communist Party of India: A Study in the Postwar Evolution of International Communist Strategy* (Cambridge, Mass.: The Technology Press of M.I.T., and New York: John Wiley and Sons, 1956).

ernizing movements that share numerous characteristics with non-Communist modernizing movements, such as the social composition of their leadership and of their following, their acceptance of Western ideologies and Western models, and their goals of rapid industrialization. In developing this interpretation I did not lose interest in the role of Marxism-Leninism or of Soviet foreign policy as elements accounting for some of the Communists' changing behavior; but I sought to place even these unique aspects of Communism into the broader context of the politics of development.

Thus all modernizing movements in underdeveloped countries, led as they almost invariably are by Western-educated or influenced intellectuals, take their inspiration from some more or less well-formulated Western ideology. Marxism, which in underdeveloped countries, is attractive by no means only to Communists, is but one of these Western ideologies, along with various forms of British, French, and American democratic thought. All of them, if they are to serve the needs of practical politicians, have to be adapted to the realities of the underdeveloped environments to which they are being transferred. Leninism was such an adaptation of Western Marxism, and Maoism and Castroism are further adaptations. In this process of adaptation, however, the old Western words of the ideology are not given up; they remain as treasured symbols that stand for political myths. And these myths do affect the behavior of those who believe in them. Thus Marxism must indeed be taken into account by anyone seeking to explain the behavior of Communist parties in underdeveloped countries, but its doctrines must be seen as myths and the functions that these myths serve must be discovered. We must not assume, as do those who are themselves caught up in the myth, that the doctrines can be studied as guides to action.

In its general relation to the politics of modernizing movements and their intellectual leaders, Marxism is not completely different from the thought of Locke, Rousseau, and Jefferson or of Sidney Webb, Jean Jaurès, and Franklin Roosevelt. Their words, too, have served as important symbols and as myths that inspire political behavior. They cannot, therefore, be ignored by anyone seeking to understand the actions of a Nehru, Ben Bella, or Nkrumah, a Nasser, Touré, or Sukarno. Yet no one studies the American Declaration of Independence as the Communist Manifesto has been studied, expecting to find a guide to their specific policies; no one writing a book on Asian or African politics begins with a chapter on Western political thought, whereas all too few books on the Soviet Union do not begin with a chapter on Marxism.

If prerevolutionary Russia is itself seen as an underdeveloped country and the Communist revolution as a revolution of a modernizing intellectual-led movement, then Soviet policy, too, can be seen in the context of the politics of development rather than merely as an alien force acting on the underdeveloped world from the outside. Its changes are themselves the results of the impact of industrialization on politics, notably with respect both to the growing power of the Soviet Union in international affairs and to the change in the Soviet elite from a revolutionary to a managerial intelligentsia. These changes produced different Soviet policies vis-à-vis other modernizing movements in other developing countries, and hence different attitudes toward Communist parties in these countries.

On the one hand, then, as I gradually discovered, one can usefully study Communism, including even the unique aspects of its Marxist-Leninist ideology and of its links to Soviet foreign policy, as a phenomenon of the politics of development. On the other hand, Communist parties, particularly those that follow the Soviet lead, have become less and less clearly distinguishable from non-Communist modernizing movements. This is true because, as we shall see, the former support more and more the policies of the latter and subordinate themselves to their leadership, in a few cases even merging with them. It is true also because non-Communist modernizing movements, facing conditions that are in some respects similar to those faced by Communist ones, advocate and follow similar policies, for example, nationalization of foreign property and government organization of agriculture or, more generally, opposition to colonialism and to traditionalism.

It follows that Communism, even apart from the related development of polycentrism and the Sino-Soviet split, has ceased to be a well-defined concept. To put it more bluntly and to oversimplify, there is no one such thing as Communism—a point to which I shall return in my concluding essay. To deal with the phenomena that can, in view of their past, more or less adequately be described as Communist in the context in which I like to study them requires therefore not a book on Communism but a book—or perhaps several books—on the process of political change under the impact of modernization. I am now working on such a project that seeks to evolve generalizations about the politics of development based on the experience of Communist as well as non-Communist countries and deals with both Communist and non-Communist modernizing movements.

In the meantime, however, given the widespread interest in Communism, there may still be room in the literature for a book on Communism such as the present one. I hope it can usefully serve as a forerunner and an introduction to my future work in which the treatment of Communism is to be merged with that of the politics of development. Not only does the present book reveal the evolution of my own interpretation of the subject—a matter of greater interest to me than to the reader—but it also stresses the evolution of Communist policy over the past two decades. Thus it shows both how Communist and non-Communist modernizing movements have tended to converge and how this process can be explained in terms of the politics of development.

It will now be understandable why I am reprinting even my earliest articles virtually in their original form. To revise them in the light of my present thinking would have required me to write the new book I mentioned. It, however, would be quite a different book from this one and would not serve the same functions. Obviously, then, I do not now fully subscribe to every line of thought and every formulation I put on paper years ago. I could hardly claim to do so without admitting to a deplorable lack of intellectual growth. On the other hand, I feel no need to disavow what I wrote in the past as long as it is seen as expressing past thinking based on data available to me then and perhaps also reflecting different atmospheres prevailing in the fields both of international politics and of political science. An alert reader may become aware, perhaps more than I am, of changes in my attitudes conditioned by changes from the immediate post-Stalin era of cold war to that of Brezhnev's peaceful coexistence. I, on the other hand, am more aware than most readers will be of changes in my own political science approach under the impact of what is sometimes inadequately labeled the "behavioral revolution" in this field.

For better or worse, then, the articles and papers in this book are reprinted virtually in their original form. Since they appeared at various times and in various publications and were addressed to somewhat different audiences, they are, on certain points, occasionally repetitive. I have reluctantly decided not to edit them in order to eliminate repetition but rather to maintain the continuity of my argument within each article as I originally developed it and also to show in this manner how later articles are built on points made in earlier ones.

Only the following minor changes in the original articles have been made. In three cases I have altered the titles under which articles were originally published. I have made minor stylistic changes here and there.

I have modified chronological references, such as "in the past decade" or "last year," which would now, years after the articles were written, be confusing. And I have in some cases added and in others omitted references to my own writings now appearing in this book or have substituted page references to the location in this book for them. I have also changed a few footnotes to refer to sources that are now more easily available than are those originally cited and I have here and there taken the opportunity of restoring passages and footnotes contained in my original manuscripts that editors had removed before publication. In a few cases I have also added footnotes in brackets to indicate my present disagreement with an earlier formulation or to bring it up to date.

The articles are, with one minor exception, arranged in the chronological order of their original appearance in print or of their presentation as papers so as to reflect changes both in the subject matter and in my interpretation since the early 1950s. I have introduced each piece with some remarks that seek to place it in the context of my present thought on Communism in underdeveloped countries and to relate it to others to help tie all of them into a coherent whole.

1. The New Strategy
of International Communism*

Introductory Note. The first two articles reprinted here grew out of my research in 1953 and 1954 on the relation of the Communist Party of India to Moscow, which subsequently resulted in my *Moscow and the Communist Party of India.*[1] My chief aim was to stress that a new strategy had been developed by the Communists and to illustrate its adoption and the tactical variations played on the new strategic theme by tracing interaction between Moscow and one Communist party. I felt that the novelty of the Communist approach needed to be emphasized at a time when it was still commonly held that Communism stood for anticapitalism and was invariably committed to the use of violent methods. Now, two decades after the new strategy was first advanced for Communism all over the world, this still needs to be stressed, for non-Communists are as persistently attached to the old myths of Communism as are the Communists themselves.

However, it is now clear, as it was not when these articles were written, that what I then regarded as merely a new strategy turned out to be only the beginning of a trend toward the convergence of Communism with non-Communist modernizing movements. This trend has vitally changed the character of Communism and is dealt with at length in subsequent articles. The relationship between Communism and the politics of development is recognized only in passing in these early articles and had not yet become the focus of my thought on the subject as it did later. Analyzing changes in Communism largely apart from the changes in its environment, these articles strike me as somewhat superficial from my present point of view.

* Reprinted from *The American Political Science Review*, XLIX, No 2 (June 1955), 478–486, by permission of The American Political Science Association. This article had its immediate origin in research done by the author at the Center for International Studies, Massachusetts Institute of Technology. He is thus indebted to the Center, which bears, of course, no responsibility for the substance of the article. The same is true of his former colleagues, Morris Watnick and Bernard Morris, to whom he wishes to express his appreciation for contributing greatly to the development of many of the ideas presented here.

[1] Cambridge, Mass.: The Technology Press of M.I.T., and New York: John Wiley and Sons, 1956.

The diagnosis of what I then called the "new" strategy of international Communism is still important as the identification of the first step of a major development, but that development has also rendered these early articles out-of-date. For one thing, the new strategy has grown from one of opposition to non-Communist movements into one of alliance and even merger with them, thus becoming similar to the old "right" strategy (a fact only dimly visible when these articles were written but noted by me in footnote 13 of the first article and in the last sentence of the second one). However, its "all-class" character, stressed in these articles as its novel feature, remains a more vital element of Communist thinking than ever. For another thing, the new strategy and other developments have resulted in the disintegration of international Communism, making the very concept, which I still freely used in the 1950s, obsolete and rendering incorrect today some of the premises of these early articles, like that stated in the very first sentence of the first article, which were correct when they were written.

In short, these articles are included here, because they deal with early phases of that evolution of Communism which is the theme of this entire book. They deal with them, however, from a perspective available to me at the time when they developed rather than from the better perspective of hindsight from which I would regard them now and which is reflected in some of my later articles. Read by themselves, they do not adequately represent my present conception of the subject; read in conjunction with later articles, however, they still contribute to its understanding.

The first article, on "The New Strategy of International Communism," is useful as an introduction to this book, because it seeks to define sharply—perhaps too sharply in the light of subsequent developments— the "new" strategy and to distinguish it from the two older "right" and "left" ones. It thereby sets the stage for the story to be told in the rest of this book by stressing the major departure executed by the Communists in the late 1940s from their traditional policies. Since that policy change had gone virtually unnoticed even by the time when I wrote this article, I sought to call attention to it and to provide the criteria by which analysts of Communist policy could distinguish the new from the old in spite of the persistent tendency of both Communists and their enemies to insist that Communist policy is "basically" unchanging and to obscure change by the use of unchanging symbols.

Communist international organizations and Communist parties the world over tend to follow a single strategy, which is always determined primarily by the needs of Soviet foreign policy paramount at the time. Corresponding to the requirements of the Soviet Union's "cold war" against the United States, a new strategy was gradually adopted by international communism beginning in 1947. Often non-Communist observers and sometimes even the Communists themselves seem unaware of the novelty of this strategy and they frequently obscure it by the use of terms more descriptive of older strategies, such as "united front" and "popular front." It is the purpose of this essay to distinguish sharply between the various Communist strategies with a view to clarifying the characteristic features of the new strategy. It would, of course, be both easy and tempting to document and enliven such an attempt with innumerable examples from history and quotations from Communist literature. However, it would go beyond the intended scope of this brief analysis to do more than draw the broadest generalizations from the record of thirty-five years of international communism.[2]

The central problem of Communist strategy has always been to determine who is, at any time, to be considered the principal enemy and consequently what classes should be accepted as allies of communism and what type of alliance should be entered into with them. These three factors, and especially the latter two, furnish the crucial distinctions between different Communist strategies. Two alternative solutions of this problem formed the bases of the two strategies followed by international communism during its first thirty years as an organized movement. In the Communists' own terminology,[3] we may refer to them here simply as the "left" and the "right" strategies.

The "left" strategy, which can perhaps be called the classical strategy of communism and is often erroneously thought to be still in effect, considered capitalism as its main enemy. Even in underdeveloped areas, the native bourgeoisie was looked upon as an enemy on a par with foreign imperialism and native feudalism, i.e., the landlords and the nobility. This strategy envisaged the socialist revolution as its immediate goal. Even in societies which, according to the Marxian schema of his-

[2] It may also be noted that to a large extent Communist terminology is used in the following discussion of the distinguishing characteristics of the various Communist strategies, since it is both derived from and intended to be applied to the analysis of Communist writings. It must be remembered that, though quotation marks will be omitted for the sake of simplicity, the meaning to be attached to such terms as imperialism, feudalism, bourgeoisie, socialism, or national liberation is that given to them by the Communists.

[3] Used particularly while one strategy was in effect to condemn as deviationists the followers of the other one.

torical stages, had not yet traversed the capitalist stage, the next revolution was presumed to lay the basis for socialism and to merge with or even skip some of the phases of the so-called bourgeois-democratic revolution.

This "left" strategy was an attempt to form a "united front from below." It was based on appeals to workers and also poor peasants and petty bourgeois elements, both as individuals and in local organizations affiliated with socialist or "bourgeois" parties, or in the underdeveloped countries, the so-called bourgeois-nationalist movements. The appeals were designed to induce the rank and file to leave these parties and to join the Communists, either directly or by cooperating with them in "united action." Such appeals were therefore always coupled with violent denunciations of the top leaders of the other parties as servants of the bourgeoisie and of imperialism and as traitors to the interests of their rank-and-file followers. Similar tactics were followed in the trade union field in pursuance of this "left" strategy.

The "right" strategy of communism, on the other hand, regarded as its main enemy not capitalism as such but fascism and similar movements and, in underdeveloped areas, feudalism and foreign imperialism. The professed immediate aim of this strategy was the establishment or defense of democracy or national liberation, to which social revolution had to be subordinated. It therefore looked forward to a revolution in two stages: first a bourgeois-democratic revolution directed against fascism or imperialism and feudalism, followed later by a proletarian-socialist revolution directed against the bourgeoisie and capitalism, with the Communists participating in the first as well as in the second.

Not being anti-capitalist, the "right" strategy called for an alliance of the Communist party with other parties, which were recognized as anti-fascist or anti-imperialist and anti-feudal and which might include both labor and bourgeois parties.[4] Its most important characteristic, which easily distinguished the "right" strategy from the other Communist

---

[4] The "popular front" was broad enough to embrace both of these, while the "united front from above," in the narrower sense of this term, was an alliance of the Communist party only with a labor or socialist party. In practice this distinction is not too important, for the really difficult decision for Communists was to ally themselves with any strong party and particularly with their most hated enemies, the democratic socialists. Since these latter are, in any case, regarded as lackeys of the bourgeoisie, once this decision was made, it was easy and usual to extend the alliance to at least some left-wing bourgeois parties. We may therefore overlook the distinction here and refer to both the popular front and the united front from above by the latter term.

strategies, was thus that it involved a united front "from above," a "top alliance" with other parties arrived at in agreement with their national party leadership. Similar alliances or even mergers of Communist trade unions with socialist and nationalist trade unions were also advocated as part of this policy.

It is clear then that the "left" and "right" strategies were designed for diametrically opposite objectives: the united front from below was intended to weaken and split the very groups with which the Communists sought to enter an alliance when they were committed to a united front from above. The unfortunate fact that the Communists referred to both of these strategies as "united front" policies has given rise to much confusion and can obscure shifts from one to the other. The fact is all too often overlooked that, in a sense, Communists always follow a united front policy. To state no more than this, as is frequently done, without distinguishing between the united fronts from above and below, is merely to inform us that they, like all political parties, seek to increase their strength.

Different as the two strategies were, it must be emphasized that under both of them the Communist party insisted that it was a proletarian party, representing the interests of the workers and of the poor peasantry and petty bourgeoisie, but not those of the capitalists. It remained anti-bourgeois even when it entered into alliances with certain bourgeois parties and groups in a united front from above.

Until after the Second World War, the "left" and the "right" strategies were the only ones pursued by international Communism. Both found application during the early 1920's. Then the "left" strategy was followed throughout the late twenties and early thirties. It was replaced about 1935 by the "right" strategy, which remained in use until 1947, interrupted only be a return to the "left" strategy during the period between the conclusion of the Stalin-Hitler Pact in August, 1939 and the Nazi invasion of Russia in June, 1941. During the war, however, the Chinese Communists under the leadership of Mao Tse-tung developed a strategy which is fundamentally different from the two traditional ones, though it combines certain of their features.

As it has since come to be applied by international communism, this new strategy, like the "right" one, singles out foreign imperialism and, where applicable, feudalism, as its main enemy. Also like the "right" strategy, therefore, it expects the revolution to take place in two stages: first as an anti-imperialist struggle for national independence or an anti-feudal bourgeois-democratic revolution, and only later as a socialist revolution.[5] The range of forces to be united under Communist leadership, consequently, also corresponds to that grouped in the united front from above and particularly the popular front embracing the so-called "bloc of four classes," i.e., the proletariat, the peasantry, the petty bourgeoisie, and the anti-imperialist sections of the bourgeoisie.[6] To some extent, this union is to be attained by the methods of the united front from above, i.e., by a "top" alliance with other parties, but these are generally parties weaker than the Communist party and frequently fronts set up by the Communists. Principally the new strategy follows the method of the united front from below of the "left" strategy. The large parties, which more or less actually represent the classes to be united and with which the Communists would be allied in a united front from above under the "right" strategy (e.g., the socialist, liberal, and Christian-Democratic parties in the West and the nationalist parties, like the Kuomintang and the Indian Congress, and the socialists in the underdeveloped areas) are denounced as traitors to the interests of these classes and as servants of foreign imperialism. The same policy is applied by the Communist trade unions.

The Communist party (alone or in conjunction with its "united front" of subsidiary and front-parties) now claims to represent the interests of the entire peasantry and the anti-imperialist capitalists, as well as those of the proletariat, the poor peasantry, and the petty bourgeoisie. Having confined their appeal under both traditional strategies to these latter three "exploited" groups, the Communists were able to attract sections of these groups only through the united front from below. However—and this is crucial—they could seek the support also of sections of the bourgeoisie and of the entire peasantry only through the united

[5] Cf. particularly Mao Tse-tung, *On the New Democracy* (January 19, 1940), *Selected Works* (New York: International Publishers, 1954), III, 106–156. The attempt, by *ex post facto* rationalizations, to fit the Eastern European "People's Democracies" and the Chinese "New Democracy" into the Marxian scheme of two revolutions has brought some confusion into this subject and resulted in the expectation of varying numbers of stages or sub-stages of the revolution, always, however, more than one stage, under the new strategy.

[6] Sections of the bourgeoisie are first explicitly included and strikingly pro-capitalist statements appear in Mao Tse-tung, *On Coalition Government* (April 24, 1945) *ibid.*, IV, 244–315, especially pp. 273–276, and 299. For a useful summary of the Chinese Communists' attitude toward the bourgeoisie, with several long quotations from Mao, see Yu Huai, "On the Role of the National Bourgeoisie in the Chinese Revolution," *People's China*, I, No. 1 (Jan. 1, 1950), 7–10.

front from above. It is because of the radical innovation of appealing directly to the interests of all four classes that the new strategy can apply the method of the united front from below to a range of groups so wide that it could formerly be encompassed only in the united front from above.

We need not be concerned with the theories according to which the bourgeoisie is divided into a pro-imperialist and an anti-imperialist wing.[7] What matters is merely that the dividing line between the friends and enemies of the Communist party is now drawn not short of the bourgeoisie but bisecting it. In practice, of course, the division is made not so much along economic or sociological lines, as is implied by the terms used to describe the two sections, but along political lines. Those businessmen who, for whatever reasons, are willing or likely to be willing to follow the lead of the Communist party are considered anti-imperialist capitalists. Those who are and are likely to remain opposed to the Communists, even if they have no ties with foreign interests and have only small businesses, are condemned as allies and servants of imperialism. Just as the working class is frequently made synonymous with the Communist party, so here too the Marxist materialist conception of history is turned upside down; class affiliation is deduced from ideology rather than vice versa.

As the new strategy was developed in China by Mao Tse-tung and more recently in some countries of Southeast Asia, its most important characteristics appeared to be not the appeal "from below" to the bourgeoisie, but reliance on the peasantry rather than the industrial working class as a mass base in the struggle for power[8] and resort to guerrilla warfare. This has tended to obscure the fact that it is the essentials of this new strategy that are being applied by international Communism throughout the non-Communist world today. Actually, neither of the two specifically Chinese features is an essential characteristic of the

[7] The terminology used in Communist literature to describe the various sections of the bourgeoisie is not always consistent. Those capitalists who are only slightly or not at all tied to imperialism and can thus help form the "bloc of four classes" are generally called the "national," "medium," "middle," or "liberal" capitalists or bourgeoisie (although the term "national" may also be used simply as a synonym for "native"), while that section of the bourgeoisie which is regarded as a firm ally of imperialism is referred to variously as "comprador," "bureaucratic," "big," or "monopolistic."

[8] For an excellent discussion of this point, see Benjamin I. Schwartz, *Chinese Communism and the Rise of Mao* (Cambridge, Mass.: Harvard University Press, 1952), especially pp. 72–78 and 189–204.

new strategy. In China, the peasants were the Communist party's main target; elsewhere other groups can be substituted, as has been the case not only in the West, but also in Japan and to some extent even in India. On the other hand, some reliance on the peasantry is not a new Communist policy. In practically none of the underdeveloped countries have the Communists in any real sense of the word been a working-class party. Rather they have been largely intellectuals seeking a popular base where they could find it. In this search, even under the old "right" and "left" strategies, they have never looked exclusively to the industrial working class (which in its Marxian sense of an urban stratum cut off from its rural moorings has, at least until recently, been virtually non-existent in most underdeveloped countries). Instead, they have also sought out the petty bourgeoisie and at least some sections of the peasantry who can easily be characterized as exploited classes in underdeveloped countries. They have attempted to conceal this fact, just as Maoism has in China, by speaking of working-class hegemony, which always means their own hegemony. In other words, they substituted themselves for the working class by a process of mental transposition.

Similarly, the use of armed force is neither characteristic of the new strategy alone nor does it necessarily accompany that strategy. Obviously important as it is, the use or absence of violent methods does not constitute the basic distinction among Communist strategies, which is rather, as we have seen, to be found in the extent and type of alliances made by the Communists with non-Communist elements.[9] Attempts to identify one or the other of the three strategies with a "hard" or "soft" line, though frequently made, are therefore misleading. Thus it is often implied that the "right" strategy is necessarily coupled with a "soft" line. It is, of course, true that under many circumstances an alliance between the Communist party and labor and bourgeois parties is inconceivable where the Communist party engages in violent activities. But in other circumstances its allies, too, may be engaged in or approve of such activities as, for example, during the Spanish Civil War, the wartime

[9] A simple and perhaps oversimplified test to determine which of the three strategies the Communists pursue at any one time consists of the following one or two questions: Are the Communists making a serious attempt to form an alliance with the top leadership of the socialist party? If the answer is yes, they are following the "right" strategy; if it is no, a second question must be asked: Are there any capitalists among the groups to whose interests the Communists are appealing? If the answer to this question is no, they are following the "left" strategy; if it is yes, they are adhering to the new strategy.

resistance in Western Europe, or colonial revolts against the mother country. On the other hand, the "left" strategy, while easily adaptable to armed violence, need not necessarily employ that tactic. Thus it was, with certain exceptions, used peacefully in Western Europe before 1935. Finally the new strategy, too, though developed in conjunction with guerrilla warfare, can also be combined with a "soft" line, as is illustrated by the present tactics of the Communists not only in Western Europe and Latin America but also in India and Indonesia. Each of the three strategies can be applied in a violent or a peaceful manner. The use of armed force is a matter not of strategy but of tactics, which can be changed according to conditions while the strategy remains unchanged; it can even be in effect in some parts of a country while peaceful methods are applied in others at the same time.

The essential characteristic of the new strategy, which distinguishes it from both its "left" and its "right" predecessors, is its direct appeal "from below" (i.e., not through bourgeois parties) to the bourgeoisie. This appeal is made quite openly; it is defended on theoretical grounds and is expressed in propaganda emphasizing the interests held in common by workers and capitalists as against the foreign imperialists. Unlike reliance on the peasantry or on armed force, it is startlingly new to Communists. The proposition that the Communist party, the party of the exploited toilers, represents also the interests of the capitalists, who are, by Marxian definition, the exploiters, that the two classes between which the class struggle is supposed to be raging can be united in the Communist party, is hardly traditional Communist doctrine. It can, however, be considered an extraordinary but logical extension of "proletarian internationalism," i.e., the identification of the interests of the proletariat everywhere with those of the Soviet Union: the party of the proletariat is to unite all classes, regardless of their class interests, provided they are opposed to imperialism, meaning the United States.[10] In short, the class struggle has been replaced by the cold war.

[10]The only conceivable further extension of this anti-imperialist alliance could be made by adding feudal elements to the bloc of four classes. Since the immediate goal is presumably an anti-feudal, though not an anti-capitalist revolution, this is an even more extraordinary step than the inclusion of capitalists. Yet even it has been taken. "The scale of this national front [of the Chinese people] embraces workers, peasants, intellectuals, the petty-bourgeoisie, the national bourgeoisie and even the progressive gentry," Liu Shao-chi, *Internationalism and Nationalism* (Peking: Foreign Languages Press, no date; written 1948). "The motive forces of the Viet-Nam revolution at present are the people comprising primarily the

Indeed if the "left" strategy was the strategy of anti-capitalism and the "right" strategy that of anti-fascism, the new strategy is the strategy of anti-Americanism. Before 1947 the new strategy as it had been developed in China was of little interest to Moscow and probably was hardly known there. With the beginning of the cold war, however, the "right" strategy of cooperation with the principal bourgeois and labor parties and with the governments formed by them was given up, since these were generally pro-American. During the following years, which also saw the rise to prominence of the Chinese Communists and their strategy in the world of international Communism, there was some difference of opinion in Moscow and in some Communist parties as to whether the "left" or the new strategy was to replace the discarded "right" one.[11] It soon became clear, however, that the "left" alternative, by regarding capitalism as an enemy, unduly limited the range of the Communists' potential supporters to the so-called exploited classes—the workers, the poor peasantry and some petty-bourgeois elements—while in Moscow's eyes there was no reason, except the negligible one of Marxist theory, why exploiters too should not be mobilized on its side against the United States. The "left" strategy, though traditionally "internationalist," even entailed the serious danger that each Communist party would concentrate on the bourgeoisie in its own country as its main enemy rather than on Moscow's chief opponent, the United States, thus, from the Soviet point of view, "fighting the wrong war against the wrong enemy at the wrong time."

The new strategy, on the other hand, is admirably suited to the needs of Soviet foreign policy. Under it, the Communists frankly invite the cooperation of "all classes, parties, groups, organizations, and individuals,"[12] including capitalists and even feudal elements, the sole test of

---

workers, peasants, petty-bourgeoisie and national bourgeoisie, followed by the patriotic and progressive personages and landlords." "Platform of the Viet-Nam Lao Dong Party," *People's China*, III, No. 9 (May 1, 1951), Supplement. "The right of patriotic landlords to collect land rent in accordance with law shall be guaranteed," "Manifesto of the Viet-Nam Lao Dong Party," *ibid.*

[11] This point is developed and documented in the author's *Moscow and the Communist Party of India, op. cit.*, Chs. 2 and 3. This work also contains numerous quotations to document the advocacy of the new strategy with its appeal to the bourgeoisie by Soviet, Chinese, and Indian Communists.

[12] "Speech by Liu Shao-chi at the Conference of Trade Unions of Asia and Oceania," *For a Lasting Peace, for a People's Democracy!*, Dec. 30, 1949, p. 2, also translated from *Pravda* of Jan. 4, 1950, in *Soviet Press Translations*, V, No. 6 (March 15, 1950), 168–172. The phrase has since come into frequent use in Communist literature

their eligibility being friendliness to the Soviet Union and antagonism to the United States.[13] Thus this strategy, like the "left" and "right" ones in earlier periods, has gradually been adopted by international Communism throughout the non-Communist world. It is obvious that this is true in Asia, where the Communist parties have been urged by both Peking and Moscow to take the "Chinese path," in some countries in its violent, in others in its peaceful form.[14] It is also the case in the other underdeveloped areas and particularly in Latin America, where the Communists openly employ the strategy of the bloc of four classes, including the "national bourgeoisie."[15] However, since the Communists depict even the countries of Western Europe as colonial spoil of "American imperialism,"[16] a strategy containing the essential elements of the

---

on Asia. For a later corresponding Western expression of the new strategy, see the statement of the French Communist Party's Central Committee of October 22 and 23, 1953. "We Communists declare that we are ready, with all Frenchmen, whoever they may be,—we say advisedly, whoever they may be—who, like us, do not want a new Wehrmacht, to take part in all political activities which can and must be organized in a mighty campaign throughout the length and breadth of France." Jacques Duclos, "France Moves,' *Labour Monthly*, XXXVI, No. 2 (Feb. 1954), 63–70, p. 70.

[13] While, as we mentioned, the approach of the new strategy to other parties is generally one "from below" (i.e., antagonistic), this can, in conformity with the dominant anti-American motive behind the strategy, be changed to one "from above," where a party becomes sufficiently anti-American and pro-Soviet, as has happened in Indonesia and under the Arbenz regime in Guatemala, thus constituting a return to the "right" strategy in relation to that party. The Communist party's direct appeal to the bourgeoisie, however, is likely to continue in any case.

[14] For discussion and documentation, see Kautsky, *Moscow and the Communist Party of India, op. cit.*, Chs. 4 and 5, and also the article "The Postwar Development of Indian Communist Party Strategy," pp. 22–41 below.

[15] For some typical statements, see articles by the leaders of the Communist parties of Brazil, Chile, and Argentina in the Cominform journal, *For a Lasting Peace, for a People's Democracy!*, June 5, 1953, p. 3; Dec. 18, 1953, p. 3; and Jan. 15, 1954, pp. 3–4, respectively, and especially the "Draft Program of Communist Party of Brazil" *ibid.*, Feb. 26, 1954, p. 3. See also Daniel James, "Lessons of Guatemala," *The New Leader*, XXXVII, No. 28 (July 12, 1954), 3, who says: " . . . what we think we have been fighting is classic Leninist-Stalinist Communism, whereas what we really had to contend with in Guatemala, and must now face throughout the Hemisphere, is the more formidable doctrine of Maoism."

[16] "In view of the policy of expansion pursued by the American monopolies, the struggle for national independence and economic development has now become a necessity not only for the peoples of the colonial and semi-colonial countries but also for those in the developed capitalist countries." "Decisions of Third World Trade Union Congress," *For a Lasting Peace, for a People's Democracy!*, Oct. 30, 1953, p. 2.

new strategy has come to be applied in these countries too.[17] This is
clear from the Communist parties' concentration on the United States
rather than on capitalism as their main enemy and their call "from
below" for cooperation with all elements, regardless of class, coupled
with attacks on the governments and leading parties who would be
their allies in the united front "from above" of the "right" strategy.
The so-called "peace" movement with its anti-American appeal to all
classes, the emphasis in Communist propaganda on the injury done by
"American imperialism" to the national economy and the interests of
labor and capital alike, and the outright attempts to attract capitalists
by vistas of East-West trade, notably expressed by the Moscow Economic Conference of 1952, are all manifestations of the new strategy
in evidence as much in the West as in the underdeveloped areas.

That the new strategy of Communism involves a radical departure
from Marxism is obvious and has already been indicated. It is, however,
only a logical development of Leninism. The doctrines of Mao Tse-tung,
even better than Lenin's prototype, serve to elucidate the implications
of Leninism. To Marx and Engels the working class itself was the revolutionary agent, as it was matured by the inevitable historical development
of society. The party, along with the trade unions, was conceived to
be only a tool of the class in its class struggle and it could not therefore,
any more than the unions, rely on elements which, by Marxian definition,
were the enemies of the workers. Lenin, however, took the crucial step
of divorcing the party from the class, shifting the emphasis from the
latter to the former as the agent of a no longer inevitable historical
development, and in effect making the working class the tool of the
party. Once this step was taken, there was no longer any reason why
some other class could not also become the tool of the party. This can

[17] For Western Communist statements explicitly including sections of the bourgeoisie
among potential allies see Jacques Duclos, "Historic Example of October Revolution
and Middle Strata," *ibid.*, Nov. 2, 1951, reprinted with a highly relevant and
perceptive introductory note in *Problems of Communism*, I, No. 1 (1952), 1–5,
and the speeches by Duclos and Thorez at the 13th Congress of the French Communist Party in *For a Lasting Peace, for a People's Democracy!*, June 11, 1952.
Statements making the same point implicitly by the Italian Communist leaders
Palmiro Togliatti and Luigi Longo, the Austrian Johann Koplenig, and the West
German Max Reimann may be found *ibid.*, Dec. 18, 1953, p. 2; May 7, 1954,
pp. 3–4; May 21, 1954, p. 3; and July 2, 1954 p. 3, respectively. Even in the
United States, the Communist Party is appealing to some "groups of capital" to
join its "popular coalition movement." "New U.S. Red Line Seeks 'Coalition,'"
The New York Times, March 7, 1954, p. 1.

be the peasantry, as it was in China and to some extent in Russia, but it can even be the capitalists, as is now possible under the new strategy.[18] From the Marxist emphasis on the working class we have, via Lenin's reliance on the party, now arrived at a party, independent of all classes and representing none, seeking a base for the realization of its own ambitions in any class where it can find support. The end of Marx's party—the class struggle—has been abandoned for the means—the party in its quest for power.

[18] This point is well made by Morris Watnick, "Continuity and Innovation in Chinese Communism," *World Politics*, VI, No. 1 (Oct. 1953), 84–105, particularly pp. 94–96. It is also further developed by me in "Neo-Maoism, Marxism and Leninism," pp. 42–55 below.

2. The Postwar Development
of Indian Communist Party Strategy*

Introductory Note. The preceding article sought to define three alternative Communist strategies, particularly the new one, in very general terms as they appeared all over the world. The next article on "The Postwar Development of Indian Communist Strategy" tries to apply the criteria developed in the first article in an analysis of Soviet and Indian Communist Party documents. It thereby focuses on shifts in the line of one particular Communist party from one strategy to another and shows how these are related to earlier changes of line in Moscow.

While my main purpose in writing this article was to point up the evolution of the so-called new strategy in Moscow and its subsequent adoption in India, my research also threw some interesting light on the relationship between Moscow and a Communist party at a time when the concept of international Communism with its implication of centralized control was still far more viable than it is today. Even then, when the Indian Communists were eagerly looking to Moscow for guidance and anxious to follow its lead, communications between Moscow and the CPI were remarkably poor. There were periods when there was disagreement in Moscow as to what the line of the CPI should be, when Moscow authorities did not want to or did not bother to call their line to the attention of the CPI when they did agree on one, and when the CPI leadership was unable to understand the line that was finally called to their attention. Thus, as this article shows, the relatively smooth evolution of the new strategy in Moscow (1947 to 1949) is reflected in a much longer development interrupted by several violent upheavals in the CPI (1947 to 1951).

As a postscript I have added a few paragraphs that were written four years later in a review of Gene D. Overstreet and Marshall Windmiller,

* Reprinted, by permission, from *Pacific Affairs,* XXVIII, No. 2 (June 1955), 145–160, and originally entitled "Indian Communist Party Strategy Since 1947." This article is based on research done by the author at the Center for International Studies, Massachusetts Institute of Technology, in 1953–1954. Its complete and documented results are available in his *Moscow and the Communist Party of India* (Cambridge, Mass.: The Technology Press of M.I.T., and New York: John Wiley and Sons, 1956). The author wishes to express his deep appreciation of the advice he has received from Morris Watnick and Bernard Morris.

Communism in India. These bring the story of the relationship between the Indian Communist Party and Nehru and his Congress Party farther up to date and indicate how, under Soviet prodding, the Communist Party has moved more and more to support the non-Communist modernizing movement, a trend that has generally continued in India and in other underdeveloped countries and has led to the subordination of Communist parties to their erstwhile non-Communist rivals.

E ver since its beginning, the Communist Party of India has sought to adhere to international Communist strategy as determined in Moscow, though it has not at all times been equally prompt or successful in making the required changes. It has always attempted to give the same answers as Moscow to the three main questions determining Communist strategy: who was, at any time, the main enemy and consequently what classes and groups were eligible as allies of Communism and what type of alliance was to be formed with them. A study of CPI strategy thus throws light on the development of international Communist strategy in general, particularly in the period since the end of World War II when changes in the CPI line have been much more clearly marked than some of the corresponding shifts in Moscow.

Organized as an all-India party as late as 1933, the Communist Party of India began its career following the "left" strategy of Communism as it had been laid down by the 6th Congress of the Communist International in 1928. This strategy characteristically considered capitalism and the native bourgeoisie as enemies at least as important as feudalism and foreign imperialism and therefore looked forward to an early "socialist" revolution merging with, or even skipping, the "bourgeois-democratic" revolution. It sought a united front "from below" by appealing to workers and also the poor peasantry and petty bourgeoisie as individuals or in local organizations to leave nationalist, labor and bourgeois parties and work with the Communists. Though it thereby isolated itself from the great Indian nationalist movement, the CPI, according to this "left" strategy, denounced the National Congress as "a class organization of the capitalists" and the Congress Socialist Party as "Social Fascists."[1]

---

[1] For a short history of the CPI during the prewar and war periods, with many quotations from Communist documents illustrating the Party's attitude, see Madhu Limaye, *Communist Party, Facts and Fiction* (Hyderabad, India: Chetana Prakashan, 1951), pp. 18–50. A fuller treatment of these periods, also useful for its quotations and notes, is M. R. Masani, *The Communist Party of India, A Short History,*

When Moscow finally recognized the danger posed by German Fascism and changed its foreign policy and, correspondingly, the strategy of international Communism, the CPI, too, after some delays, obediently switched to the "right" strategy as it had been ordered to do at the 7th Comintern Congress of 1935. This strategy regarded imperialism and feudalism (or, in Western countries, Fascism) as the Communists' main enemies and therefore envisaged first a "bourgeois-democratic" and only later a "proletarian-socialist" revolution. It called for an alliance of the Communist Party with anti-imperialist and anti-feudal (or anti-Fascist) parties, both labor and bourgeois, a united front "from above" or popular front. Accordingly, the CPI began to seek unity with the Indian Socialists and the Congress, now referred to as "the principal anti-imperialist people's organization," although, it may be noted, these groups, unlike the Communists' new popular front allies in the West, were much more anti-British than anti-Nazi or anti-Japanese.

Although it was rather unnecessary (because of this last-mentioned peculiar Indian situation), the CPI, like all Communist parties at that time, shifted back from the "right" to the "left" strategy after the conclusion of the Stalin-Hitler Pact of August 1939, once again "unmasking" its erstwhile allies as "reformists" and "agents of imperialism" and denouncing the war against the Axis as "imperialist." While this line proved not unpopular in India, the return to the "right" after the German invasion of Russia in June 1941, which eventually resulted in such growth in Communist strength and prestige in the West and in Southeast Asia, proved disastrous for the CPI's reputation in India, for the Party's new ally was to be Britain, still widely regarded as India's main enemy. Only under great pressure, especially from the Communist Party of Great Britain, long the CPI's mentor, could the Party be prevailed upon to shift from the line of "imperialist war" to that of "people's war."

In accordance with the continuing wartime alliance of the Great Powers and the participation of Communists in Western coalition governments, Moscow apparently expected the CPI, too, to persist in the postwar period in its adherence to the "right" strategy of cooperation not only with the Congress and Socialists but also the Moslem League, and even to combine this, at least until the end of 1945, with a relatively

(London: Derek Verschoyle; New York: Macmillan, 1954), Chs. 1–5. A later, more thorough history of the CPI is Gene D. Overstreet and Marshall Windmiller, *Communism in India* (Berkeley and Los Angeles: University of California Press, 1959). The prewar and war periods are covered *ibid.*, pp. 19–222.

friendly attitude toward the British. Emerging from the war isolated and demoralized and receiving little or no guidance from Moscow (which was then preoccupied with Europe rather than Asia), the CPI could, in view of these utterly unrealistic expectations, only follow a hesitant, bewildered "right" course,[2] for the groups with which it was expected to form a united front were strongly opposed both to the Communists and to each other. For a period in 1946 a faction gained the upper hand in the leadership of the frustrated CPI which, as was especially indicated in the Central Committee resolution "Forward to Final Struggle for Power" (*People's Age*, Bombay, August 11, 1946), even switched its strategy temporarily back to the "left." This was a fact of some importance because it was during this period that the Communists seized the leadership of a peasant uprising in the backward Telengana district of Hyderabad, which was destined to continue for five years and to play a crucial part in CPI strategy discussions. This "left" anti-Congress line was not, however, acknowledged by Moscow which, though clearly anti-British by now, remained uncertain in its attitude toward the Congress.[3] By the end of 1946, the CPI had returned to the "right" strategy of attempted cooperation with the "progressive" wing of the Congress and also the Moslem League, and, when the Mountbatten Plan of 1947 announced the forthcoming division of India as well as during the subsequent communal riots, the CPI repeatedly pledged its support to Nehru and "the popular Governments" of India and Pakistan, notably in its so-called Mountbatten Resolution (*People's Age*, June 29, 1947).

In the meantime, however, Moscow, along with its policy of more conciliatory relations with the West, was giving up the "right" strategy for international Communism. In June 1947 a session on India of the USSR Academy of Sciences strongly denounced—at the very time when the CPI was praising part of it—the entire Congress, including Nehru, as an ally of imperialism and opposed to it an anti-imperialist movement led by the Communists. While thus agreeing on the abandonment of the "right" strategy of cooperation with the Congress "from above," this

[2] See the draft and final versions of the CPI's election manifesto, "For a Free and Happy India," *World News and Views,* December 1, 1945, p. 391, and "Final Battle for Indian Freedom," *ibid.*, March 10, 1946, p. 78.
[3] For a very useful analysis with many quotations of Soviet statements on India during the postwar years, see Gene D. Overstreet, *The Soviet View of India, 1945–1948,* Columbia University (unpublished M.A. thesis in Political Science), 1953.

session also marked the beginning of a striking disagreement in Moscow—probably not even noticed at the time—on the strategy to be substituted for it. V. V. Balabushevich and A. N. Dyakov, the two chief Soviet experts on India, identified the entire bourgeoisie with imperialism and thus, by implication, favored a return from the "right" to the "left" strategy with its proletarian, anti-capitalist approach.[4] E. M. Zhukov, the head of the Academy's Pacific Institute, on the other hand, condemned only the "big" bourgeoisie,[5] thus leaving the way open to cooperation by the "working class" (i.e., the Communists) not only with peasants and the petty bourgeoisie, as under the "left" strategy, but also with the so-called "medium" or "progressive" capitalists. This was to be accomplished, not as under the "right" strategy through a united front "from above" with the capitalists' parties, but rather through the united front "from below" against these parties, an approach hitherto associated only with the "left" strategy.

Zhukov thus introduced the essential element of a strategy until then unknown to international Communism, but destined to become within only a few years its almost universally applied line. This strategy had first been developed in China by Mao Tse-tung during World War II as the anti-imperialist and anti-feudal strategy of the "bloc of four classes" leading to the "new democracy" rather than immediately to the "socialist" revolution. It implied that the Communist Party itself, not in alliance with the major bourgeois and labor parties, was now considered the true representative of the interests not only of the exploited classes but also of the capitalists. The "left" Dyakov-Balabushevich line and the new Zhukov line existed side by side in Moscow for about two years, strongly suggesting that the differences between them and the general import of the new strategy were not yet appreciated there and perhaps also that Moscow at that time seriously underestimated the Chinese Communists' prospects of victory.

Far from clarifying its switch of strategy for the Indian Communists, Moscow, less interested then in Asian affairs than later, did not even inform the CPI of it, but let it continue its reluctant adherence to the unsuccessful "right strategy" for six months after the Academy session

---

[4] Akademia Nauk SSSR, *Uchenye zapiski tikhookeanskogo instituta,* Moscow, 1949, Vol. II.

[5] E. Zhukov, "K polozheniiu v Indii," *Mirovoe Khoziaystvo i Mirovaya Politika,* July 1947.

of June 1947. Only through the much more publicized speech by Zhdanov on "The International Situation" (*For a Lasting Peace, for a People's Democracy!*, November 10, 1947) to the founding meeting of the Cominform in September 1947 did the CPI become aware of the change in the international line. That speech, expounding the thesis of the division of the world into two camps, did not, however, clearly favor either the "left" or the new alternative to the "right" strategy. It was almost exclusively concerned with the situation in Europe and the role of the United States, though its general anti-imperialist (rather than anti-capitalist) tenor could be interpreted as favoring the new strategy, a possibility generally overlooked at the time, when any abandonment of the "right" strategy of international Communism was widely regarded as necessarily tantamount to a return to the "left." At any rate, the Zhdanov thesis was interpreted as calling for a turn to the new strategy in an important article by Zhukov on "The Growing Crisis of the Colonial System" (*Bolshevik*, December 15, 1947), which, this time, expressly included the "middle bourgeoisie" in the Communist united front "from below." Nevertheless, both Balabuchevich and Dyakov continued to champion the "left" strategy for India; the uncertainty between the two strategies in Moscow had apparently not yet been resolved or perhaps even recognized.

Weakened by lack of guidance from abroad, by factionalism and by internal discontent with the "right" strategy, the CPI leadership eagerly executed what it interpreted to be the change of line desired by Moscow. In December 1947, soon after the full text of Zhdanov's speech had become available to it, the Central Committee of the CPI met and adopted a resolution, "For Full Independence and People's Democracy" (*World News and Views*, January 17, 1948), signaling the abandonment of the "right" strategy and containing all the essential elements of the "left" strategy. It sharply attacked both the entire Congress (thus turning from the "right" strategy) and the entire bourgeoisie (thus failing to follow the new strategy) as allies of imperialism, favored a united front "from below" against them, looked forward to an early anti-capitalist revolution (another characteristic of the "left" strategy alone) and implied that the use of violent methods was in order, as Zhdanov's speech, too, had done with reference to the colonial areas.

B. T. Ranadive, who at the December meeting took over effective control of the CPI from P. C. Joshi, its General Secretary, was clearly convinced that the formation of the Cominform and Zhdanov's report to it heralded Moscow's return to the "left" strategy.[6] That he should have remained unaware of the uncertainty actually prevailing on this point in Moscow is not surprising when it is considered that he had only Zhdanov's vague and largely inapplicable language to guide him He must have felt sure, however, that he was expected to discard the "right" strategy, and, like many of the CPI leaders, he was in any case inclined to be "leftist" and had never known any but the "left" alternative to the "right" strategy. Even when Zhukov's application of the Zhdanov thesis to the colonial areas must have become known in India, Ranadive, like Balabushevich and Dyakov in Moscow, persisted in giving that thesis a "left" interpretation, probably not so much in reliance on those two Soviet experts and in defiance of the Zhukov view as simply in ignorance of the difference between them. Moscow apparently neither supported nor rebuked Ranadive, who is likely to have emerged as the CPI's new leader more because he had long been the outstanding "left" rival of Joshi, whose "right" policy was discredited by the Zhdanov speech, than as a result of any direct intervention by Moscow.

The switch from "right" to "left" in the CPI's line through the little-publicized December 1947 resolution was publicly confirmed at its Second Congress held in February-March 1948 in Calcutta. This, following immediately upon the Moscow-sponsored Southeast Asia Youth Conference in the same city, has often mistakenly been regarded as the turning point in CPI strategy. The Second Congress formally replaced Joshi by Ranadive as General Secretary and adopted a *Political Thesis* (Bombay, 1949), which was essentially an elaboration of the December resolution, though somewhat more explicit on the use of violent methods and making even clearer Ranadive's fantastic belief, derived from Zhdanov's two-camp thesis, in the imminent outbreak of revolution in India and throughout the world. It is only on the basis of this expectation that CPI policy during the next two years can be understood.

There was a striking absence of comment in Moscow on the Second CPI Congress. Throughout 1948 the international Communist leaders neither clearly approved nor disapproved of the CPI's new "left" strategy. As yet the new strategy, as it had been advocated by Zhukov and earlier developed by Mao, had not become dominant in Moscow,

[6] See P. C. Joshi, *Views,* Calcutta, May 1950, p. 27. This first and only issue of Joshi's periodical is an extremely revealing collection of anti-Ranadive statements made by Joshi after his ouster from the CPI.

for Balabushevich and others continued to include statements in their writings implying adherence to the "left" strategy. While they now sometimes confined their condemnations to the "big" bourgeoisie, thus approaching Zhukov's line, they did not, like the latter, take the crucial step of including any section of the bourgeoisie among the forces led by the Communist Party.

Thus again left without clear direction from Moscow but no doubt in the belief that it enjoyed Soviet support, the CPI, following its Second Congress, embarked on a policy of violent strikes and terrorism, especially in large urban areas. This resulted in heavy loss of support for the Party and growing dissatisfaction and factionalism within it, but that merely led Ranadive to engage in further adventures and intra-Party repression, bringing the CPI close to complete collapse. Only the Telengana uprising was fairly successful during this period. It was led by the Andhra provincial committee of the CPI, which had long enjoyed considerable autonomy and now, because of its independence and the relative success of its program of rural violence, became the most dangerous rival of Ranadive whose policy of urban violence was failing. The ensuing conflict between the two reflected in an extreme fashion the uncertainty between the "left" and the new strategy then prevailing in Moscow.

In June 1948 the Andhra Committee submitted an anti-Ranadive document to the CPI Politburo advocating adherence to the new strategy.[7] Basing themselves completely on the Chinese Communist example, as was only natural for Asian Communists engaged in armed clashes and leaning on peasant support mobilized through a program of agrarian reform, the Andhra Communists stood for both the specifically Chinese elements of that strategy (rural guerrilla warfare and chief reliance on the peasantry) as well as its essential elements (concentration on imperialism and feudalism, rather than capitalism, as the main enemies; a "democratic" but not "socialist" revolution in the near future; and the inclusion of a section of the bourgeoisie as well as the "middle" and even the "rich" peasantry in the united front "from below").

Just as the Andhra document had gone well beyond Zhukov's analysis

---

[7] The full text of this document has not been available to the author but its main features can be reconstructed from "Struggle for People's Democracy and Social-ism—Some Questions of Strategy and Tactics," *Communist*, Bombay, June–July, 1949, pp. 21–89; and from "Statement of Editorial Board of *Communist* on Anti-Leninist Criticism of Comrade Mao Tse-tung," *ibid.*, July–August 1950, pp. 6–35.

in its adherence to the new strategy, so Ranadive's reply to this challenge, formulated at a Politburo session lasting from September to December 1948 and published in the form of four statements appearing between January and July 1949,[8] reached a point in its uncompromising advocacy of the "left" strategy never approached by Dyakov and Balabushevich in Moscow. The native Indian bourgeoisie, rather than foreign imperialism and feudalism, was now depicted as the main enemy, not only in the cities but (in the role of the rich peasantry) even in the countryside. The united front "from below" against the Congress, therefore, could be based only on the urban and rural proletariat and poor peasantry and could include some middle peasant and petty bourgeois elements, but in no case any part of the bourgeoisie or the rich peasantry. Correspondingly, the coming revolution would be a "socialist" one. The issue between the "left" and the new strategy was thus joined in the conflict between Ranadive and the Andhra Communists and the differences between the two were clearly brought out, while their similarities—the reliance on the approach of the united front "from below" against the Congress and the possible use of violent tactics—also emerged by implication from the discussion.

However, Ranadive went further and, no doubt, in order to ingratiate himself in Moscow, where he apparently expected an early shake-up of the international Communist leadership, he sharply accused various unnamed "advanced" Communist parties for having been guilty of "revisionism" since the end of World War II. By this he meant all forms of cooperation with bourgeois elements, whether "from above" with bourgeois parties, as applied in the "right" strategy in Western Europe in the immediate postwar years, or "from below," as used in the new strategy of Mao Tse-tung in China against the Kuomintang (hitherto considered the principal bourgeois party)—two very different approaches which, as a doctrinaire "leftist," Ranadive was unable to distinguish. Finally, in the last of the four Politburo statements, Ranadive went even beyond this point and, relying heavily on Zhdanov's Cominform speech, attacked Mao Tse-tung by name, ridiculing the assertion that he was an authoritative source of Marxism, mentioning him in one breath with Tito and Browder and describing some of his passages

[8] "On People's Democracy," *ibid.*, January 1949, pp. 1–12; "On the Agrarian Question in India," *ibid.*, pp. 13–53; "Struggle Against Revisionism Today in the Light of Lenin's Teachings," *ibid.*, February 1949, pp. 53–66; "Struggle for People's Democracy and Socialism," *loc. cit.*

advocating the promotion of capitalism as "in contradiction to the world understanding of the Communist Parties," "horrifying" and "reactionary and counterrevolutionary."[9] Whether Ranadive actually enjoyed the support in Moscow of which he, the leader of a small and unsuccessful Communist Party, must have felt sure to go out of his way to launch such an attack on the powerful Mao on the eve of his victory in China and whether Moscow or one faction in Moscow, such as one representing the now dead Zhdanov, was opposed to Mao and approved of or even encouraged Ranadive's step are questions on which it is fascinating to speculate[10] but on which no evidence is available.

Whatever Moscow's attitude toward Mao, it was Ranadive's misfortune that by the time he had reached the high point of his opposition to the new strategy, Moscow had finally, after two years of uncertainty, given its support to the latter. Quite apart from any influence the Chinese Communist victories may have had, the Soviet leaders no doubt realized that the "left" line, by regarding capitalism as an enemy, unduly limited the range of the Communists' potential supporters in their cold war with the United States to the so-called exploited classes and thus entailed the serious danger that each Communist party would concentrate on the bourgeoisie in its own country as its main enemy, to that extent ignoring Moscow's main enemy, the United States. It is even possible that both Ranadive's practical course in 1948 and 1949 and his theoretical formulations in his conflict with the Andhra Committee contributed to this realization in Moscow and to the recognition that the new strategy with its willingness to cooperate with virtually everyone regardless of

[9] "Struggle for People's Democracy and Socialism," *loc. cit.,* pp. 77–79. It is fascinating to note that Ranadive also attacked Maoism for placing its entire reliance on the Communist Party instead of the working class, *ibid.,* p. 88, partly quoted in Robert C. North, *Moscow and the Chinese Communists* (Stanford: Stanford University Press, 1953), p. 242. He thus puts his finger on a real weak spot (from the point of view of Marxian theory) of Maoism. What Ranadive remained unaware of is that he was here attacking the very basis of Leninism, that it was Lenin, not Mao, who first "deviated" from Marx on this fundamental point and that Maoism, being an adjustment of Marxism to an even more undeveloped country than Tsarist Russia, is but Leninism in a more developed form. Both Leninism and Maoism seek to obscure their perversion of Marxism by defining the working class, in a most un-Marxian manner, in terms of its adherence to Communist ideology, thus generally identifying the Party and the class, a trick which Ranadive by distinguishing between the two very uncautiously laid bare in his attack on Maoism.
[10] See Franz Borkenau, "The Chances of a Mao-Stalin Rift," *Commentary,* XIV (August 1952), 117–123; Ruth Fischer, "The Indian Communist Party," *Far Eastern Survey,* XXII, No. 7 (June 1953), 79–84.

class against its main enemy, foreign imperialism, was far better suited to the needs of the Soviet Union's anti-American foreign policy.

The adoption of the new strategy in Moscow was marked by two concurrent events in June 1949. One was the publication in *Pravda* of a pamphlet (*Internationalism and Nationalism*[11]) by the foremost Chinese Communist theoretician, Liu Shao-chi, written as early as November 1948. The cause of the delay in its appearance in Moscow could hardly have been its main contents, which, being directed against Tito, would have been welcomed earlier, but is likely to have been a passage at its very end in which the Communists in colonial and semi-colonial countries, including India, were expressly told that they would be committing "a grave mistake" if they did not "enter into an anti-imperialist alliance with that section of the national bourgeoisie which is still opposing imperialism." At the very time when this vigorous directive to the Asian Communist parties to adopt the new strategy appeared in the pages of *Pravda,* a meeting of the Soviet Academy of Sciences on the colonial movement was taking place. It differed sharply from the similar meeting held two years earlier. The reports delivered (as well as another set of reports presented to the Academy later in 1949[12]) showed that not only Zhukov but also the former champions of the "left" strategy, Balabushevich and Dyakov, who dealt specifically with India, favored the inclusion of some bourgeois elements in the united front "from below," though it is interesting to note how much more grudgingly and reluctantly the latter two took this step than Zhukov and some other Soviet writers represented in these reports. During the months following June 1949, the Cominform journal and *Pravada* also showed clearly that the new strategy now had Moscow's approval by featuring pronouncements of Mao Tse-tung and Chu Teh advocating it.

A showdown between Moscow and the CPI now became inevitable. The situation, in which Ranadive, who had always thought of himself as a faithful follower of Moscow, was now hopelessly doomed, did not

[11] *Pravda,* June 7, 8 and 9, 1949, in *Soviet Press Translations,* IV, No. 14 (July 15, 1949), 423–489; also Liu Shao-chi, *Internationalism and Nationalism* (Peking: Foreign Languages Press, no date).

[12] *Colonial Peoples' Struggle for Liberation* (Bombay: People's Publishing House, 1950); also condensed from *Voprosy Ekonomiki,* August and September 1949, in *Current Digest of the Soviet Press,* I, No. 49 (January 3, 1950), 3–10; and *Crisis of the Colonial System, National Liberation Struggle of the Peoples of East Asia,* Reports presented in 1949 to the Pacific Institute of the Academy of Sciences, USSR (Bombay: People's Publishing House, 1951).

lack elements of drama. The end, however, was not to come for several months. Ranadive seems to have long remained unaware of the most recent change in Moscow; in fact his most violent attack on the new strategy appeared in print a month after Moscow had publicly embraced it. In November 1949 Moscow utilized the meeting in Peking of one of its international front organizations, the World Federation of Trade Unions, to dramatize and publicize to the Asian Communist parties the fact that Moscow's and Peking's views on Communist strategy now coincided. Sounding the keynote of this meeting and, indeed, of the subsequent history of Asian Communism, Liu Shao-chi in a speech reprinted in the Cominform journal of December 30, 1949, directed the various colonial Communist parties in the most unequivocal language to take "the path" of China and of Mao Tse-tung and defined this path as union of the "working class . . . with all other classes, parties, groups, organizations and individuals who are willing to oppose the oppression of imperialism" in a broad united front, but as requiring "armed struggle" only "wherever and whenever possible." That India was not considered a country where armed struggle was possible (a fact of crucial importance in the next phase of the CPI's history) was implied in the Manifesto issued by the Peking meeting and printed in the Cominform journal of January 6, 1950, and had already been suggested earlier in Zhukov's reports to the Academy of Sciences.

Even the clear call of the Peking WFTU Conference was ignored by the CPI. Ranadive seemed too blindly convinced of the correctness of his "left" strategy to understand any but the most direct orders from Moscow and was, in any case, by now too deeply committed to that strategy to be able to give it up without admitting that his intra-Party rivals had been right and thus losing power to them. More immediate intervention by Moscow finally came in the form of an editorial in the Cominform journal of January 27, 1950, entitled "Mighty Advance of National Liberation Movement in the Colonial and Dependent Countries," telling the CPI to take the Chinese "path" of forming the broadest united front with all anti-imperialist classes and elements, but again pointedly omitting India from the list of countries where the use of armed violence was appropriate. The editorial thus did substantially no more than repeat the message of the WFTU Conference, but it was addressed directly to the CPI and, above all, it emanated not from Peking, which Ranadive despised as a source of Communist strategy, but from the very Cominform on which he had placed his main reliance.

Once he was thus publicly abandoned by Moscow, Ranadive's fate was sealed and his Party rivals began to close in on him, which they had not ventured to do in spite of the utter failure of his policies as long as he could claim Moscow's support. Still he sought desperately to cling to his authority. Instead of issuing the statement of abject "self-criticism" called for by Communist etiquette in this situation, Ranadive, writing in the February-March issue of *Communist,* hailed the Cominform editorial but subtly reinterpreted it to justify and even praise his own strategy. Whether this was the result of his inability to understand the import of the editorial or a desperate gamble to gain time, Moscow did not accept his statement and, by remaining silent, allowed the Andhra faction to press its attack against the hated Ranadive. On April 6, Ranadive issued one more statement, far more self-critical than its predecessor but apparently still an attempt to remain in power. This, too, failed to regain Moscow's support for him, and, at a meeting held in May and June 1950, the Central Committee "reconstituted" itself and the Politburo and replaced Ranadive as General Secretary with Rajeshwar Rao, the leader of the Andhra faction. A CPI Central Committee statement (appearing a full half year after the Cominform editorial had initiated the shake-up) announcing the change in both leadership and policy was published in *Pravda* and *Izvestia* of July 23, 1950,[13] and was thus given Moscow's stamp of approval which had been denied to Ranadive's efforts to remain at the helm.

The leadership of the CPI had fallen into the Andhra Communists' hands because they had long been the foremost champions of the new strategy in India and the only well-organized opposition to Ranadive within the Party and not because they had been selected by Moscow for their clear understanding of what was desired there. In a series of statements published after their assumption of the CPI's leadership in the July-August 1950 issue of *Communist,* they not only mercilessly criticized Ranadive's "left" strategy and restated the fundamentals of their own new strategy but also made it clear that, deeply committed as they were to the type of peasant guerrilla warfare they had been carrying on in Telengana, they misunderstood Moscow's and Peking's references to the "Chinese path" as including the specific Chinese Communist tactics of such warfare, as well as the essential four-class element of the new strategy. The continuation by the Andhra leaders of

[13] *Current Digest of the Soviet Press,* II, No. 30 (September 9, 1950), 31.

Ranadive's emphasis on violent methods, though their focus was now being shifted entirely from urban to rural areas, led to further disintegration of a Party already on the brink of ruin and to what a September 1950 circular of their Politburo called "a state of semi-paralysation."[14]

Three months earlier, a Chinese Communist statement, "An Armed People Opposes Armed Counterrevolution," had appeared in the Peking *People's Daily* of June 16, 1950, and in English in *People's China* of July 1, 1950, thus being available to the CPI. After referring to the WFTU Conference and the Cominform editorial and specifically to the Indian Communists, it had pointed out that "armed struggle . . . can by no means be conducted in any colony or semi-colony at any time without the necessary conditions and preparations." However, this pointed warning was ignored by the CPI, for even its Andhra leadership, though it took the Chinese Communists as its example, looked to Moscow alone for directives. Yet Moscow, in spite of the admittedly disastrous situation within the CPI, seemed again in no hurry to provide specific guidance on how its order to adopt the new strategy was to be implemented.

Finally, in December 1950, such guidance arrived in the form of an open letter, published in the CPI's *Cross Roads* on January 19, 1951, from R. Palme Dutt, the British Communist leader of Indian descent who had in years past often served as Moscow's voice for the CPI. The Party was now told in some detail that its "present paramount task is . . . the building of the peace movement and the broad democratic front." Here it was also suggested that Nehru's neutralism, again and again "unmasked" by the CPI since December 1947 as subservience to "Anglo-American imperialism," was "a very important development." In the same month the CPI's Central Committee met to enlarge itself and reconstitute the Politburo by adding adherents of the new strategy in its peaceful form to its violent followers of the Andhra faction. While it was openly admitted that "differences on vital tactical issues have yet to be resolved" (*Cross Roads,* December 29, 1950, p. 5), a number of statements made at this meeting and in subsequent months reemphasized the themes struck in Dutt's letter and thus underlined the ascendancy of the peaceful over the violent form of the new strategy in the CPI. This shift in policy, quite unlike the earlier ones from Joshi's "right" to Ranadive's "left" and from the "left" to Rajeshwar Rao's

---

[14] Quoted in Limaye, *op. cit.,* p. 75.

new strategy, was a gradual one. The leaders of both factions shared power, an arrangement inconceivable in the earlier cases, which indicates that the differences between violent and peaceful tactics, though more spectacular, are far less fundamental than those among the three strategies of Communism.

In April 1951, the CPI leadership published a new Party program (reprinted in the Cominform journal of May 11, 1951) which, in strict accordance with the new Communist strategy, did not demand a united front with the Congress as had the "right" strategy, and explicitly rejected the anti-bourgeois revolution called for by the "left" line. It called for replacing "the present anti-democratic and anti-popular Government by a new Government of People's Democracy, created on the basis of a coalition of all democratic anti-feudal and anti-imperialist forces in the country." The May Day Manifesto of the same period defined these forces as consisting of Socialists who oppose their anti-Communist leaders, "other Leftists, honest Congressmen, and above all, the *lakhs* of workers, peasants, middle classes, intellectuals, non-monopoly capitalists and other progressives,"[15] a perfect statement of the new strategy's united front "from below" uniting workers and capitalists. By April 1951, however, the Party's leadership was also sufficiently consolidated around the Moscow line not merely to reaffirm its adherence to the new strategy but also to issue an authoritative *Statement of Policy*[16] on the tactics by which this strategy was to be achieved. Both Ranadive's urban insurrections and the Andhra Communists' guerrilla warfare were specifically rejected and "the correct path" was now proclaimed, "a path which we do not and cannot name as either Russian or Chinese." The view which Moscow and Peking had been hinting at for well over a year, that armed violence on the Chinese model was not applicable in India, was then elaborated at some length, though the use of violence in principle in the more distant future was not rejected.[17] The immediate tasks of the Party were again described as the formation of the broadest

[15] "May Day Manifesto of Communist Party of India," *Cross Roads,* April 27, 1951, p. 3. A lakh is one hundred thousand.
[16] Bombay, 1951; also *Cross Roads,* June 8, 1951, pp. 3, 6, and 16. Most of the important passages are reprinted in Democratic Research Service, *Communist Conspiracy in India* [Bombay: Popular Book Depot, (distributed in the U.S. by the Institute of Pacific Relations, N.Y.) 1954], pp. 20–23.
[17] See "Tactical Line," in *Communist Conspiracy in India, op. cit.,* pp. 35–48, and in Masani, *op. cit.,* pp. 252–263. This supposedly secret document on which the *Statement of Policy* was based makes the last-mentioned point more frankly but in essence does not differ substantially from the published Policy Statement.

possible united front against the Congress and Socialist Parties and the building up of the peace movement, both of which are intimately related to the essential element of the new strategy, its "four-class" appeal.

The *Statement of Policy* marked the defeat of the violent application of the new strategy as advocated by the Andhra faction, a fact confirmed when the Central Committee in the following month replaced Rajeshwar Rao with Ajoy Ghosh as the Party's new leader and when, after the failure of efforts at negotiations with the government, the Party in October 1951 nevertheless called off the fighting in Telengana.[18] The changes in leadership and the Party's documents setting forth the new line were finally ratified by an All-India Conference of the CPI in October 1951 and, in a Politburo statement appearing in the Cominform journal of November 2, 1951, were hailed as settling all differences and disputes that had torn the Party during the preceding years. Though harmony was by no means established among the CPI leaders, the Party leadership has, ever since 1951, been firmly settled on the new strategy in its peaceful form and, most important for its stability since then, was for the first time in at least two (and possibly four) years successful in comprehending Moscow's wishes concerning both strategy and its violent or peaceful execution.

That the CPI's strategy did, after 1951 enjoy Moscow's approval is indicated by the publication in the Cominform and Soviet press of CPI documents, which had been strikingly absent during the preceding years, and of five major articles within two and a half years in the Cominform journal by Ghosh, the new General Secretary,[19] an honor not once accorded to Ranadive or Rajeshwar Rao. Palme Dutt and several Soviet writers also praised the CPI's new line in the year following its adoption. Finally, at a session of the Soviet Academy of Sciences in November 1951, which offered the clearest indication up to that time of the Soviet view of Communist strategy in underdeveloped countries in general and in India in particular,[20] both Zhukov and Balabushevich very clearly

---

[18] "C.P.I. Ready for Negotiated Settlement in Telengana," *Cross Roads*, June 15, 1951, p. 3; "C.P.I. States Basis for Telengana Settlement," *ibid.*, July 27, 1951, pp. 1–2; "Congress Game in Telengana," *ibid.*, August 10, 1951, p. 8; "C.P.I. Advises Stoppage of Partisan Action in Telengana," *ibid.*, October 24, 1951, pp. 1, 3.

[19] On October 19, 1951; March 28, 1952; November 7, 1952; February 5, 1954; May 21, 1954.

[20] *Izvestia Akademii Nauk SSSR*, History and Philosophy Series, IX, No. 1 (January-February 1952), 80–87, in *Current Digest of the Soviet Press*, IV, No. 20 (June 28, 1952), 3–7 and 43; and in *Labour Monthly*, XXXV, No. 1 (January 1953), 40–46; No. 2 (February 1953), 83–87; No. 3 (March 1953), 139–144.

distinguished between the essential four-class element of the new strategy, which was applicable everywhere, and its specific Chinese element of armed violence, which was applicable in some countries but was explicitly and vigorously rejected for India.

With agreement on the new strategy in its peaceful form reached in 1951, only differences on tactics remained to plague the CPI leadership. A full discussion of these would be beyond the scope of this article,[21] but some of the difficulties the CPI has faced in executing the new strategy during the four years after 1951 may be noted. One of the most pervasive of these seems to be "sectarianism," i.e. the reluctance of party members to cooperate with the many non-Communist elements who must be drawn into the united front of the new strategy. Another is the tendency to form that united front primarily from above by entering into alliances with various relatively small "left" parties, in which the CPI's identity is in danger of being submerged, rather than from below by winning members away from the major anti-Communist parties, the Congress and the Socialists. Still another problem, related to that of sectarianism, is the continued hostility on the part of wide circles in the CPI toward the broad non-party peace movement which the Communists sought to build up after 1951.

All these difficulties were aired at the CPI's Third Congress held in January 1954 in Madurai. The last mentioned issue appeared in the form of a conflict over whether Britain or the United States was to be regarded as the main enemy.[22] Those who held the primarily anti-British view, notably the Andhra Communists, were also the ones who wished to emphasize the "national liberation movement" and to concentrate on building a strong Party and who, being "sectarians," tended to look down on the peace movement where they were expected to cooperate with non-Communists. The anti-American attitude, on the other hand, was closely associated with emphasis on the peace movement and definitely seemed to be closer to Moscow's desires. Why, then, could the conflict between the two not be resolved clearly in favor of the

---

[21] The divisions of the CPI in the early 1950's are well summarized in Marshall Windmiller, "Indian Communism Today," *Far Eastern Survey,* XXIII, No. 4 (April 1954), 49–56.

[22] *Communist Conspiracy in India, op. cit.,* pp. 12–19 and 51–52; Ajoy Ghosh, *On the Work of the Third Congress of the Communist Party of India* (New Delhi: Jayant Bhatt, 1954); Ghosh, "Third Congress of Communist Party of India," *For a Lasting Peace, for a People's Democracy!,* February 5, 1954, p. 5; *Political Resolution* (New Delhi: Jayant Bhatt, 1954).

latter, but was in fact treated with the greatest caution by the leadership? The answer is suggested by Ghosh's reports on the Third Congress, when he said that the anti-American position would lead to "full support" of the Nehru government, which the CPI seemed to regard as basically pro-British and anti-American. Such a step, the CPI leadership recognized, would involve another shift in strategy to a united front "from above" with the Congress. Moscow, however, did not (at any rate not yet) seem to regard the Nehru government as sufficiently anti-American and pro-Soviet to warrant CPI efforts at cooperation with it.* Obviously, Nehru's neutralist foreign policy posed a dilemma for the Indian Communists.[23] This was confirmed when their Central Committee, perhaps in response to an editorial in *Pravda* praising Nehru, blamed the CPI's disastrous defeat in the Andhra elections of February 1955 primarily on the Party's failure to emphasize sufficiently the "important part of India was playing in recent times in the international arena in favor of world peace and against imperialist warmongers."[24]

The new strategy of international Communism was the Soviet Union's reaction to the cold war, an adjustment of Communist policy to a situation where the major parties in a country, both bourgeois and labor, were relatively pro-American and anti-Soviet and where the Communists yet wanted to unite all the classes represented by these parties against the United States. In the mid-1950's this situation prevailed throughout most of the non-Soviet world, and the new strategy was applied throughout it, not only in the underdeveloped areas of Asia and Latin America, but even in the West. In countries, however, where the governments and some major parties are neutralists, difficulties of the type just mentioned as besetting the CPI may arise. Whether Moscow and the Communist parties will be able to adjust to such a situation remains to be seen. Guatemala under the Arbenz regime and Indonesia, where the united front "from below" was given up for that "from above" with

---

* [This sentence, hesitantly as it is phrased, now seems to me to have been outdated when it was written in 1955. Moscow was by then in favor of CPI cooperation with the Nehru government, but the CPI leadership and particularly certain factions within it consistently lagged behind Moscow on this issue.]

[23] See the very interesting discussion of the CPI's attitude toward Nehru in Madhu Limaye, "Indian Communism: The New Phase," *Pacific Affairs*, XXVII, No. 3 (September 1954), 195–215.

[24] Quoted in A. M. Rosenthal, "Indian Reds Admit Error in Andhra," *New York Times*, March 31, 1955. The CPI's failure to pursue "correct" united front tactics before the election also was criticized by the Central Committee.

anti-American parties, point one way, whereas Burma, where the Communists have for years fought a civil war against a neutralist government, suggests another direction.[25]

Postscript[*]

In the 1950's, the Indian Communist Party found itself in a quandary from which it could not escape for some time. While it benefited from its role of opposition to the Nehru government, its strength, like that of any Communist party, also depended on the support and prestige of the Soviet Union. But Moscow, for reasons of its own, lent its support and prestige increasingly to the Nehru government. The short-run goal of Soviet policy—and it is doubtful that anything beyond the short run was of much concern to it—was, after all, not the success of the ultimate Communist program for a new social order but the reduction of Western and especially American power. It followed that a neutralist government like Nehru's was more vital to Soviet plans than the fate of Indian Communism.

The CPI thus found itself compelled to give increasing support to Nehru's foreign policy. By 1954, Moscow began to hint that the Indian Communists might also back the government's domestic policy, particularly its Soviet-supported program of industrialization. Nevertheless, it was not until its Palghat congress in April 1956 that the CPI acknowledged, rather equivocally, that some conditional support for Nehru's domestic policies was unavoidable. By that time, voices from Moscow were speaking of the Nehru government's "progressive" contribution toward "people's democracy" and even of its "socialism." Yet, even at its congress at Amritsar in March–April 1958, the CPI gave its support only to those government measures which had received Soviet endorsement; it continued its opposition to other phases of government policy, and particularly to the Congress administrations in the Indian states where it could exploit local discontents.

Many of the Party's gains in the 1950's probably stem from what opposition to the ruling Congress it still maintained. How, by way of contrast, the CPI may suffer from Soviet support for Nehru is shown

[25] [As the later articles in this book stress, it became clear soon after this was written that Moscow and Communist parties generally chose the path they had followed in Guatemala and Indonesia.]

[*] Reprinted, by permission, from my review article, "From Proletarianism to Nationalism," *Commentary*, XXVIII, No. 1 (July 1959), 86–90, copyright © 1959 by the American Jewish Committee.

by its defeat in the 1955 elections in Andhra. A principal campaign document used by the Congress was a *Pravda* editorial, published just before the election, which praised Nehru's foreign and domestic policies.[26]

Throughout the 1950's, the CPI's dilemma provoked continual intra-party crises. Even at its 1958 congress, the General Secretary reported that the "ideological homogeneity of the Party is seriously weakened." Obviously, strong forces in the CPI insisted on continued opposition to the Congress government. Yet, in view of the Soviet attitude, the Party had to go far in offering Nehru support. If it was to go much farther, it would be forced to give up what was left of its opposition policy, which it could ill afford to do. The farther Nehru moved in a pro-Soviet direction and the more he was praised and supported by Moscow, the less of a role was left for the CPI to play in Indian politics. In short, the Indian Communists suffered from the very successes of Soviet foreign policy to which they were expected to contribute.

[26] [For references to Soviet statements of 1956 suggesting that India could move toward "socialism" under Congress Party (i.e., "bourgeois") rule and CPI objections to this threatening implication, see p. 111 below.]

3. Neo-Maoism, Marxism, and Leninism[*]

Introductory Note. Originally written for a different audience, the article on "Neo-Maoism, Marxism and Leninism" is largely an elaboration on the final paragraph of my earlier piece on "The New Strategy of International Communism." It repeats my definition of the new Communist strategy, which I here called, as in my book on *Moscow and the Communist Party of India,* the "neo-Maoist" strategy. It also supplements the earlier articles on this subject by providing numerous quotations from Communist statements appealing to capitalists and thus illustrates the most striking aspect of the new strategy.

The article is included in this collection, above all, however, because it moves beyond the mere description and definition of the new strategy. As it explores some of its implications, the outlines of a new interpretation of the phenomenon of Communism begin to take shape. On the one hand, I here link the subject of neo-Maoism with a subject of interest to me in my earlier work, the relationship of Leninism and Communism to Marxism. On the other hand, even in doing this, I strike a number of themes, some of them only in passing, that become central in my later writing on Communism. Thus Leninism is seen not merely as a perversion or misunderstanding of Marxism but more specifically as an adaptation of an ideology born in an industrial environment to the conditions of an underdeveloped one. The Russian Revolution is interpreted as a movement of intellectuals in an underdeveloped country, and Communist parties in other such countries are similarly regarded as intellectual-led groups seeking to gain broad support across class lines in pursuit of their objectives of anti-imperialism and rapid industrialization. There is also some concern with the use of Marxian and proletarian symbols by such a movement and some hint that their use involves not mere deceit but that the symbols can serve the function of myths.

[*] Reprinted, by permission, from *The New Leader,* XL, No. 50 (December 16, 1957), 12–16. Certain passages and footnotes eliminated from the original manuscript for publication have been restored here. The article is expanded and revised from an earlier version published as "From Marx To Mao," *Soviet Survey* (London), No. 16–17 (June–July 1957), 35–40.

After thirty years of following strategies initially inspired by conditions in advanced industrial countries, international Communism, in its fourth decade, adopted a strategy well suited to areas where industralization is still in its beginnings or a mere aspiration. In this process, Communism had to abandon the very essentials of Marxism, though its present strategy in underdeveloped countries is a further development of Leninism. Thus, Leninism now appears in a new perspective which accounts for its appeal in underdeveloped areas.

Until after World War II, Communist parties throughout the world regarded themselves as primarily the parties of the industrial proletariat. They sometimes claimed to represent also the interests of the poor peasantry and the petty bourgeoisie, but never those of the capitalists. This was true not only under the anti-capitalist "left" strategy, but also under the anti-Fascist "right" strategy of the Popular Front, which called for "top alliances" with other parties, including bourgeois ones. Both these strategies were faithfully followed by Communist parties throughout the world, even though in underdeveloped countries the very basis for their successful application was generally absent, for an industrial proletariat hardly existed there.

After the onset of the cold war, a third and entirely new strategy was adopted by international Communism. Its main enemy was neither capitalism nor Fascism but "imperialism," i.e., the United States. Like the "right" strategy, it sought the cooperation of non-Communists groups, both labor and bourgeois. If some major parties were sufficiently "anti-imperialist" (i.e., anti-American and pro-Soviet), this cooperation could be sought through the "united front from above." However, conditions of this kind did not prevail, with such relatively few and temporary exceptions as in Guatemala under Arbenz, Iran under Mossadeq, Indonesia under Sukarno, and possibly in India under Nehru.*

Generally, Communists appealed against the major parties and their leaders directly "from below," not only to the proletariat, the petty bourgeoisie and the poor peasants, as under the "left" strategy, but also to the rich peasants, the capitalists and even "feudal" elements. Under this new strategy, then, the Communist party claims to be the true representative not only of the "exploited" classes but also of their "exploiters" and seeks to unite them all against their supposedly common

---

* [Here, as in the two preceding articles, I still regarded as exceptional what was in fact going to become the rule.]

enemy, American "imperialism" and the governments regarded as subservient to it.

This new strategy was first developed by Mao Tse-tung during World War II[1] (and is therefore referred to here as the neo-Maoist strategy), and its adoption in Moscow coincides with the conquest of China by the Communists. But the chief reason for its acceptance in Moscow lies not in Chinese Communist influence but in the fact that it proved to be the strategy best suited to Soviet foreign-policy needs in a period of cold war. In any event, neo-Maoism became the strategy of Communist parties in all underdeveloped countries[2] and its characteristic appeal "from below" to all groups of the population, regardless of class, for the liberation of the country from American "imperialism" and its native servants has even been adopted by the Communist parties in the West.[3]

Unlike the two older strategies, neo-Maoism is well adjusted to the needs of Communist parties in underdeveloped countries. Foreign imperialism, unlike capitalism and Fascism, is an enemy widely known and widely hated in these countries. With a strategy openly appealing to "all classes, parties, groups, organizations, and individuals,"[4] the Communists are no longer tied to a non-existent proletarian base or obliged to attack the native bourgeoisie or, for that matter, any other native groups except those closely connected with "imperialist" interests. They can thus ally themselves with and make use of any group to whom their program of "national liberation" appeals.

The main plank of this program is the promise of rapid industrializa-

---

[1] See especially "The Chinese Revolution and the Chinese Communist Party" (1939), *Selected Works of Mao Tse-tung, op. cit.*, III, 72–101, and the works of Mao cited on p. 14 above.

[2] For the story of its imposition on the Indian Communist Party see my *Moscow and the Communist Party of India, op. cit.*, pp. 95–117, and for numerous Soviet, Chinese and Indian Communist statements espousing it, see *ibid., passim*. Its adoption throughout the underdeveloped world is discussed and illustrated by quotations from a number of Asian and Latin American Communist sources in Bernard S. Morris and Morris Watnick, "Current Communist Strategy in Nonindustrialized Countries," in John H. Kautsky, ed., *Political Change in Underdeveloped Countries: Nationalism and Communism* (New York: John Wiley and Sons, 1962), pp. 282–292. See also Walter Z. Laqueur, *Communism and Nationalism in the Middle East* (New York: Frederick A. Praeger, 1956), pp. 271–272.

[3] See Bernard S. Morris, "Some Perspectives on the Nature and Role of the Western European Communist Parties," *The Review of Politics*, XVIII, No. 2 (April 1956), 163–167.

[4] "Speech by Liu Shao-chi at the Conference of Trade Unions of Asia and Oceania," *For a Lasting Peace, for a People's Democracy!*, December 30, 1949, p. 2.

tion on the Soviet and Chinese model, which arouses vistas not only of economic and political independence from Western influence but also of welfare, wealth and power. While these would supposedly benefit, above all, the vast poverty-stricken masses of the underdeveloped countries, the Communist program for industrialization has, in fact, its chief attraction for the intellectuals. They are the only group capable of grasping the implications of industrialization and they hope that such rapid economic change would provide a leading role for them in the new order which has been frequently denied to them in the colonial economy.[5]

While no doubt of far less importance in terms of its success, in a consideration of the development of Marxist and Leninist thought the direct Communist appeal to the capitalists is the most startling innovation of neo-Maoism. In underdeveloped areas some capitalists may be potential supporters of Soviet foreign policy, because they suffer from competition from Western countries or are drawn by promises of trade with Communist countries. The expectation of rapid industrialization under Communist auspices may also hold some attraction for them. They lack the background and attitudes of the bourgeoisie of Western Europe which rose independently of and sometimes in opposition to government policies. The industrialists in countries still in the early stages of industrialization are always more or less dependent on their governments' support; they may, therefore, in many cases, not be particularly frightened by prospects of being converted into a Communist government's industrial managers and bureaucrats.

On the other hand, the Communists have learned a good deal since, on the eve of his coup d'état, Lenin thought that accounting and control of production and distribution "have become the extraordinary simple operations of checking, recording and issuing receipts, which anyone who can read and write and who knows the first four rules of arithmetic can perform."[6] They know that the realization of their plans for industrialization will require trained specialists, that these are scarce in their

[5] For amplification of this point crucial to my argument, see Morris Watnick "The Appeal of Communism to the Underdeveloped Peoples, "in Kautsky, ed., *op. cit.,* pp. 316–334, and Laqueur, *op. cit., passim* and pp. 272–275. See also Eduard Heimann, "Marxism and Underdeveloped Countries," *Social Research,* XIX (September 1952), 322–345, and Eugene Staley, *The Future of Underdeveloped Countries* (New York: Harper & Brothers, 1954), pp. 174–178.
[6] V. I. Lenin, "The State and Revolution," *Selected Works* (New York: International Publishers, 1943, 12 vols.), VII, 92–93.

underdeveloped countries, and that a chief source for them are the present capitalists.

Hence the Communists' appeals to the capitalists make sense in underdeveloped countries. Three fascinating examples of such appeals may serve to illustrate this. Shortly after the completion of the Communist conquest of China, Liu Shao-chi is reported to have addressed Chinese businessmen along the following lines:

> As Communists we consider that you are exploiting your workers; but we realize that, at the present stage of China's economic development, such exploitation is unavoidable and even socially useful. What we want is for you to go ahead and develop production as fast as possible and we will do what we can to help you. You may be afraid of what will happen to you and your families when we develop from New Democracy to Socialism. But you need not really be afraid. If you do a really good job in developing your business, and train your children to be first-class technical experts, you will be the obvious people to put in charge of the nationalized enterprise and you may find that you earn more as managers of a socialized enterprise than as owners.[7]

In 1952, an Indian Communist propagandist returned from China had this message for Indian capitalists:

> Supposing, therefore, Communism of the Chinese type comes to India, a majority of our capitalists and, particularly, the industrialists would not only survive but receive every possible encouragement from Government in the interest of production. In fact, the national bourgeoisie, or patriotic capitalists who have not tied themselves with Anglo-American cartels, would have every reason to welcome such a changeover.[8]

Finally, a very interesting report by a Soviet correspondent on a Shanghai "academy for capitalists" contains this passage:

> The people's state has an economic stake in supporting the national bourgeoisie. We will use private capital to reconstruct the economy, develop production, train technical specialists, to avoid unemployment, to expand the turnover of goods, and for many, many other purposes.[9]

[7] Quoted by Michael Lindsay in Otto B. van der Sprenkel, ed., *New China: Three Views* (London: Turnstile Press, 1950), p. 139.
[8] R. K. Karanjia, *China Stands Up* ('Bombay: People's Publishing House, 1952), p. 160.
[9] G. Borovik, "Shanghai Capitalists," *Ogonyok*, No. 50 (December 1956), 26–28.

Needless to say, none of this means that Communists, once in power, represent the interests of the capitalists. As Chinese experience proves, their class and their organizations are atomized, and they are used as individuals for the purposes of the regime. But this does not prove that the Communists are still at heart proletarian anti-capitalists. It merely indicates that to be crushed and manipulated by the regime is the fate of *all* classes, including the proletariat, once the Communist party has attained power.

It is clear, then, that the current neo-Maoist strategy of international Communism is well adjusted to conditions in underdeveloped countries. Just by virtue of this fact, this new strategy demonstrates, better than the old "left" and "right" ones, how far Communism has departed from Marxism and puts the relationship between the two into sharp focus.

A strategy demanding, as Liu Shao-chi did in 1949 of Asian Communists, that "the working class must unite with all classes, parties, groups, organizations, and individuals"[10] has obviously for all practical purposes given up the basic Marxian concept of the class struggle. Under neo-Maoism, the international class enemy of the proletariat has openly been replaced by the national enemy of the Soviet Union; the class struggle has been replaced by the cold war.

A few quotations from Communist directives in various underdeveloped countries will make clear how far Communism has travelled along this path. In 1947, Mao Tse-tung, in language more reminiscent of that of an employers' association than that of Marx, sharply condemned "the advocacy of uneconomically high standards in working conditions; excessively high income-tax rates; . . . the taking of a short-sighted, one-sided view of the so-called 'welfare of the toilers' instead of making our objective the development of production, the prosperity of our economy, the taking into account of both public and private interests and benefits to both labour and capital."[11]

The Indian Communist Party promised that a Communist-dominated government in India would "develop India's industry . . . cooperating with private industrialists who will be guaranteed profits stipulated by law and whose interests will be guaranteed"[12] and demanded that "the

[10] "Speech by Liu Shao-chi . . . ," *op. cit.*
[11] Mao Tse-tung, "On the Present Situation and Our Tasks," van der Sprenkel, ed., *op. cit.*, pp. 167–168.
[12] "Election Manifesto of Communist Party of India," *For a Lasting Peace, for a People's Democracy!*, August 31, 1951, pp. 3–4.

working class must come out for the protection of national industries against the competition of the imperialists."[13] To emphasize the community of interest between capital and labor, the Indian Party's Politburo suggested that in Party propaganda, "the demands of the working class in each industry should be linked with demands of the industry itself so that the working class can come before the people as the builder and defender of national economy, which monopoly interests subservient to foreign powers are ruining."[14]

The Vietnamese Communist Party declared that "the national bourgeoisie shall be encouraged, assisted and guided in their undertakings in order to contribute to the development of the national economy. The right of patriotic landlords to collect land rent in accordance with the law shall be guaranteed."[15] Similarly, the leader of the Brazilian Communist Party stated as early as 1946 that "even among the landlords a good proportion of the liberals can work with us . . . we back the progressive national bourgeoisie when it wishes to liquidate the remains of feudalism, to develop capitalism, with the collaboration of the proletariat."[16]

Among numerous Chinese Communist statements in a similar vein, the following one well illustrates the strikingly non-Marxian view of class relations underlying this approach: "Even at the present stage of Socialist Revolution, an alliance is still maintained with the national bourgeoisie, their legitimate interests are looked after . . . . For at a certain stage of revolution and under given historical conditions the interests of the working class are identical with the interests of certain democratic classes."[17]

As these pronouncements show, Communist parties in underdeveloped

[13] Communist Party of India, *Political Resolution,* Third Congress of the CPI, Madurai, December 27, 1953 to January 4, 1954 (New Delhi: Jayant Bhatt, 1954), pp. 28–29. The same demand already appeared in the 1951 "Draft Programme of the Communist Party of India," *For a Lasting Peace, for a People's Democracy!,* May 11, 1951, p. 3.

[14] CPI Politburo resolution of August 1952, "Post Election Situation and our Tasks," *New Age,* I (Madras), No. 1 (September 1952), 44.

[15] "Manifesto of the Viet-Nam Lao Dong Party," *People's China,* III, No. 9 (May 1, 1951), Supplement.

[16] Luis Carlos Prestes at the 1946 Party Conference, *A Classe Operaria* (Rio de Janeiro), July 20, 1946, quoted in Robert J. Alexander, "Brazil's CP: A Case Study in Latin American Communism," *Problems of Communism,* IV, No. 5 (September–October 1955), 19–20.

[17] Chang Chih-yi in *Ta Kung Pao* (Peking), March 31, 1957.

countries want to cooperate with the capitalists because they need them for industrialization. And this simply makes no sense in Marxian terms. To Marx and Engels, the Communist party was conceivable only as the representative of the industrial proletariat, which, of course, was created only by an industrialization already achieved. The suggestion that a Communist party take power in a non-industrialized country in order to industrialize it and thus create a proletariat would, therefore, have struck them as preposterous.

The entire notion of a Communist party coming to power in a country without a strong proletariat is quite incompatible with the Marxian view of social development. According to that view, social classes and their ideologies evolve only as a result of the growth of material productive forces. A political party representing the ideology and interests of a class, can therefore not come to power before that class has matured, much less before even the material foundations for its growth have been laid. The *Communist Manifesto* stated that "the first direct attempts of the proletariat to attain its own ends, made in times of universal excitement, when feudal society was being overthrown, these attempts necessarily failed, owing to the then undeveloped state of the proletariat, as well as to the absence of the economic conditions for its emancipation, conditions that had yet to be produced, and could be produced by the impending bourgeois epoch alone."[18]

It is passages of this kind that are typical of the materialist conception of history which is the foundation of the Marxian theory of social development in general and of social revolution in particular. They are reaffirmed in the later works of Marx and Engels, until, shortly before his death in 1895, Engels wrote with reference to the expectation of their youth of a quick socialist revolution which would be led by a conscious socialist minority followed by the backward masses: "History has proved us, and all who thought like us, wrong."[19]

The time of surprise attacks, of revolutions carried through by small conscious minorities at the head of unconscious masses, is past. Where it is a question of a complete transformation of the social organization, the masses themselves must also be in it, must themselves already have grasped what

[18] Karl Marx and Frederick Engels, *Manifesto of the Communist Party*, Karl Marx, *Selected Works* (New York: International Publishers, preface dated 1933, 2 vols), I, p. 237.
[19] Frederick Engels, Introduction of 1895 to Karl Marx, *The Class Struggles in France, 1848–50, ibid.*, II, 176.

is at stake, what they are going in for with body and soul. The history of the last fifty years has taught us that.[20]

Consequently, ". . . Socialists are realizing more and more that no lasting victory is possible for them, unless they first win the great mass of the people. . . ."[21]

Lenin, no less than Marx and Engels, believed that the Communist party had to be the representative of the proletariat. Thus, in one of his earliest directives on Communist strategy in underdeveloped countries drawn up for the Second Comintern Congress, he went as far as to advocate that "all the Communist Parties must assist the bourgeois-democratic liberation movement in these countries . . . ," but went on to insist that they "must not merge with it, and must unconditionally preserve the independence of the proletarian movement even in its most rudimentary form."[22] How he might have felt about the neo-Maoist appeal by the Communist party to all classes as the true representative of their interests can perhaps be gathered from his sharp admonition in *Two Tactics:* "A Social-Democrat must never, even for an instant, forget that the proletarian class struggle for socialism against the most democratic and republican bourgeoisie and petty bourgeoisie is inevitable. This is beyond doubt. From this logically follows the absolute necessity of a separate, independent and strictly class party of Social-Democracy."[23]

However, while Lenin maintained the Marxian belief that the Communist party must be linked to the proletariat, he gave up the Marxian idea underlying this belief, that a proletariat and its party can mature only in a highly industrialized country. This link between party and class, a logical necessity in Marxian theory, became a non-essential element in Communist thought.

The basic break that has so obviously occurred somewhere in the long development of ideas from Marxism to neo-Maoism, came neither with Mao nor with Stalin. It came when Lenin began to adjust Marx's theory of socialist revolution to his desire to see and make such a revolution in industrially backward Russia. The fact that Lenin retained Marxian language—and no doubt sincerely believed that he retained

[20] *Ibid.,* p. 187.
[21] *Ibid.,* p. 188.
[22] V. I. Lenin, "Preliminary Draft of Theses on the National and Colonial Questions" (dated June 5, 1920), *Selected Works, op. cit.,* X, 236–237.
[23] V. I. Lenin, "The Two Tactics of Social Democracy in the Democratic Revolution," *ibid.,* III, 100.

its Marxian content—is here of no more significance* than the theories with which he justified his seizure of power. Today we can dismiss these theories of breaking the chain of imperialism at its weakest link and of a Russian revolution bringing about revolutions in the West which would ultimately save it. Not only were they based on a faulty analysis of the situation in the West, but they were really no more than tortuous rationalizations designed to show that the existence in one part of the world of Marx's prerequisites of a socialist revolution could justify such a revolution in another part of the world where the prerequisities were lacking.[24]

Lenin's impatient desire to skip one of Marx's inevitable stages of history inexorably led him back to ideas which Marx and Engels thought they had overcome in their "scientific" socialism. These are typical of socialist thought in times and countries where both industry and the labor movement are still quite backward and were held by such diverse thinkers as the Utopian Socialists, Blanqui and Bakunin. They all imply that the workers do not know their own long-run interests and are by themselves incapable of grasping them, that is, of becoming socialists, and of carrying through a socialist transformation of society. Only a minority of intellectuals can do these things, either in the workers' place, as with the Utopians, or on their behalf, as with Blanqui and Bakunin, or as their vanguard, as with Lenin.

The contrast between Marx and Lenin on this point becomes very clear by a comparison of Lenin's famous statement that the workers by their own efforts can only develop trade-union consciousness and that socialist consciousness has to be brought to them from without by intellectuals[25] with the following little known remarks reported to have been made by Marx in an interview with a German trade union official:

If the trade unions are to fulfill their functions, they must never be connected with or made dependent on a political organization. To do this is to give them a death-blow. The trade unions are the schools for socialism. In the trade unions, the workers are educated to become socialists, because

* [In a later article, I made clear that in another context Lenin's retention of Marxian language and commitment to Marxian concepts is of the greatest significance. See pp. 121–144 below.]

[24] See the excellent treatment of the transformation of Marxism at the hands of the Russians by John Plamenatz, *German Marxism and Russian Communism* (London: Longmans, Green & Co., 1954), pp. 238–240.

[25] Lenin, "What Is To Be Done?" (1902), *Selected Works, op. cit.,* II, 53.

there they have the struggle with capital before their eyes day after day. All political parties, whichever they may be, inspire the mass of workers only temporarily; the unions, however, tie the mass of the workers to themselves permanently, only they are able to represent a real labor party and to oppose the power of capital. The greater mass of the workers has attained the insight that their material situation must be improved, may they belong to any party they like. But if the material situation of the worker is improved, he can devote himself better to the education of his children, his wife and children need no longer go to the factory, he himself can better cultivate his mind and look after his body, he becomes a socialist without having an inkling of it."[26]

Marx believed that socialism would grow out of existing material conditions and that the working class itself would be the revolutionary agent introducing socialism at a time when both the economy and the proletariat itself would have reached the necessary maturity. At the root of Lenin's thought on the other hand, as at that of all the impatient pre-Marxian socialists from Babeuf to Bakunin, lay the notion that the realization of socialism was a matter not of historically conditioned prerequisites, but merely of insight, will, and, above all, of the conquest of political power. He thought of the Communist party, a "shock-troop" of intellectuals, rather than of Marx's "mass of the workers" as the "maker" of revolution and of a now no longer inevitable historical development. To Marx, the party had been the instrument of the proletariat; to Lenin, the proletariat became a tool of the party.

The Communists, since Lenin's day, have tried to conceal this significant shift by identifying their party with the proletariat and often, in effect, by referring to the party as the working class, by playing what Morris Watnick has called "the role of a proletariat by proxy."[27] They define the working class in terms of an ideology rather than of economic and social criteria, an approach which would have amazed Marx and which can also result, as John Plamenatz has noted in an incisive passage, in the formation of "proletarian" parties establishing or aiming to estab-

---

[26] Quoted from *Volksstaat* (Leipzig), 1869, No. 17, by Karl Kautsky, "Sekte oder Klassenpartei?," *Die Neue Zeit*, XXVII/2 (1909), 7. Cf. also this passage from the *Communist Manifesto*: "The Communists do not form a separate party opposed to other working class parties. They have no interests separate and apart from those of the proletariat as a whole. They do not set up any sectarian principles of their own, by which to shape and mould the proletarian movement." Karl Marx, *Selected Works, op. cit.*, I, 218.

[27] Morris Watnick, "Continuity and Innovation in Chinese Communism," *World Politics*, VI, No. 1 (October 1953), 94.

lish "proletarian" states in countries like Mongolia, where no proletariat exists.[28]

This ill-concealed switch in the roles of the proletariat and "its" party, initiated by Lenin, is crucial. Once it is accomplished, there is no longer any compelling theoretical reason why the party, which by definition always acts for the proletariat, regardless of whether the latter agrees or even exists, cannot use some other class in its quest for power. Lenin himself was already quite willing to use the peasantry in Russia and Mao relied on it practically exclusively as the mass basis for his party until finally his peasant troops conquered the cities to provide him with his proletarian base.[29]

Perhaps the ultimate point in this development was reached when first Mao and then all of international Communism accepted the capitalists, too, as proper tools of the party—a party which was once supposed to fight the proletarian class struggle against capital. Better than anything, this demonstrates how Communism, following Lenin's substitution of his party for Marx's proletariat, has developed a party composed of an élite of intellectuals representing no given social class but seeking a base for the realization of its ambitions in any class from which it can draw support.

Russia is too close to Western Europe and Lenin was too close to Marx for these implications to have become clear either to him or to most of his generation. The real meaning of the perversion he introduced into Marxism as a result of transplanting it to his backward native land has become fully clear only with its further transplantation to countries even less developed than early 20th-century Russia. In neo-Maoism, which seeks to appeal to nomadic herdsman and capitalist alike and which has brought the proletarian revolution to the jungles of Malaya and the plateaus of Tibet, Leninism has reached its fullest development; it has become more Leninist—and therefore less Marxist—than Lenin himself could ever be.

Of course, neo-Maoism, like Leninism, contains remnants of the Marxian vocabulary. Communism still has a hankering for "socialist" and "proletarian" language, although Marxian terms such as "proletariat" and "working class" are being replaced more and more by the "toiling people," the "people's masses," "all peace-loving people," struggling, not

---

[28] Plamenatz, *op. cit.*, pp. 237–238.
[29] See the highly relevant discussion by Benjamin I. Schwartz, *Chinese Communism and the Rise of Mao, op. cit.*, pp. 189–199, and "On the 'Originality' of Mao Tse-tung," *Foreign Affairs*, XXXIV, No. 1 (October 1955), 73–76.

for any class interests, but in the "national interest" for "national independence." Nevertheless the continued use of Marxian terminology, even if the original content has been drained from it, and the invocation of Marx and Engels, as well as Lenin and Mao, as the prophets of present-day Communism are by no means without significance, for they deceive both Communists and anti-Communists.

Thus, some Western anti-Communists still believe the half-truth that Communists appeal chiefly and most effectively to the poor and exploited. On the other hand, some anti-Communists in underdeveloped areas might be repelled by Communism merely because of what proletarian trappings it still maintains. Finally, some Communists, especially those not in the top leadership of their parties, themselves took these trappings so seriously that they were very reluctant to consider themselves the true representatives of all classes of the population and especially of the capitalists. This explains the repeated and widespread difficulties Communist parties had under the neo-Maoist strategy with what, in their language, is referred to as sectarianism.

It may now be time to abandon the categories of thought in which Lenin conceived of himself and his revolution and in which most of his contemporaries, both friends and foes, were almost necessarily entrapped. After our own experience with neo-Maoism, it now appears more clearly than ever that Lenin was not voicing the ideology of an industrial proletariat but was a spokesman of a part of the intelligentsia in an underdeveloped country, of a group in quest of political power and in search of a short-cut to industrialization. The Bolshevik revolution, then, is to be understood not as the first proletarian-socialist revolution but as the first successful seizure of power by such an intelligentsia.

From its very beginnings in Leninism, Communism has been a highly relevant doctrine for underdeveloped countries, but has been irrelevant for the advanced countries which have, by definition, already solved the problem of industrialization, the problem Communism proposes to solve in a manner so attractive to the intelligentsia. Here lies the secret of the relative success of the Communist appeal in underdeveloped areas and of its relative failure in the advanced countries.[30]

[30] Of all industrialized countries, only France and Italy have strong Communist parties. This is not the place to attempt an explanation of this phenomenon, but it is significant that industry is relatively backward in these countries, that Communism appeals strongly to their intellectuals, and that in the working class it appears as the heir not of Marxism but of its ancient enemy, anarcho-syndicalism.

Some writers have thought they discovered the ultimate proof of Marx's failure in the paradox that Marxism, an ideology of and for the industrialized West, first came to power in the backward East. The Communists, on the other hand, embarrassed by it, have sought to rationalize it away. In fact, this is no paradox at all, but merely an irrelevancy: What came to power was simply not Marxism but Leninism—which quite illegitimately but very successfully claimed the Marxian heritage by assuming the name "Marxism-Leninism"—and its legitimate successor, neo-Maoism.

4. From Proletarianism to Modernizing Movement*

Introductory Note. Several of the themes in the preceding article are fully elaborated in my next piece, here entitled "From Proletarianism to Modernizing Movement." This consists principally of the chapter on "Communism" in my "Essay in the Politics of Development." The object of this essay was not primarily to analyze Communism but to present in very brief form a set of interrelated generalizations about the impact of industrialization on politics. It was my first attempt to deal with the politics of development and to place the analysis of Communism into this broader framework.

Since I was concerned with the relationship of Communism to modernizing movements in general, I am here also reprinting some excerpts from the chapter on "Nationalism." These excerpts are included here only to place the discussion of Communism in its context. They are, by themselves, an inadequate treatment of the subject of "nationalism," but this is not the place to present a more complete analysis, which would, indeed, have to go far beyond what I attempted to do in my essay and would differ from it in some respects. I might merely note that I would now no longer use the term "nationalism" with reference to underdeveloped countries. I would substitute for it the concepts of anti-colonial and modernizing movements to stress even more than I did that these are quite different from the nationalist movements of Europe with respect to the aspects of politics that matter most to me— their composition in terms of groups and interests.

However, the main point I make in the excerpts reproduced here, that Communist and non-Communist modernizing movements tend to converge, still seems valid to me today and has, I believe, been borne out by developments since my essay was written in 1960 (some of which I note in subsequent writings reprinted below).[1]

* Reprinted from "An Essay in the Politics of Development," in John H. Kautsky, ed., *Political Change in Underdeveloped Countries: Nationalism and Communism* (New York: John Wiley and Sons, 1962), pp. 38–51, 53, 55–89.

[1] This point, and some others in my essay not relevant here, was thoughtfully criticized in an excellent review article by Richard Lowenthal, "Communism and

Nationalism as Anti-Colonialism

In the absence of a common language, culture, religion, or race, what is it that provides the focus for the unity among politically conscious elements from all strata of the population that is characteristic of nationalist movements in underdevloped countries? Speaking of underdeveloped countries in general, there would seem to be no positive factor at all, but rather the dislike of a common enemy, the colonial power. However, nationalist movements are not confined to territories that are or were until recently administered by foreign powers as colonies, like India and most of Africa. Quite similar movements have appeared in independent underdeveloped countries like Turkey, China, and Mexico and, more recently, Egypt, Iraq, and Cuba. Unless they are virtually inaccessible, underdeveloped countries almost by necessity stand economically in a colonial relationship to industrial countries, in which the former serve as suppliers of raw materials (often made available by cheap native labor) and sometimes as markets for the industries of the latter. Anti-colonialism, then, must here be understood as opposition not merely to colonialism narrowly defined but also to a colonial economic status.

It is opposition to colonialism so defined and to those natives who benefit from the colonial relationship that constitutes nationalism in underdeveloped countries.[2] As such, nationalism can unite not only people of quite different language and cultural background, but also people of all the major economic and social classes, even though it is directed against certain economic policies. The social tensions which modernization and industrialization produce everywhere and which in Europe were necessarily turned inward, resulting in conflicts dividing societies, are, in underdeveloped countries, largely turned outward. Instead of

---

Nationalism," *Problems of Communism*, XI, No. 6 (November–December 1962), 37–44. Subsequently, Lowenthal felt that later Communist policy was more in line with my predictions. See footnote 5 on p. 146.

[2] An impressive attempt to generalize about the nature of nationalism in Asia and Africa, providing both a wealth of data and much thoughtful interpretation, is Rupert Emerson, *From Empire to Nation* (Cambridge, Mass.: Harvard University Press, 1960). For excellent detailed studies of the bases of nationalism in two underdeveloped areas, see James S. Coleman, *Nigeria: Background to Nationalism* (Los Angeles and Berkeley: University of California Press, 1958) and some of the articles in Walter Z. Laqueur, ed., *The Middle East in Transition* (New York: Frederick A. Praeger, 1958).

blaming each other for the difficulties growing out of modernization, the various social strata all blame the colonial power, the result being, not internal conflict, but that internal unity of anti-colonialism which is the basis of nationalism in underdeveloped countries.

This may be illustrated in somewhat more detail by a quick survey of the effects of colonialism on the major social strata and of their attitudes toward nationalism. The peasants are the group in which the greatest number of those indifferent to nationalism may be found. This is so both because they form by far the largest of the social strata in underdevloped countries and because, in their isolation and ignorance, they tend to be indifferent to politics beyond the local level generally. To the peasant in an isolated village, depending neither on export to nor import from the outside world, it may make very little difference whether a foreigner or a native of the larger territory in which his village happens to be located occupies the government palace in the far-off capital. He may, indeed, not even know the difference or even that there is a government and a capital city.

However, such peasant communities unaffected by and indifferent to the outside world are no longer the rule in most underdeveloped countries. Colonialism itself has put an end to their isolation. Through the extension of its influence, the peasant has become integrated into a wider money economy—even in the absence of various kinds of forced labor or of any compulsion to pay taxes in cash rather than in kind. He would want to buy those products of foreign industry which are superior to his own. In order to get the money to pay for them, he has to export his agricultural goods, which he can do effectively only by concentrating on the production of a single product that he can produce most efficiently. This, in turn, makes him more dependent on imports for the other necessities of life, which he himself can no longer produce. The peasant now becomes subject to vast impersonal forces which he can neither understand nor control since they reach far beyond the primitive village community which bounded his horizon for generations. This situation inevitably gives rise to intense frustrations. The peasant comes in contact with the outside world through middle-men and money-lenders some of whom may become "big" peasants appropriating the land of their indebted fellows. In any case, they, or tribal or village chiefs who (under colonial laws) appropriate communally owned land as their private property, can easily exploit the peasant in his weak economic and political condition. Clearly, much of the peasants' consequent frustration and resentment is, or can easily be, directed against the colonial power and its representatives who brought the change from the familiar and, in that sense, secure life of the village to the incomprehensible and insecure life as a small part of a wider economy. Thus while the peasants themselves, because of their apolitical way of life, are very unlikely to initiate any nationalist movement, they can become an important mass base for such a movement led by others, notably by intellectuals.

A second old, i.e., pre-industrial, class is that of the tradesmen and craftsmen of the towns. Wherever industry advances or even where its products become available, this old middle class is threatened. The small shopkeepers cannot successfully meet the competition of large commercial organizations nor the craftsmen that of cheaper and often better mass-produced goods. As they face the end of their way of life and the loss of the relatively high status they enjoyed in the old society, being doomed to descend into the lower classes by forces they can hate but not stop, they are, as a group, likely to become embittered and even desperate. This political mood was one of the important elements contributing to the rise of Fascism in Central Europe in the interwar period and it continues to play a significant role in the politics of some Western countries, especially in France, where its most striking recent manifestation was that of Poujadism.

What led to deep divisions and conflicts in the now more advanced industrialized countries, has, in the underdeveloped countries, contributed to nationalist unity, for the modernization which ultimately dooms the old middle class is brought by colonialism; the large commercial and industrial enterprises which threaten it are usually owned by citizens of the colonial power. The decline of the old middle class, then, which is a general phenomenon accompanying industrialization, feeds anti-colonialist nationalism in the underdeveloped countries.

The third of the old classes, the aristocracy, is also ultimately doomed in its old way of life by advancing industrialization and modernization. Colonial governments have frequently found it less convenient to uproot aristocrats and replace them with their own administrators, than to govern the natives through them. Under such arrangements of "indirect rule," some form of which is almost inevitable (especially at the local level), and which have been the way most past empires were formed and administered, the colonial power clearly benefits. However, it must, in turn, protect the aristocracy, and the old order in which its power is rooted, from the native forces desiring modernization (to be discussed shortly), who are themselves a product of colonialism.

Colonialism is thus not only a modernizing influence, but also a conservative force. In some instances, where the modernizing forces among the natives have become strong enough, it may in the end be only the colonial government that maintains the old aristocracy in power. Thus, the princely governments in India could not outlast British rule by more than a few months. Nor does this type of relationship prevail under formal colonial administration alone. In independent underdeveloped countries, too, the aristocracy's position is protected by economic colonialism, as is negatively illustrated by the fate of the large landowners in the Mexican and Cuban revolutions. It is clear that an aristocracy, whose privileged status depends on the continuance of colonialism, cannot be expected to join the anti-colonialist movement. The claim of nationalism to represent the interests of "the" people must therefore be rejected and it must be recognized that some of the most powerful native forces in underdeveloped societies—the aristocracy and the frequently still numerous people whom it can influence—may, in effect, be allies of colonialism and enemies of nationalism.

However, while the conservative side of colonialism preserves the aristocracy, its modernizing aspects threaten its power. Many a formerly absolute ruler now has to accept the "advice" of a colonial official and many a native landowner has had to give up his land to settlers from the colonial power. More generally and more importantly, modernization undermines the traditional society on which the power of the aristocracy rests. The aristocracy and its allies, particularly among the religious officials—the priests and holy men, the monks, mullahs, and medicine men—have almost everywhere fought a rear guard action against modern Western dress and customs, against the type of education and the outlook on life characteristic of industrial societies—just as they did in Europe for some centuries. Those who adopt the perspectives of an industrialized society, which means, above all, those who become familiar with the notion of economic and social change, unheard of in static agrarian societies, are not likely to accept unquestioningly, as generations before them did, the status of an aristocracy based merely on age-old tradition. Yet these perspectives so threatening to the aristocracy are brought to the underdeveloped countries by colonialism (the more so, by and large, the more industrially advanced the colonial power). No wonder that among the aristocracy, too, there may be important forces who join the ranks of the nationalist movement and who, in fact, often lead its traditionalist wing.

The new social groups, which are a product of the growth of commerce and industry, and of the advancement of communications and education that accompany it, in this sense owe their very existence to colonialism. It does not by any means follow, however, that they are more favorably disposed toward it than the older groups from which they were recruited. Thus the industrial workers, like labor everywhere in the early stages of industrialization, form a group with many grievances. The shift to a money, and often a one-crop, economy forced many peasants to go to work in the plantations and mines, and in the factories of the growing cities. At present, these workers are frequently less than a generation removed from their ancestral villages and tribes, where life, although—or because—extremely limited materially and intellectually, provided a high degree of security for the individual. Suddenly torn from the bonds of such a small, highly integrated society and thrown into the anonymity of life in an industrial plant and an urban slum, where not only the physical surroundings, but also many values and behavior patterns, are utterly alien, the worker is bound to be subject to maladjustments, tensions, and frustrations of various kinds.[3]

Furthermore, since the worker is as yet largely defenseless politically and economically, his working and living conditions are likely to be poor, his wages low and hours long, and his wife and children may be compelled to work. The owners of the enterprise and their representatives, whom the worker blames and possibly hates for this situation, are likely to be corporations and citizens of the colonial power. The conflict between labor and capital, then, which in Europe gave rise to radical movements of the left, like anarchism, syndicalism and early socialism, and thus became a prime source of domestic division in the age of industrialization, in underdeveloped countries furnishes more recruits and an important mass base for anti-colonialist nationalism.

Unlike the peasants, who, because of their physical isolation, narrow intellectual horizon, and conservatism, can often be reached and persuaded only with some difficulty by urban intellectuals in search of a mass following, the workers in the cities are relatively easily accessible and organizable and, having been torn from their familiar environment, receptive to ideas advocating radical change. It is therefore

[3] On some effects of urbanization, see Lucy P. Mair, "Social Change in Africa," *International Affairs,* XXXVI, No. 4 (October 1960), 447–456.

not surprising that trade unions, such as they are in underdeveloped countries, have everywhere, under intellectual leadership, tended to become adjuncts of the nationalist movement.[4] This may also be one—though only one—reason for the frequent vague identification of nationalism in underdeveloped countries with "socialism," a term which has by now lost virtually all specific meaning, but retains plenty of emotional overtones.

If labor is anti-colonialist, one might expect the opposite of the native capitalists in commerce and banking, who developed from the old traders and money lenders, and also of the few native industrial capitalists who may have emerged. Undoubtedly, many of them are so closely tied to the colonial economy through their business relations that they favor its continuation. They may therefore become anti-nationalists like some of the aristocracy, to which they may also have social and economic ties. On the other hand, the native capitalists may also suffer from, and hence resent, competition from banking, commercial, and industrial establishments owned by citizens of the "mother" country and located either there or in the colony. They may well feel that the removal of colonialism would enhance their opportunities to expand their own businesses and deal more successfully with their foreign competitors or, indeed, get rid of them altogether. Thus the native capitalists, a group of no great size in any underdeveloped country but of growing political importance in some of them, may also join the nationalist movement for reasons of their own.

The Role of the Intellectuals

The third of the new groups produced by modernization are the intellectuals. The peculiar importance of this group in the nationalist movements of underdeveloped countries requires that somewhat more space be devoted to it than to the others. For our purposes, we do not include among the intellectuals the scholars trained along traditional, usually religious (such as Islamic or Confucian) lines in the old society, but, on the other hand, our definition is a much broader one than that usually applied in advanced countries. Like the latter, it embraces persons with advanced standing in the humanities, sciences, and social sciences. How-

[4] See George E. Lichtblau, "The Politics of Trade Union Leadership in Southern Asia," in Kautsky, ed., *Political Change in Underdeveloped Countries*, pp. 265–281, and the same author's *The Politics of African Trade Unionism* (New York: Frederick A. Praeger, 1967).

ever, it also includes all those natives in underdeveloped countries, most likely to be found among the aristocracy and the businessmen, who have, through the contacts afforded by colonialism become aware of the world beyond their own culture area, and have obtained an advanced education appropriate to an industrial country, or who are at present students obtaining such an education.

In some underdeveloped countries, especially those where such an education qualified a native to serve in the administrative service of his government, whether independent, as in Latin America, or colonial, as in India, significant numbers of natives have, for some decades, studied in industrialized countries in Western Europe, and increasingly in the United States and the Soviet Union, and in institutions of higher learning conducted according to European-American standards in their own countries. In other underdeveloped countries, only a handful of natives have been involved. Thus, there were said to be only 16 native college graduates in the entire population of about 13 million in the Belgian Congo when it became independent in 1960.

For our purposes of generalization, an image of the intellectuals will be conveyed which is, no doubt, often far too monolithic. For the study of any particular country or situation, it is subject to revision and refinement. Thus, one might have to draw distinctions and even note conflicts between intellectuals educated at home and those who studied abroad, between civilian and military intellectuals, and between the successive generations of nationalist intellectuals.[5]

The key role of the intellectuals in the politics of underdeveloped countries is largely due to their paradoxical position of being a product of modernization before modernization has reached or become widespread in their own country.[6] In the universities, the intellectuals

---

[5] For a more complete discussion of the definition of intellectuals in underdeveloped countries, as well as some of the distinctions among intellectuals, see Edward Shils, "The Intellectuals in the Political Development of the New States," in Kautsky, ed., *op. cit.* pp. 195–234, and Harry J. Benda, "Non-Western Intelligentsias as Political Elites," *ibid.*, pp. 235–251. See also Edward A. Shils, "The Intellectuals, Public Opinion, and Economic Development," *Economic Development and Cultural Change,* VI, No. 1 (October 1957), 55–62.

[6] The leading role of the intellectuals is excellently stressed in Hugh Seton-Watson, "Twentieth Century Revolutions," *The Political Quarterly*, XXII, No. 3 (July–September 1951), 251–265, an article all the more valuable for relating, as we shall try to do, developments in Russia and Southeastern Europe to those in the present underdeveloped countries. See also the same author's *Neither War Nor Peace* (New York: Frederick A. Praeger, 1960).

absorb the professional knowledge and skills needed by an industrial civilization; they become students of the humanities and social sciences qualified to teach in universities, and they become lawyers and doctors, administrators and journalists, and increasingly also scientists and engineers. When they return from the universities, whether abroad or not, the intellectuals find, all too often for their taste, that in their old societies their newly acquired skills and knowledge are out of place. Not only is there as yet little need—though it is often rapidly growing—for engineers and scientists where there is little industry, but professors will find few advanced students and lawyers will find few clients in a society still operating largely through simple face-to-face contacts. Although there is plenty of sickness, most patients might prefer the traditional herb-doctor or medicine man to the trained physician and, in any case, could not pay him. Few administrators are needed where the sphere of government activity is still very limited and fewer still where all higher posts are occupied by representatives of a colonial power. Where the bulk of the population is illiterate journalists are confined to writing for their few fellow intellectuals. As a result, intellectuals in underdeveloped countries are frequently unemployed or underemployed, especially since, for all their "industrial" education, they are likely to have retained the aristocratic attitude that manual labor is demeaning and hence will refuse to do other than intellectual work.

During their studies, the intellectuals are likely to acquire more than new knowledge. They also absorb the values of an industrial civilization, above all the notion that continuing material improvement of the life of the mass of the population through continuing technological progress and popular participation in government is both possible and desirable, and they become admirers of the political systems and ideologies embodying these values, whether they be American liberalism, Western European democratic socialism or Soviet Communism. On their return, they discover that these values, too, are inappropriate to the old society. Continuous and cumulative technological progress, which is so typical of an industrial system, is absent from purely agrarian economies. Until industrialization (and changes in agricultural techniques resulting from industrialization) are introduced, a belief in any substantial improvement in the standard of living of the mass of the population is, in fact, unrealistic. At the same time, advocacy, based on such a belief, of ideals of democracy, equality, and social justice, which arose out of an industrial environment, is subversive to the existing order of government by the native aristocracy and the foreign colonial power and is therefore not likely to endear the intellectuals to these powerful forces.

To the extent, then, that a native intellectual has substituted for the values of his traditional society those of an industrial one—a process which need by no means be complete in each case—he becomes an alien, a displaced person, in his own society. What could be more natural for him than to want to change that society to accord with his new needs and values, in short, to industrialize and modernize it? A number of motivations intermingle to produce the intellectuals' drive for rapid modernization. Most obviously, there is their desire for gainful and satisfying employment, for an opportunity to use the knowledge and to practice the skills they have acquired. But beyond this relatively narrow motive, there may be the more or less clear realization that only through industrialization can an eventual end be put to the poverty prevalent in underdeveloped countries, that only rapid industrialization can solve the problem posed by increasing populations, and that only industrialization can produce the "better" society at home which the intellectuals have come to admire abroad.

The peasant's typical response to overpopulation and his consequent hunger for land (if he is sufficiently politically conscious and organizable to respond effectively at all) is the demand for land reform. The intellectuals stimulate and support that demand, for one thing, because it is in accord with their new ideas of justice and equality. These ideas also make it desirable for them to become the leaders of a mass movement, of "the people." Since most of the people are peasants, they are inclined to seek peasant support, and advocacy of land reform is the most obvious way of mobilizing such support. Intellectuals may favor land reform also because a higher standard of living for the peasantry would create a better market for, and thus further the growth of, native industry. Finally, they press for land reform not because of anything it will do *for* the peasants, but because of what it will do *to* the aristocracy. The latter is the intellectuals' only powerful domestic enemy, and land reform strikes at the very root of its economic and social position.

However, where overpopulation is greatest, as in China, redistribution of land by itself is no longer an adequate solution to the problem, because there is simply not enough arable land to go around. Thus there is underemployment among the peasantry, which in turn tends to depress the wages of labor in the cities. Sooner or later only industrialization can satisfy the "rising expectations" in underdeveloped countries which are first and foremost, the expectations of the intellectuals, though they have spread them to the poorer strata accessible to them in the rural and especially in the urban areas. Only through industrialization can the intellectuals hope to realize their various dreams of democracy, equality, and social justice, of liberalism, socialism, or Communism in their own countries.

As the only ones in their societies who can even visualize a new, and, to them, a better order, the intellectuals naturally think of themselves as the leaders of the future society and of the transition to it. Thus a more narrowly political motivation is added to the others underlying their desire for modernization. Modernization serves to undermine and ultimately do away with the leadership of the old aristocratic ruling strata, and replace it with that of the intellectuals. Similarly, industrialization is the only road to the economic independence and military strength that can eventually provide freedom from colonial domination for their "country," that is, their government, which means more power for its new leaders, the intellectuals. Their anti-colonial nationalism thus makes the intellectuals desire industrialization.

It is equally true, however, that it is their desire to industrialize that makes the intellectuals nationalists. They see colonialism as opposed to industrialization, in part because the colonial power does not want industries in the colony to compete with its own industries for the colonial supply of raw materials or for the colonial market, and more generally because, as we have seen, modernization in the colony constitutes a threat to colonialism. Hence colonialism is regarded as an obstacle in the intellectuals' path to modernization as well as in their path to power. This helps explain the apparent paradox of intellectuals in underdeveloped countries who were trained in the West and came to admire it and yet turn against the West in their policies. They do so exactly because they admire it and at the same time see the West as denying them, through colonialism, the opportunity to make their own country more like the West.[7] To the intellectuals in underdeveloped countries nationalism and modernization have become inextricably intertwined as means and ends. Each has become an essential aspect of the other.

---

[7] The intellectuals' ambiguous attitudes are well discussed and documented in Mary Matossian, "Ideologies of Delayed Industrialization: Some Tensions and Ambiguities," in Kautsky, ed., *op. cit.*, pp. 252–264. The ambivalence of the nationalist intellectuals toward the West is also noted by Rupert Emerson, "Paradoxes of Asian Nationalism," *The Far Eastern Quarterly*, XIII, No. 2 (February 1954), 131–142.

In Western Europe, during the process of industrialization, the intellectuals played an important role in developing the ideology of liberalism, but industrialization itself was accomplished by industrial capitalists. In underdevleoped countries, the intcllcctuals, in effect, play the roles of both groups. A native class of industrial capitalists is virtually or completely absent, and sufficient wealth for the development of industry is not available in private hands—or, if available in the hands of aristocrats, is, for cultural and ideological reasons, not likely to be invested in industry. Under these circumstances, the government appears to be the only possible major domestic source of capital, and the intellectuals—if they want to industrialize their country—must wrest control of it from the native aristocracy and the colonial administrators who oppose industrialization. This need to control their government in order to industrialize provides another reason both for the intellectuals' anticolonialist nationalism and for the appeal of various "socialist" ideas, whether Communist or not, to them. Thus, Nehru and U Nu, Nhrumah and Touré, Castro and many other nationalist intellectuals regard themselves as "socialists."

That intellectuals should almost invariably emerge as the leaders of the heterogeneous nationalist movements in underdeveloped countries is not difficult to explain. As long as modernization has not set in to any large extent, what native intellectuals there are, are likely to be not merely the leaders of the nationalist movement, but to be *the* movement. Even as, with progressing modernization, members of other strata, for reasons indicated for each of them earlier, join the movement, the intellectuals remain dominant. The peasants, the old traders and artisans, and the industrial workers who become nationalists are too poor and downtrodden, too ignorant and limited intellectually and too used to accepting leadership from above to challenge the intellectuals, though occasionally a few of them may rise into the ranks of the intellectuals themselves. Generally, their nationalism is more likely to be caused by negative resentment induced by their particular grievances than by a positive vision of a new society. The old aristocrats, insofar as they become nationalists at all, are, in a rigidly stratified society, often prevented from leading a mass movement by virtue of their own upper class position. The same may be true of what new businessmen there are, but they are also often handicapped by lack of prestige in societies where money-making does not provide high status.

The intellectuals assume the leadership of nationalist movements, because, unlike the other groups, they have broken out of the rigid class lines of the old society, they have a vision of the future and some ideas, however vague or impractical, of how to attain it, and they are, almost by definition, skilled in the use of the written and spoken word. Furthermore, the intellectuals have the simple advantage over members of other groups of having free time on their hands. Unemployed or underemployed and yet often receiving enough support from their wealthy families to be able to live, they have time to devote to politics, to speaking, reading, writing, to agitating and organizing, and time to spend in jail or in exile and, often soon thereafter, in the government.

Since colonialism serves, at one and the same time, a modernizing and a conservative function in the underdeveloped countries[8] and since nationalism in these countries consists of anti-colonialism, it follows that the nationalist movement unites both those who oppose colonialism because they feel that it introduces modernization too rapidly and those who oppose it because in their view it delays and obstructs modernization. Nationalism encompasses both those who want to retain or regain the old order—some of the aristocracy and religious officials and their followers among the peasants and the old middle strata—and those who want to replace that old order as rapidly as possible with a modern industrial one—the native industrialists, if any, the incipient labor movement and, above all, the intellectuals.

However, while the nationalist movement is composed of different groups looking, broadly speaking, in two different directions—backward to the old society and forward to a new one—the power relationship among these various groups does not remain constant. Those who desire modernization are likely to gain strength and gradually to eclipse those who dream of a return to the tribal or highly stratified society of agrarianism. It is the peculiar form of nationalism, which looks at steel mills both as symbols of anti-colonialism and as its instruments, that is becoming characteristic of nationalism in underdeveloped countries. This is so not only because the intellectuals are the leaders of the entire nationalist movement, but above all because modernization itself, as it progresses, strengthens them and their supporters among the native

[8] On the effects of nationalism, both before and after the attainment of independence, of this dual character of colonialism, see S. N. Eisenstadt, "Sociological Aspects of Political Development in Underdeveloped Countries," *Economic Development and Cultural Change,* V, No. 4 (July 1957), 289–307.

industrialists and the labor movement, while weakening the hold of the old aristocracy on the society and disintegrating the peasantry and old middle strata.

As a result, the nationalism of underdeveloped areas has more and more become identical with the nationalism of their intellectuals. It may now be defined as the drive of intellectuals for industrialization, industrialization that has to be as rapid as possible and as independent as possible of aid from the former colonial powers. It must be rapid, since the needs of the intellectuals and the needs of their countries, as the intellectuals see them, are felt to be pressing, and it must be independent of aid from the colonial powers, since its motivation is, after all, nationalist, that is, anti-colonialist.

Pre-Revolutionary Russia as an Underdeveloped Country

If the dominant form of present-day nationalism in underdeveloped countries can be defined as the drive of a relatively thin stratum of intellectuals, who absorbed the skills and values of advanced countries, toward rapid modernization in opposition to the aristocracy and independently of the colonial industrial powers, then the Russian Revolution may be viewed as one of the most important manifestations, and certainly the most successful one, of this form of nationalism.[9] This is not to insist that the Russian Revolution can only be understood as a nationalist movement. It can, perhaps with equal validity, also be seen as a proletarian movement, a peasant movement, an atheistic movement, a messianic movement, or an internationalist movement. We merely suggest that an attempt to demonstrate what the nationalist movements in underdeveloped countries have in common with the Russian Revolu-

[9] This important but widely ignored point, to be developed in this essay, was made very briefly some time ago by Hugh Seton-Watson. "Communism, as developed by Stalin and Mao Tse-tung, is only the most important example of a wider phenomenon, the revolt of the backward peoples, led by a section of their intelligentsia, against the West," "Twentieth Century Revolutions," *The Political Quarterly*, XXII, No. 3 (July–September 1951), 259. See also Hugh Seton-Watson, *From Lenin to Khrushchev: The History of World Communism* (New York: Frederick A. Praeger, 1960), p. 340. Theodor H. von Laue, "Die Revolution von aussen als erste Phase der russischen Revolution 1917," *Jahrbücher für Geschichte Osteuropas* (Munich), IV, No. 2 (1956), 138–158, also places the Russian Revolution in one category with the revolutions in backward countries. This theme is greatly elaborated in the first five chapters of the same author's *Why Lenin? Why Stalin?* (Philadelphia: J. B. Lippincott Co., 1964).

tion may also yield significant hypotheses and may provide some interesting insights into the role and characteristics of both nationalism and Communism, and the relation between the two.

It is only for this purpose that the interpretation of the Russian Revolution and of Communism presented here is offered.[10] It is developed with the advantage of hindsight, and, to the extent that factors important also in present-day nationalism are elaborated and other factors are de-emphasized, some of the present is even read into the past. If the present did, indeed, exist in the past, this approach is quite justified. Perhaps, in any case, it is almost unavoidable for any interpreter of past events, and it permits him to go beyond the insights of earlier generations. The fact that it was the purpose of some of the participants in the Russian Revolution to introduce proletarian socialism is an important datum for the historian, but the Revolution need not be interpreted solely in this light. It may be equally valid to view it differently in the light of subsequent events, including its own effects. The revolutionaries of 1917 could hardly share our image of the Russian Revolution as a nationalist movement, and we are not implying that they were, consciously or unconsciously, motivated by the same anti-colonialist bias found among the nationalists in underdeveloped countries today. We merely point out that the actual results of the Russian Revolution were, in many respects, similar to those accomplished and particularly to those desired by nationalists in such countries today. This is especially true of Stalin's "second revolution" of 1927 with its drive for rapid industrialization and its anti-Western overtones.[11]

[10] See G. F. Achminow, *Die Macht im Hintergrund. Totengräber des Kommunismus* (Grenchen/Ulm: Spaten-Verlag, 1950). Along with points of dubious validity, Achminow's analysis of the Russian Revolution, pp. 48–123, contains some important insights. Their relevance to the present chapter may be gathered from two quotations: "The positive goal of modern Communism is not to remove social conflicts or to create a classless society but to overcome the backwardness of the country in question. Communism assumes in the history of some nations the role fulfilled in the advanced countries by early capitalism." (*Ibid.*, pp. 56–57). ". . . this program [of industrialization] opens up almost infinite opportunities for advancement to hundreds of thousands of new people who must administer the factories, enterprises, power stations and everything that goes with them. . . . Not the workers but the propertyless intelligentsia, the future general managers, directors, etc., constitute the social force that—under certain conditions, of course—is induced by its position to profess Communism, to support it and to pave the way for it." *Ibid.*, p. 89.
[11] Achminow, *ibid.*, pp. 122–123, states; "The Soviet system as we know it today crystallized, not during the revolution of 1917, but during the Stalinist 'revolution from above' that was carried out in the period from 1927 to 1933. . . . The

The broad generalizations we have so far made about politics in under-developed countries* do by and large apply to early twentieth century Russia, simply because Russia was then an underdeveloped country. In Russia then as in underdeveloped countries now, the bulk of the population consisted of peasants, poor, ignorant, illiterate, living in the isolation of their village communities, hence unorganizable and without any active role in national politics. In Russia, as in other underdeveloped countries, the people whose interests were taken care of in national politics were the aristocracy, represented by the Tsar and his court, the Orthodox Church, the military, and the bureaucracy. As in other underdeveloped countries, too, there had been for centuries a high de-gree of instability of personnel at the top of the government, as court intrigues, coups d'état, and assassinations followed one another, masking a high degree of stability in the interests served by the government.

As in other underdeveloped countries, modernization, resulting from contact with Western Europe, brought significant changes to the setting of politics in Russia. As elsewhere, it brought dislocations and discontent to the peasants' villages. Industrialization produced no large class of native capitalists, for the new industry was owned largely by Western capital. It did produce an industrial labor movement, which, as in other underdeveloped countries, was small in relation to the total population and subject to the influence and leadership of intellectuals. However, industry was concentrated in a few localities and was highly advanced for its day, having been organized on a large scale and employing great numbers of manual workers. The labor movement was therefore quite well organized and had a high degree of political consciousness. In view of their poor working conditions and the hostility of Tsarist auto-cracy, the workers could easily turn revolutionary. The existence of a class-conscious, revolutionary labor movement had some crucial effects in the realm of ideology, for it permitted Russian intellectuals to adopt the proletarian doctrines of Marxism, which had little appeal in other underdeveloped countries until they had been transmuted into Leninism.

Communists of today desire not the Communism of which Marx once dreamt but the one that Stalin made. . . . The Stalinist 'revolution from above' was the revolution of the 'future general managers,' for they profited the most from it. . . ."

* [See also Chapter I of my "Essay in the Politics of Development" not reprinted here. The generalizations offered there are much more fully developed in my forthcoming book on *The Politics of Traditional Societies* (New York: John Wiley and Sons).]

Finally and most importantly, the key group in the nationalist movements in underdeveloped countries, the intellectuals, had the key role
in the Russian Revolution, too.[12] Even more than in other underdeveloped countries, because of Russia's long history of cultural contact with
the West and perhaps because Russians were "European" in race,
language, and religion, some of the wealthier families in Russia had
given their sons a Western education—either in the West or in Russia—
long before industrialization arrived there. The results were the same
as in other underdeveloped countries. The intellectuals absorbed values
and ideologies, which had grown out of an industrialized environment
in the West, such as various types of liberalism and socialism, that made
them feel like aliens in their own country. The presence of significant
numbers of Jewish intellectuals further contributed to this situation.
They felt doubly alien in Russia, not only as intellectuals with Western
values, but also as Jews with their distinct culture, subject to discrimina-
tion and ghetto-segregation.

To bring Russia into accord with their ideals, the intellectuals had to
favor modernization and democratization, which, under Tsarism, meant
that they had to be revolutionary. Since Tsarism appeared as the main
obstacle to the realization of the intellectuals' goals (and also because
of Russia's status as a Great Power in world affairs), the revolution
was chiefly anti-aristocratic rather than anti-colonial and anti-foreign
in character. It has therefore not commonly been referred to as a nationalist movement.* Yet its carriers, the intellectuals, were the same
as those of anti-colonial nationalism and so was one of their enemies,
the native aristocracy. Also, a significant number of the Russian intellectuals harbored the ambivalent feelings of love and hatred for the West
which we found characterizing much of the intelligentsia in present-day
underdeveloped countries; they were anti-Western to be free to become
more like the West. The Marxists among them, in particular, combined

[12] See the excellent collection of essays by Richard Pipes, ed., *The Russian Intelligentsia* (New York: Columbia University Press, 1961). In one of these, particularly
relevant to our discussion, "The Intelligentsia in Communist China: A Tentative
Comparison," Benjamin Schwartz concludes that "the phenomenon of the intelligentsia is a universal concomitant of the confrontation of a 'traditional' society
with the modern West." *Ibid.*, p. 176. He also emphasizes "certain overriding
differences," between the Russian and the Chinese intelligentsia, however, particularly the disassociation from nationalistic aspirations" of the former until the
rise of Stalin. *Ibid.*, p. 177.
* [The term "modernizing movement" is better suited than "nationalist movement"
to stress what Communism and anti-colonialism have in common.]

love of Western industrialization with hatred of Western capitalism,[13] and even now the Communists are anti-American in order "to catch up with and overtake America."[14]

Finally, the Russian intellectuals—or at least those who were ultimately to succeed in the Revolution—shared their chief goal of rapid industrialization with the intellectuals in underdeveloped countries today. Lenin indicated this when he defined Communism as "soviet power plus electrification," but the goal was to be achieved only under Stalin in his "second revolution," beginning in 1927. Like intellectuals in other underdeveloped countries, Stalin envisaged industrialization as the principal method of ensuring independence from the West.[15] It is therefore no coincidence that it was mainly under him that Communism assumed its nationalist form when he, in effect, substituted the power and security of the Soviet Union for world revolution as the goal of Communism.* As in other underdeveloped countries, industrialization and nationalism went hand in hand. Industrialization was to enhance the power of the state, and the state had to be powerful to speed industrialization.[16]

[13] Adam B. Ulam, in his stimulating essay, *The Unfinished Revolution* (New York: Random House, 1960), and in an earlier article, "The Historical Role of Marxism and the Soviet System," *World Politics*, VIII, No. 1 (October 1955), 20–45, argues that the appeal of Marxism in Russia and in all countries going through the early stages of industrialization stems from "its ability to combine anarchism—the most violent protest against industrialism—with an intense cult of technology and a conviction of the historical necessity and blessings of industrialism." *Ibid.*, p. 29.

[14] Three decades ago, Stalin expressed this anti-Western Westernism when he said, addressing a conference of Soviet industrial managers in 1931: "We are fifty or a hundred years behind the advanced countries. We must make good this distance in ten years. Either we do it, or they crush us." J. Stalin, "The Tasks of Business Executives," *Problems of Leninism* (Moscow: Foreign Languages Publishing House, 1945), p. 356.

[15] Cf. Stalin's statement made at the Fourteenth Party Congress in 1925: "The conversion of our country from an agrarian into an industrial country able to produce the machinery it needs by its own efforts—that is the essence, the basis of our general line," and his own subsequent comment on this statement, showing the anti-Western rationale behind it: "The industrialization of the country would ensure its economic independence, strengthen its power of defense and create the conditions for the victory of Socialism in the U.S.S.R." *History of the Communist Party of the Soviet Union (Bolsheviks). Short Course* (New York: International Publishers, 1939), p. 276.

* That the world revolution continues to serve as a myth and, in this sense, a goal for Communism is explained on pp. 121–144 below.

[16] The nationalist character of the other three Communist revolutions is much clearer: In China, Yugoslavia, and Vietnam, the Communists appeared, above

Marxism, Leninism, and the Russian Revolution as a Nationalist Movement

One of the ideologies produced by Western industrialism that appealed to Russian intellectuals was Marxism. It taught that every social system grows out of the conditions created by the preceding system, that it therefore cannot appear until these conditions are "ripe," but must inevitably appear when that point is reached. Specifically, socialism is said to grow out of the large-scale industry created by capitalism and to be brought about by the industrial proletariat which, as a class encompassing the great majority of the population, is itself a product of

---

all, as nationalists fighting a foreign enemy. As to the nationalist character of Communism in Eastern Europe, see the fascinating study by R. V. Burks, *The Dynamics of Communism in Eastern Europe* (Princeton, N.J.: Princeton University Press, 1961), which distinguishes between three types of Communist parties. The first two, based on Gabriel A. Almond, *The Appeals of Communism* (Princeton, N.J.: Princeton University Press, 1954), are the sectarian or deviational parties, found in the most advanced Western industrial countries, and the mass proletarian parties, found in France and Italy. "The third type of party, the national and anti-Western, flourishes in countries which are poor and backward. Such a party is comprised mainly of professional people, formally trained or self-taught, with some large element of Western education or influence. It is so comprised because the intelligentsia is the conductor through which Western influences penetrate non-Western cultures and because this party, to win and hold power, must provide a ruling class capable of governing in the conditions of that rapid industrialization and cultural metamorphosis which we call Westernization. Such a party is a national party because its basic aim is national power through the development of modern industry." (Burks, *op. cit.*, p. 186). Burks concludes from his study of eight Eastern European Communist movements, based heavily on interviews and quantitative data, that these movements on the whole "fit the deviant and proletarian types less well than they do the national." *Ibid.*, p. 187. He notes that ". . . . in the East European area as a whole it was the more backward provinces . . . which in general developed the stronger Communist movements. . . . This . . . we inferred to be the result of the contrast between conditions in Eastern Europe and those prevailing in the most industrial nations of the West. This contrast achieved its social imprint through students and teachers who had received a Western education, either in schools of the area or abroad, and who found themselves overtrained and perhaps even unemployable in their native environment. From this situation followed the decisive role of what the Russians would call the intelligentsia, the lawyers, teachers, doctors, and other professionals who provided three-fourths of the Communist leadership." *Ibid.*, p. 191. Burks also connects this situation ". . . with the marked tendency of East European Communist parties to industrialize their respective countries under forced draft and to modernize their agriculture; to create, so to speak, a society in which overtrained surplus professionals can find appropriate employment." *Ibid.*, p. 192.

capitalism. The socialist revolution, accordingly, presupposes a highly industrialized society, and Marx consequently expected that revolution to break out in the West.

Some intellectuals in Russia, as elsewhere, were attracted by Marx's attempt to develop a science of society and of history and by the Marxist claim to be able to predict, on this basis, mankind's inevitable evolution. To adhere to Marxist teachings and to relate them to the Russian environment, they had to predict that the revolution which would overthrow Tsarism would be "bourgeois" rather than "proletarian" in character, advancing the growth of capitalism and of the proletariat and, in the political arena, of democracy, thus laying the groundwork for the eventual emergence of the next historical stage, that of socialism. In the area of organization and tactics, the Mensheviks therefore advocated the creation of a mass labor party, on the model of the German Social Democratic Party, to support the bourgeois-capitalist revolution and at the same time seek to advance labor's interests, which were held to lead inevitably to socialism. Although the existence of a relatively strong revolutionary labor movement in Russia lent some substance to the Mensheviks' theory and strategy, they put too much faith in the leading revolutionary role of the bourgeoisie, a class which in fact was not a very powerful independent factor in Russia. When the Revolution did break out in 1917, its leadership was drawn from among the intellectuals, as it is in most modern revolutions, but it also represented merely that group, not the capitalists. The mass following came from the only possible source of a mass following in underdeveloped countries, the peasantry, including soldiers, who were peasants in uniform—though workers, too, played a significant role. The Mensheviks proved ineffective as Western-influenced intellectuals in an underdeveloped country must be if they are faithful to a theory that grew on a foreign soil and is irrelevant to their own environment.

Not all Western-trained intellectuals in underdeveloped countries follow this path. The Sukarnos, Nkrumahs, and Castros, too, made their revolutions inspired by ideals that developed in industrialized countries, but finding them irrelevant in their own countries, rather quickly adapted their tactics and the governments they established—though generally not their professed ideologies—to conditions prevailing there. In short, the intellectuals who absorb ideologies from industrialized countries generally fall into two categories, with the difference between them probably explicable by differences in personality. Some insist on adhering to the unadulterated, and hence irrelevant, ideology at the expense of gaining power. The others seek power at the expense of the pure ideology. And typically, each accuses the other of treason to the principles of the revolution.

Among the Russian Marxists, too, there was a group, which, in the eyes of most Western Marxists and of the more Westernized Russian Marxists, bought its success by betrayal of the faith, but which, at any rate, was successful. More in the native tradition of the Russian revolutionary intelligentsia than the Westernized Mensheviks, the Bolsheviks were attracted not so much by the "scientific" aspects of Marxism promising the *inevitable* revolution as by its promise of an *early* revolution. But to turn Marx's promise of a workers' revolution in the West into a promise of an intellectual-led revolution in Russia, Marxism had to be transmuted into Leninism. Leninism is an adaptation of Marxism, a product of the industrialized West, to the conditions of an underdeveloped country. But while Lenin—certainly in his practice and to a significant extent also in his theory—carried through that adaptation, he was never sufficiently aware of what he was doing to recognize that the Marxian model of revolution was irrelevant to Russia. He could not see his own revolution as one of intellectuals bent on modernizing an underdeveloped country, that is, by our definition, as a nationalist movement.

Unlike the Mensheviks, Lenin often looked to an alliance of the workers and peasants, rather than the workers and the bourgeoisie, to make the revolution in Russia. This introduction of the peasantry as allies of the workers is in itself a significant modification of Marxism, influenced by a realistic assessment of conditions in underdeveloped Russia. To be sure, in his writings over a period of decades, Lenin is quite inconsistent on the role he expected the peasantry to play in the revolution and, indeed, on the character of that revolution—whether it would be "bourgeois," "proletarian," or "permanent" (i.e., developing without interruption from the bourgeois to the proletarian stage). His inconsistency is explained by tactical considerations as conditions changed, but above all by the fact that these were not the questions that interested Lenin most.

What mattered most to Lenin, and what was therefore the one point on which he remained consistent in virtually all his writings, no matter how he varied on other points, was the role of the intellectuals and hence of the Party in the revolution. Whether bourgeoisie or peasantry were to support the proletariat in the revolution, whatever the character of that revolution, Lenin always insisted that it must be led by the proletariat, which, however, unable to understand its own interests, itself had to be guided by intellectuals, organized as its "vanguard," the Communist Party.[17] It is probably significant that the split among the Russian Marxists into the Menshevik and Bolshevik factions did not occur over the nature of the expected Russian Revolution, that is, the question whether Russian society was basically like that of the West or like that of the underdeveloped world—a question on which the Mensheviks were wrong and Lenin never attained clarity. Rather, the break came over the question of organization, where the Mensheviks' advocacy of a mass labor party stood in sharp contrast to the Bolsheviks' insistence on a small, secret, highly centralized and disciplined "shocktroop" of professional revolutionaries, i.e., of intellectuals, a matter on which Lenin was very clear indeed.

This insistence on the leading role of the intellectuals, organized in the Party, and their substitution for Marx's proletariat as the agents of history and the makers of revolution, constitutes the core of Leninism. It is also the essence of Lenin's adaptation of Marxism to underdeveloped countries, where the proletariat is non-existent or small and weak and the intellectuals are the chief group driving for revolution.

Lenin, however, compelled by pressures for orthodoxy engendered perhaps by his personality and certainly by his political situation, concealed the magnitude of this change—and thereby the process of adaptation—from himself and his followers. He did so by claiming that the intellectuals organized in the Party represented the "true" interests of the workers, that they, indeed, embodied that proletarian class-consciousness which Marx had ascribed to the workers, but which Lenin said workers were by themselves unable to attain.[18] From there it is but a step to the claim that the Communist Party is the "true" working class, even where it contains no workers, and where the actual workers are non-Communist—or do not exist. It is in this fashion that Communist

---

[17] These points emerge well from an excellent scholarly analysis of Lenin's thought, Alfred G. Meyer, *Leninism* (Cambridge, Mass.: Harvard University Press, 1957).

[18] His best known statement to this effect is found in V. I. Lenin, *What Is To Be Done?*, in *Selected Works* (12 vols., New York: International Publishers, n.d.), II, 53.

theory explains the existence of "proletarian" dictatorship in countries like Mongolia, where there is admittedly no proletariat,[19] and it is in this sense that Communist propaganda everywhere to this day refers to the objectives of the Party as those of "the workers." Lenin himself, however, was still too much of a Marxist to take this step, nor did he need to in view of the existence of a substantial number of real workers in Russia. He always insisted that the Party remain linked to the actual working class and did not regard it as a substitute for that class, though that implication can be and has been drawn from his theory.[20]

If Lenin's theory—and practice—on the role of the intellectuals and the Party in bringing about revolution implicitly took account of the

---

[19] For a discussion in the Soviet Academy of Sciences on the question of whether Mongolia could have a proletarian government without a proletariat, see "On the Character and Attributes of People's Democracy in Countries of the Orient," translated in *Current Digest of the Soviet Press*, IV, No. 20 (June 28, 1952), 5 and 7.

[20] A relatively little known article written by Lenin in 1923, "Our Revolution," *Selected Works*, VI, 509–512, illustrates more clearly than most of his writings his view that the revolution itself rather than preceding economic development could create the prerequisites of socialism—industrialization and, with it, an industrial proletariat. It was hence a revoluton of intellectuals meant to anticipate the historical development which Marx expected to come only as a result of the growth of industry and a proletariat. The article also shows the extent to which Lenin links his revolution to those in underdeveloped countries as well as his limited ability to distinguish these sharply from the Western revolutions Marx had used as a model. To appreciate these points, one must read the entire short article, but a few quotations will illustrate them:

". . . Russia stands on the borderline between civilised countries and . . . all the Oriental, non-European countries; . . . therefore Russia might and was indeed bound to reveal certain peculiarities, which, while of course following the general line of world development, distinguish her revolution from all previous revolutions in West European countries, and which introduce certain partly novel features in the passage to the countries of the East.

"Infinitely commonplace . . . is the argument . . . that . . . the objective economic premises for socialism do not exist in our country. . . .

"What if the complete hopelessness of the situation, by intensifying tenfold the energies of the workers and peasants, offered us the possibility of proceeding to create the fundamental requisites of civilisation in a way different from that of the West European countries? Has that changed the general line of development of world history? Has that changed the fundamental relations between the basic classes of every state that is being drawn, or has been drawn, into the general course of world history?

"If a definite level of culture is required for the creation of socialism (although nobody can tell what that definite level of culture is), why cannot we begin by achieving the prerequisites for that definite level of culture in a revolutionary way, underdeveloped character of Russia in his day, his doctrine of imperialism contains some explicit recognition of the revolutionary potential of underdeveloped societies.[21] Especially after the outbreak of World War I, Lenin was confronted by the fact that the Western European working class was not revolutionary and thus did not behave in accordance with Marx's predictions as Lenin interpreted them. Since his chief concern was revolution rather than, as with the Western Marxists (including Marx), labor's inexorable rise to political power, Lenin needed both to account for this phenomenon within a Marxian framework and to find a new agent of revolution. He did both by the theory that an influential section of the Western proletariat, a labor aristocracy, was being bribed into "social chauvinism" and the defense of capitalism by being permitted to share with the capitalists the super-profits derived from imperialist exploitation of the colonies. Carried to its logical conclusion, this theory implies that all of Western society, including the proletariat, assumes the role of exploiter or capitalist, while all of the colonial society, including its upper classes, become exploited or proletarians. Marx's domestic class struggle is thus replaced by an international conflict between the colonial powers and the colonies. The agent

---

and *then*, with the help of a workers' and peasants' government and a Soviet system, proceed to overtake the other nations?

"You say that civilisation is necessary for the creation of socialism. Very good. But why could we not have begun by creating such prerequisites of civilisation in our country as the expulsion of the landlords and the expulsion of the Russian capitalists, and then start moving towards socialism? Where, in what books, have you read that such variations of the customary historical order of events are impermissible or impossible?

"Napoleon, one recalls, wrote: *On s'engage et puis on voit*. Rendered freely that means: One must first start a serious engagement and then see what happens. Well, we first started a serious engagement in November (October) 1917, and . . . now there can be no doubt that in the main we have been victorious.

". . . otherwise revolutions could not be made at all. . . . Subsequent revolutions in Eastern countries, which possess vastly more numerous populations and are distinguished by a vastly greater diversity of social conditions, will undoubtedly display even greater peculiarities than the Russian revolution.

"It need hardly be said that a textbook written on Kautskian lines was a useful thing in its day. But it is really time to abandon the idea that this textbook foresaw all the forms of development of subsequent world history. It is time to declare that those who think so are simply fools."

[21] V. I. Lenin, *Imperialism, the Highest Stage of Capitalism*, in *Selected Works*, V, 3–119. On some of the implications of Lenin's doctrine of imperialism that are highly relevant here, see Meyer's chapter on "The Dialectics of Backwardness," *Leninism*, pp. 257–273.

of revolution in the colonial countries is no longer the proletariat but nationalism.

Again, however, Lenin's adherence to Marxism and the presence in Russia of a sizable revolutionary proletariat, prevented him from drawing these conclusions. Lenin regarded his own revolution in Russia not as a nationalist movement in an underdeveloped country but as a proletarian revolution in an imperialist country, though, to be sure, the weakest link in the chain of imperialism. Nor did he give up faith in the re-emergence of the domestic class struggle and ultimate proletarian revolution in either the industrialized or the colonial societies. Being at heart interested in revolution as such, in the overthrow of the existing order, rather than in a specifically laborite, socialist revolution, Lenin, unlike Marx, devoted some attention to the revolutionary potential of nationalism in underdeveloped countries. In order to weaken the Western powers, he even favored Communist support for the "bourgeois-nationalist" movement, though he insisted that the "proletariat," i.e., the Communist Party, must not merge with it.[22] Yet the fact remains that he looked primarily to the working class in the industrialized West and particularly in Germany for the support which he thought the Russian Revolution needed from abroad.

Most of the contemporaries of the Russian Revolution, whether Communist or not, did not and probably could not see it as a nationalist revolution in an underdeveloped country. Nationalism in the underdeveloped countries was as yet hardly recognized, although the Mexican, Chinese, and Turkish revolutions were all roughly contemporaneous with the Russian one, and the first two had broken out a few years before 1917. At a time when the socialist labor movement in the West was, by both its friends and its enemies, still regarded as the chief agent of a future transformation of society, it is not surprising that the Russian Revolution of 1917 should have been very widely viewed as the first successful revolution by an industrial proletariat intent on introducing socialism rather than as one of the first successful revolutions by intellectuals intent on industrializing a backward country independently of Western capital. Even when what proletarian elements there had been in the early Communist regime, such as the soviets of workers and the trade unions, had been eliminated from power, and when Stalin ceased to rely on the proletariat in the West for the maintenance of the Soviet

[22] V. I. Lenin, "Preliminary Draft of Theses on the National and Colonial Questions" (dated June 5, 1920), *Selected Works*, X, 231–238, p. 237.

regime, this image of the nature of the Russian Revolution persisted. It continued even when Stalin's "second revolution" of rapid industrialization made it quite obvious that developments in Russia did not fit the model of revolution Western socialists had developed, which had always pre-supposed a highly industrialized society, but did share some of the principal characteristics of nationalist revolutions in underdeveloped countries.[23]

The Communists themselves, inside and outside the Soviet Union, were too deeply steeped in the Marxist ideology to give up their view of the Revolution, nor could they do so without sacrificing a following attracted by their supposed success in realizing Marx's first goal, the socialist revolution, and by their vistas of a future classless society of peace, justice, and plenty. Conservatives everywhere, on the other hand, could gladly join in describing the Soviet regime as the first socialist one, for by focusing on the suppression and suffering it brought to many, they could discredit whatever they chose to call socialist in their own countries, identifying with the Soviet Union anything from the labor movement to river development, from social legislation to racial equality. Western socialists therefore had an interest in stressing the fact that the Russian Revolution had not been proletarian, that the Soviet regime was not socialist as they had traditionally used that term. But so much were they, too, committed to the patterns Marx had derived from Western European history, that they commonly assumed that if the Revolution had not been proletarian it must have been bourgeois. To this day, the debate continues whether the Bolsheviks were the Jacobins or the Bonapartists, whether they pushed the Revolution forward or were in fact counter-revolutionaries. Analogies with earlier revolutions can throw light on some aspects of the Russian Revolution[24] but they should not be allowed to conceal other aspects pointing to a different

---

[23] The changes in the nature of Communism that occurred as a result of its adaptation to the requirements of underdevelopment, first in Russia and then in Asia and the other underdeveloped countries, are well delineated in Robert V. Daniels' perceptive introduction, "The Evolution of the Communist Mind," to his *A Documentary History of Communism* (New York: Random House, 1960). He sums them up when he says that "the Western, international, post-industrial, anarchistic, proletarian revolution had become the Eastern, national, industrializing, totalitarian, middle-class-intellectual revolution." *Ibid.*, p. lxi.

[24] Crane Brinton, *The Anatomy of Revolution* (New York: Vintage Books, 1957), and also Isaac Deutscher, "The French Revolution and the Russian Revolution: Some Suggestive Analogies," *World Politics*, IV, No. 3 (April 1952), 369–381.

interpretation. The old middle class of traders and craftsmen was not a principal driving force in the Russian Revolution any more than it is in the revolutions of underdeveloped countries today. There is, therefore, even less justification for regarding the Russian Revolution as primarily a bourgeois revolution (as that term has been applied to the English and French Revolutions) than for regarding it as a proletarian one. The Russian Revolution, from our point of view, is best interpreted as a revolution of the intellectuals, supported by those parts of the proletariat and the peasantry that were politically conscious or stirred into consciousness by the Revolution. Its goal, or, at any rate, its result, was the destruction of the old aristocratic order of large landownership and bureaucratic and military rule, and the rapid introduction of industry without economic and political dependence on Western capital. We can, in short, classify it as a nationalist revolution in an underdeveloped country, as we defined that term earlier.[25]

The Russian Revolution and the regime it brought to power were no historical accident, as they have so often been called in an effort to explain the appearance of a "socialist" government in an underdeveloped country. Historical accidents are, in fact, generally resorted to as explanations exactly where no adequate explanations of a phenomenon are available. No such explanations of the Russian Revolution and the Communist regime could be available as long as they were sought through the exclusive application of Western European models, including the Marxian one. Perhaps we can help replace accident by regularity and mystery by understanding, which is, after all, the function of science, by fitting the Russian Revolution into the broad historical pattern of the nationalist revolutions in underdeveloped countries.

Three Decades of Proletarianism

For at least thirty years after the Russian Revolution, the Communists suffered from their inability to make as complete a break with Marxism

[25] Giorgio Borsa, "A Historical Perspective for Western Policy in Asia," *Conflence*, IV, No. 4 (January 1956), 407–420, suggests that future historians may conclude "that world communism, far from exploiting revolutionary tensions in Asia for its own purposes, was but a means by which backward stagnant societies were brought within the orbit of modern civilization." Both in Russia and in China, Communists have failed to achieve what they pretend is their main goal of egalitarianism, but they have achieved "national unity and independence; an agrarian revolution liberating the peasants from oppressive landlordism; capital investment and industrialization." *Ibid.*, p. 418.

in their thought as they had in their actions. Far from maintaining the "unity of theory and practice" to which they professed to adhere, they could not, in their theory and propaganda, as they did in their practice, entirely replace the party of the proletariat with the party of the intellectuals, the class struggle and the revolution of the proletariat with the nationalist movement and the industrialization of the underdeveloped countries. Had they been able to see themselves for what they were, in fact, more and more becoming, the Communists could have presented themselves to their fellow intellectuals in other underdeveloped countries as the first ones to succeed in attaining their common goal—rapid industrialization and elimination of the aristocracy and Western domination. Instead, they thought of themselves as the vanguard of an industrial proletariat and, therefore, of their revolution as an example to the West. The result was that they fell between two stools. In the West, where there was a proletariat, the appeal of Communism failed because its real achievement was irrelevant in already highly industrialized countries. In the underdeveloped countries, where its achievements were highly relevant, its appeal failed because it obscured that relevance by insisting on the proletarian and hence Western nature of Communism. For this reason Communist propaganda could do little or nothing to overcome Communism's general lack of progress before World War II.[26]

Not only in the Soviet Union and in the West, but also in the underdeveloped countries themselves, Communist parties, for three decades after the Revolution, kept insisting that they were parties of the

[26] Cf. Harry J. Benda's virtually identical view: "For many years, well into the 1930s and perhaps beyond, Communist progress in Southeast Asia—and for that matter in Asia generally—was seriously hampered by the Marxist blinkers through which the Russian leaders looked at world events. In spite of the success of their own revolution in an economically 'backward' country, Soviet leaders for a long time continued to expect a proletarian revolution in the West rather than Asian revolutions, to which they assigned at most a secondary significance. They were slow to grasp the nature of the revolutionary situation because of their dialectical misorientation.

"In this serious misreading of the course of events, the Soviets—not unlike the non-Communist nationalist leaders in Southeast Asia—showed their Western intellectual heritage, of which Marxism is after all only one, though the most radical offshoot. As long as the Communists adhered to this heritage, they failed miserably in the East. The inglorious collapse of Communism in China in 1927, for example, can almost certainly be largely attributed to this close reading of Marxist scriptures, which are actually quite irrelevant to Asian developments. No less striking are the failures of Communism to gain a substantial foothold in India and Japan until almost the end of the Second World War." Harry J. Benda, "Communism in Southeast Asia," *The Yale Review*, XLV, No. 3 (Spring 1956), 417–429.

proletariat. They did this even though they followed two sharply different strategies during this period, each resulting primarily from Soviet reactions to conditions in Europe, particularly in Germany.

The "left" strategy was, with some interludes in the early and middle 1920's[27] in effect until the mid-thirties. It originated in Lenin's hope for Communist revolutions in Central and Western Europe. This hope, to be realized, required first of all the destruction of the hold of social democracy on the majority of European labor. Though it was, in fact, discarded a long time ago, the "left" strategy is still widely thought to embody Communism's objectives, for it was this strategy that regarded capitalism as the main enemy and the socialist revolution as the therefore immediate goal. Since all other parties were considered capitalist or allied with capitalism, the Communists' approach to all of them, but particularly to the socialists, was that of the "united front from below," an attempt to win over their proletarian, and also poor peasant and petty-bourgeois, followers and to discredit their leadership.

The "right" strategy had its heyday from the mid-thirties until a few years after World War II, interrupted only by a brief return to the "left" during the period of the Hitler-Stalin pact (August 1939–June 1941). It stemmed from the Soviet Union's desire for cooperation with the Western powers and for collaboration between Communist and other parties against the threat of Fascism. Fascism, therefore, was now the main enemy, and the establishment and defense of democracy of the "bourgeois" variety became the Communists' main preoccupation. Not being anti-capitalist, this "right" strategy called for "top-alliances" of the Communist parties with anti-Fascist parties—which the "left" strategy had denounced—through agreements with their leadership; for a "united front from above" with socialist parties; for a "popular front" which would also include "bourgeois" parties of the left; and finally, during the War, for a "national front" which would encompass even parties of the right as long as they were opposed to the Fascist enemies of the Soviet Union.

Both "left" and "right" strategies, in spite of their European origins, were faithfully followed by Communist parties throughout the world,

---

[27] See Jane Degras, "United Front Tactics in the Comintern 1921–1928," David Footman, ed., *International Communism*, St. Antonys Papers, No. 9 (Carbondale, Ill.: Southern Illinois University Press, 1960), pp. 9–22. See also Paul Katona, "Right and Left—A Brief Survey," *Problems of Communism*, X, No. 2 (March–April 1961), 13–17.

regardless of the fact that, in underdeveloped countries, the industrial proletariat, which the Communists claimed to represent, was either non-existent or extremely weak. This proved particularly disastrous to Communist success under the "left" strategy, which emphasized "proletarian" policies and the early coming of the proletarian revolution and obliged Communist parties to attack all other parties and movements, including the nationalist ones, which, in some cases, had a substantial following. Adoption of the "right" strategy at least permitted Communist parties in underdeveloped countries to escape from this position of hopeless isolation and futility. They now entered into alliances with, or even joined, existing "bourgeois-nationalist" movements, for the nationalists' enemies—aristocratic rule and colonialism (which the Communists called "feudalism" and "imperialism")—were assumed to be also the Communists' principal enemies, corresponding to Fascism in the West; "national liberation" and a "bourgeois-democratic" revolution were now regarded as the proper goals. But even under this "right" strategy, the Communists maintained their identity as a party which claimed to represent the proletariat, and secondarily also the poor peasantry and petty-bourgeoisie, and collaborated with "bourgeois" groups only for limited and short-run purposes.

The Communists' stubborn insistence on appearing as the representatives of a largely non-existent class fighting battles against virtually non-existent capitalists was, no doubt, an important factor in their amazing failure to make headway even in those underdeveloped countries where the growth of a nationalist movement indicated the existence of a very real revolutionary potential. Thus, in India, where the nationalist Congress had 500,000 members by 1936, the Communist Party, during 1934, after 15 years of organizing efforts, increased its membership from 20 to 150! By 1939, the Congress passed the 5 million mark, while the Communist Party had a mere 5000 members by 1942.[28] Only in China, of all the underdeveloped countries, did the Communists make some significant advances before World War II and there they did so to the extent that they broke with the general "proletarian" pattern of Communism, when their failure in the cities forced them to adopt Mao Tse-tung's strategy of reliance on the peasantry.[29]

[28] Gene D. Overstreet and Marshall Windmiller, *Communism in India* (Berkeley and Los Angeles: University of California Press, 1959), pp. 155, 172, 357.
[29] See Benjamin I. Schwartz, *Chinese Communism and the Rise of Mao* (Cambridge, Mass.: Harvard University Press, 1952).

Neo-Maoism and Nationalism

The cold war between the United States and the Soviet Union compelled international Communism to develop a new strategy, which was
destined finally to bring the policies and propaganda of Communist
parties throughout the world, and particularly in its underdeveloped
parts, into line with the modernizing nationalist role which Communism
had played in the Soviet Union. It was a strategy which, in short, turned
Communism from a professedly proletarian into a frankly nationalist
movement. This new strategy was first developed by Mao Tse-tung during World War II in his battle against the Japanese. It is for this reason
that I have called it the neo-Maoist strategy, but it was adopted by
Moscow and the Communist parties, in response to Soviet foreign policy
needs, beginning about 1947.[30]

Once involved in the cold war, the Soviet Union had to mobilize
all possible forces, regardless of their class character, against American
foreign policy objectives. Yet at the same time, most of the parties that
had been the Communists' wartime and immediate postwar "national
front" allies, such as the socialist and Catholic movements in Western
Europe, were now pro-American, making continued collaboration impossible. In 1947, Zhdanov, at the founding meeting of the Cominform,
divided the entire world into two "camps," one led by the United States
and one by the Soviet Union.[31] Viewed through the black-and-white
spectacles of this doctrine, even most of the nationalist movements in
underdeveloped countries appeared to the Communists as mere stooges

---

[30] I defined the nature of the neo-Maoist strategy, illustrated its appeal by numerous quotations, and traced and documented in some detail its adoption in Moscow
and then by the Indian Communists in my book, *Moscow and the Communist
Party of India* (New York: John Wiley & Sons, 1956). See also the preceding
articles in the present book and especially Bernard S. Morris and Morris Watnick,
"Current Communist Strategy in Nonindustrialized Countries," in Kautsky, ed.,
op. cit., pp. 282–292, and also Robert J. Alexander, "Brazil's CP: A Case Study
in Latin-American Communism," *Problems of Communism*, IV, No. 5 (September–
October 1955), 17–26. The subject is brought more up to date by Hugh Seton-
Watson, "The Communist Powers and Afro-Asian Nationalism." in Kurt London, ed.,
Unity and Contradiction (New York: Frederick A. Praeger, 1962), pp. 187–206. See
also W. Z. Laqueur, "Towards National Democracy: Soviet Doctrine and the New
Countries," *Survey* (London), No. 37 (July–September 1961), 3–11, and my article
on "Soviet Policy in the Underdeveloped Countries," reprinted on pp. 145–162
below, with its references to more recent literature.

[31] A. Zhdanov, "The International Situation," *For a Lasting Peace, for a People's
Democracy!* (Journal of the Cominform), November 10, 1947, pp. 2–4.

of "American imperialism." There was no doubt, then, that the "right" strategy of cooperation with non-Communist parties had to be abandoned with the onset of the cold war. For the next two years there was uncertainty in Moscow as to whether it should be replaced by the old "left" or the new neo-Maoist strategy, while the various Communist parties pursued either one or the other. But by 1949 it had become clear that the "left" strategy unnecessarily limited Communist parties' support to the "exploited" classes in each country and concentrated their fire on local capitalists, rather than on the Soviet Union's enemy, the United States.

The neo-Maoist strategy was an attempt to appeal to all classes at a time when an alliance with most major parties, including most nationalist movements, was impossible. Under it, the Communists' main enemy was identified as neither capitalism nor Fascism, but as "imperialism," a term that has become virtually synonymous with the United States in the Communist vocabulary. Whether the opposition to foreign imperialism and its alleged native allies, such as the nationalists, was to be peaceful or violent was a matter of flexible tactics rather than worldwide strategy, but it was always to be based on what the Chinese Communists have called the bloc of four classes. That bloc consisted of the proletariat, the peasantry, the petty-bourgeoisie (which is the rather inappropriate Marxist-Western term the Communists apply to what we have designated as the old middle class, and to some extent also to the intellectuals), and, most notably, the anti-imperialist capitalists. That this latter group may, in fact, hardly exist in underdeveloped countries does not reduce the importance of its explicit inclusion by the Communists in the neo-Maoist front, for it is at this point that the wholly novel character of their new strategy becomes apparent.

Neo-Maoism did not differ much from the old "right" strategy in establishing a broad front of the four classes (to which have since been added aristocratic elements). But since the former party-allies were not available any more, the Communist appeal to all these groups now had to be directed "from below." This meant that the Communist party now had to claim to represent the true interests not only of the "exploited" classes, as it had always done, but also of their "exploiters." For the first time, Communist parties could transcend the limits imposed on them by their former "proletarianism"; they freed themselves from the proletarian myth after being prisoners to it for thirty years.

What Lenin had merely implied, as he took account of the realities of Russian underdevelopment and of the anti-colonialist movement, was now realized in neo-Maoism. This was true of the implication in Lenin's doctrine of imperialism that the colonial powers, including their working classes, were the main enemy of all classes in the colonies and that the latter would and should unite against the former. It was also true of Lenin's identification of the intellectual leadership of the Communist party with the "true" proletariat. Once this identification was accepted, the Party could use any class to attain its objectives, and its objectives would, by definition, be proletarian.[32] Lenin had still insisted on a link between the Party and the actual proletariat, though in his practice he also relied very heavily on the peasantry. Under neo-Maoism all classes, including the capitalists, became acceptable as tools of the Party. The Leninist doctrines of imperialism and of intellectual leadership, then, contained in embryonic form (or were at any rate quite compatible with) the abandonment of the class struggle and of the socialist revolution, Marxian doctrines which Communist parties in underdeveloped countries have by now fairly openly given up. Russia was too close to Western Europe, not only geographically and culturally but also in her economic development, and Lenin was too close to Marx for these implications to become apparent either to him or to most of his generation. The logic of the changes he introduced into original Marxism in transplanting it to the underdeveloped soil of his native land has become fully clear only with its further transplantation to countries even more backward industrially than was Russia at the turn of the century.[33]

The relative success of Communism in the postwar period as compared to the prewar era has been due to a number of factors in addition to its adoption of the neo-Maoist strategy. Thus, colonialism was weakened both by the war itself and by changes that had taken place in the colonies as well as in the colonial powers. Communism's prestige and power had grown as a result of the Soviet Union's victory in the war and its occupation of Eastern Europe and North Korea, and of the role Communist parties played in the anti-German and anti-Japanese resistance movements. Perhaps most important, the achievements of So-

[32] See Morris Watnick, "Continuity and Innovation in Chinese Communism," *World Politics*, VI, No. 1 (October 1953), 84–105, pp. 92–97.
[33] On the growth of an "Eastern orientation" in the Soviet view of world revolutionary development, from Lenin's day to the present, see Robert C. Tucker, "Russia, the West, and World Order," *World Politics*, XII, No. 1 (October 1959), 1–23.

viet industrialization have been far more dramatic and obvious recently than they were before World War II. Neo-Maoism, however, made it possible for the Communists to exploit fully the attractiveness of these achievements to underdeveloped countries.

With a strategy openly appealing to, in their own often-used phrase, "all classes,"[34] the Communists in underdeveloped countries were no longer tied to a non-existent or very weak proletarian base or obliged to attack the native capitalists, if any, or, for that matter, any other native groups except those closely connected with "imperialist" interests. They could thus seek support from any group to whom their anti-co-lonialist program appealed.[35] The main domestic plank of this program was the promise of rapid modernization and industrialization on the

---

[34] In the single most important directive issued jointly by Moscow and Peking to the Asian Communist parties to adopt neo-Maoism, the first point reads: "The working class must unite with all other classes, parties, groups, organizations and individuals who are willing to oppose the oppression of imperialism and its lackeys, to form a broad nationwide united front and ready to wage a resolute struggle against imperialism and its lackeys." "Speech by Liu Shao-chi at the Conference of Trade Unions of Asia and Oceania," *For a Lasting Peace, for a People's Democracy!*, December 30, 1949, p. 2. For additional quotations and comment, see Milton Sacks, "The Strategy of Communism in Southeast Asia," *Pacific Affairs*, XXIII, No. 3 (September 1950), 231–236, and Kautsky, *Moscow and the Communist Party of India*, pp. 95 ff. A more recent authoritative international Communist pronouncement similarly declares: "The urgent tasks of national rebirth facing the countries that have shaken off the colonial yoke cannot be effectively accomplished unless a determined struggle is waged against imperialism and the remnants of feudalism by all the patriotic forces of the nations united in a single national-democratic front. . . . In the liberation struggle . . . a big role can be played by the national patriotic forces, by all elements of the nation prepared to fight for national independence, against imperialism. "Declaration of Representatives of the Eighty-one Communist Parties, Meeting in Moscow, November–December, 1960," Dan N. Jacobs, ed., *The New Communist Manifesto and Related Documents* (Evanston, Ill.: Row, Peterson & Co., 1961) pp. 31, 32.

[35] This program, with its striking absence of proletarianism and anti-capitalism, is well summarized in the "Declaration . . . of the Eighty-one Communist Parties . . .": "The national democratic tasks on the basis of which the progressive forces of the nation can and do unite in the countries which have won their freedom, are: the consolidation of political independence, the carrying out of agrarian reforms in the interest of the peasantry, elimination of the survivals of feudalism, the uprooting of imperialist economic domination, the restriction of foreign monopolies and their expulsion from the national economy, the creation and development of a national industry, improvement of the living standard, the democratization of social life, the pursuance of an independent and peaceful foreign policy, and the development of economic and cultural cooperation with the socialist and other friendly countries." *Ibid.*, p. 32.

Soviet and Chinese Communist model. For the first time, the appeal of the Soviet Union having achieved the goals of intellectuals in underdeveloped countries—elimination of aristocratic rule and quick industrialization without dependence on Western capital—could be fully brought home to these intellectuals. In industrialized countries, it is difficult to appreciate the power of this appeal and the depth and urgency of the intellectuals' concern with the problem of modernization. To them the appeal is hardly weakened by knowledge of the sacrifices which the Communist path to modernization imposed on millions in the Soviet Union and China. In countries where mass starvation was a common occurrence and millions are still undernourished, sick, and illiterate, and where there is no tradition of individualism and civil liberties, such sacrifices do not weigh very heavily as against the hope of future improvements. Nor do the intellectuals expect to bear these sacrifices themselves; what makes the Soviet and Chinese example so attractive is also the fact that it put intellectuals in control, with seemingly untold opportunities to gain power and prestige.[36]

In fact, Russia in 1917 was not, like many underdeveloped countries today, overpopulated, nor did her industrialization really proceed without Western aid: it began with the foreign capital accumulated under Tsarism and continued with the support of Western credits, machinery, and technicians until the end of World War II, after which the industrial plant and specialists of the newly conquered European satellites were heavily relied upon for some time. But all this is little understood in underdeveloped countries and does not seem to reduce significantly the relevance of the Soviet—and not at all that of the Chinese—example

---

[36] On the Communist appeal to the intellectuals in underdeveloped countries, see Morris Watnick, "The Appeal of Communism to the Underdeveloped Peoples," in Kautsky, ed., *op. cit.*, pp. 316–334, an important article that anticipates some of the points made in this essay on the nature of nationalism in underdeveloped countries. For another interesting approach to the Communist appeal to intellectuals, see Eduard Heimann, "Marxism and Underdeveloped Countries," *Social Research*, XIX (September 1952), 322–345. See also Joel Carmichael, "The Nationalist-Communist Symbiosis in the Middle East," in Kautsky, ed., *op. cit.*, pp. 304–315; Eugene Staley, *The Future of Underdeveloped Countries* (New York: Harper and Brothers, 1954), pp. 174–178; Sidney Hook, "Grim Report: Asia in Transition," *The New York Times Magazine*, April 5, 1959, pp. 11, 104, 106, 108; and, for an excellent review article, G. L. Arnold, "Communism and the Intelligentsia in Backward Areas: Some Recent Literature," *Problems of Communism*, IV, No. 5 (September–October 1955), 13–17. Justus van der Kroef, "Marxism in Southeast Asia," *Current History*, XXVII, No. 159 (November 1954), 289–297, also contains some relevant points.

to the intellectuals in these countries.[37] The fact remains that the Communist revolutions in Russia and in China, like their own nationalist movements, confronted the problems of backwardness at home and weakness and dependence in international affairs, and they have already in large measure attained the goals which to the intellectuals in most underdeveloped countries are still chiefly unfulfilled aspirations. This is an appeal that the Western societies, which have been industrialized and powerful so much longer, and have acquired their industry and their power under such different circumstances, inherently have difficulty in matching.

If, as we saw earlier, nationalists in underdeveloped countries are intellectuals appealing to all strata of the population in their drive for industrialization and against colonialism, and Communists in underdeveloped countries are, as we have now seen, intellectuals appealing to all strata of the population in their drive for industrialization and against colonialism, then Communists are nationalists.[38] This conclusion sums up the vital change that the neo-Maoist strategy brought to international Communism beginning in the late 1940's. To be sure, since complete and sudden breaks in ideological development are impossible, the Communists still conceal this change from themselves and from others by their continued habit of seeking doctrinal support for their practice in quotations from Marx and Engels and by their continuing affinity for the vocabulary of the nineteenth-century Western socialist movement.

[37] The relevance to underdeveloped countries of the Soviet model, particularly in the area of economic policy, is examined by Alec Nove, "The Soviet Model and Under-developed Countries," *International Affairs*, XXXVII, No. 1 (January 1961), 29–38, and by Oleg Hoeffding, "The Soviet Union: Model for Asia?—State Planning and Forced Industrialization," *Problems of Communism*, VIII, No. 6 (November–December 1959), 38–46. See also Alex Inkeles, "The Soviet Union: Model for Asia?—The Social System," *ibid.*, pp. 30–38.

[38] "As the Chinese experience illustrates, Asian communism is not based on a class-struggle strategy or appeal; it is primarily a movement of belligerent nationalism." Robert Vincent Daniels, "The Chinese Revolution in Russian Perspective," *World Politics*, XIII, No. 2 (January 1961), 210–230, p. 229. On the relation between nationalism and Communism in an area where, because of its backwardness, proletarianism is particularly irrelevant, see Walter Z. Laqueur, *Communism and Nationalism in the Middle East* (New York: Frederick A. Praeger, 1956), and also some of the articles in Laqueur, ed., *The Middle East in Transition*. See also Victor Alba, "Communism and Nationalism in Latin America," *Problems of Communism*, VII, No. 5 (September–October 1958), 24–31; and David T. Cattell, "Communism and the African Negro," *Problems of Communism*, VIII, No. 5 (September–October 1959), 35–41.

But though words lag behind action or, to use Marxist terminology, the ideological superstructure is transformed more slowly than the material base, even in Communist propaganda and theoretical writings, the "people's masses" and "all peace-loving people"—and, most broadly, simply "the peoples"—are more and more replacing the "proletariat" and the "working class," fighting now not the "class struggle" for "class interests" and for the "socialist revolution," but in the "national interest" for "national independence."

In slowing the complete identification of Communism with nationalism, the remnants of a proletarian vocabulary have been less important than the fact that neo-Maoism was originally developed as a strategy of opposition to the major nationalist movements in underdeveloped countries which appeared to the Communists to be tools of the "imperialists," rather than genuinely anti-colonialist. In the period of the adoption of the neo-Maoist strategy, it was only in exceptional cases, such as those of the regimes of Arbenz in Guatemala, Mossadeq of Iran, and the Nationalist Party in Indonesia, that Moscow considered a nationalist government sufficiently pro-Soviet and anti-American to have the local Communist parties support rather than oppose the non-Communist nationalists.

The Convergence of Communism and Nationalism

With the adoption of neo-Maoism, Communist parties had been turned into nationalist parties with respect to their ideology and policies, but they and the Soviet Union were still opposed to the older nationalist movements in underdeveloped countries. In the early 1950's, however, even before Stalin's death, a change in Soviet and subsequently in Communist party policy became apparent.

The realization evidently grew among Soviet policy makers that their anti-American objectives could be served at least as well by the non-Communist nationalist movements and governments as by the Communist parties in underdeveloped countries. This had become true not so much as a result of changes in the policies of these non-Communist nationalist movements as of the gradual ripening of changes in Communism itself. Communist goals had now become limited to those that can be effectively served by nationalism—chiefly the elimination of American political, military, economic, and cultural influence wherever possible.

Soviet reliance on non-Communist nationalists to help carry out Soviet objectives would have been quite impossible when the Communists still thought of themselves as champions of the lower classes, and of their goal as a social revolution. Then the nationalist movements were contemptuously referred to as "bourgeois-nationalist." A generation after the Revolution, the dream of world-wide social revolution, which had conditioned even some short-run policies of Lenin and Trotsky and probably affected the long-run calculations of Stalin, had receded so far into the background as not to influence Soviet policy any longer. Statements by Soviet leaders that world Communism is their ultimate goal are of the same significance as similar statements with regard to worldwide justice and liberty made by other government leaders. They are no doubt believed by those who make them and they serve as important symbols to mobilize the loyalties and exertions of their followers, but they cannot account for any particular foreign policy decision.

This change of Soviet objectives from proletarianism to nationalism, from world revolution to the expansion of Soviet power—which, at the present time, is more or less synonymous with the reduction of American power—is to be explained in terms of changes in Soviet society and leadership. Immediately after the Revolution, that leadership consisted of "professional revolutionaries," men who had spent most of their lives dreaming and plotting revolution, philosophers, journalists, and agitators, who could make passionate appeals because they were passionately moved by what they considered injustice and misery. These men did not change their outlook after they came to power. They continued to consider themselves revolutionaries and champions of the underprivileged and looked on the country which they now controlled as the base for further advances of the revolution. But as that base was consolidated through industrialization, its society has, inevitably, changed. A new bureaucratic and managerial leadership has emerged to whom the Revolution is not something yet to be made or even completed, but something in the past, on which its own power is based, and that hence should be preserved. They are conservatives, for they wish to preserve the *status quo* in their own society. To be sure, as is true of any regime established by revolution, the symbols of the *status quo* are those of the Revolution, but this must not conceal the fact that the new leaders can maximize their power not, as their predecessors did for most of their lives, by overthrowing the government of their country, but by strengthening it.[39] They share many of the concerns of managerial and bureaucratic elites in other industrialized countries[40] and, being at the top of their own society, they have little understanding or sympathy for the underprivileged in other societies. As they seek to strengthen their power position through their foreign policies, they are, therefore, not bound, either by conviction or by any affinity of interests, to rely on the lower classes in other countries for support. Rather, they can appeal to any strata that may, for whatever reasons, be opposed to the policy objectives of the United States.

Once world Communism had, in effect, been dropped as a Soviet policy objective and replaced by the much more realistic one of expansion of the power of the Soviet Union and of those who govern it, Khrushchev could recognize the existence of a third, neutralist, "camp" in addition to Zhdanov's two.[41] In an evolution not entirely dissimilar from that of American foreign policy, which also at one time tended to regard neutralism as "immoral," Moscow came to accept and even to see advantages to itself in the existence of governments that were, if not pro-Soviet in their policies, at any rate frequently anti-American. During the 1950's, the Soviet Union acted more and more as the champion of the neutralist countries and supplied some of their regimes with

[33] Robert C. Tucker concludes his analysis of the 1961 Soviet Communist Party program, "The CPSU Draft Program: A Credo of Conservation," *Problems of Communism*, X, No. 5 (September–October 1961), 1–4, with this statement: "Despite the impression of radicalism created by its use of revolutionary phraseology, the new Communist Manifesto is, in its underlying significance, a credo of Soviet conservatism. It is the political expression of a ruling and possessing class which wants to project an image of a Soviet Russia on the march—and towards full communism at that—but which, in actuality, is concerned most of all with the preservation, without radical change, of the existing institutional structure and its associated pattern of power, policy, and privilege."

[40] See the interesting work by Clark Kerr, John T. Dunlap, Frederick H. Harbison, and Charles A. Myers, *Industrialism and Industrial Man: The Problems of Labor and Management in Economic Growth* (Cambridge, Mass.: Harvard University Press, 1960), which, in discussing "the inevitable structuring of the managers and the managed in the course of industrialization" (pp. 7–8), concludes that ". . . the similarities of enterprise management in all advanced industrializing societies are far greater than their differences." (p. 164).

[41] At the 20th Party Congress of 1956, he hailed the emergence of "a vast peace zone," "of a group of peace-loving European and Asian states which have proclaimed nonparticipation in blocs as a principle of their foreign policy." N. S. Khrushchev, "Report of the Central Committee of the Communist Party of the Soviet Union to the 20th Party Congress," February 14, 1956, in Leo Gruliow, ed., *Current Soviet Policies—II: The Documentary Record of the 20th Communist Party Congress and Its Aftermath* (New York: Frederick A. Praeger, 1957), p. 33.

increasingly significant amounts of economic and technical aid, all, of course, in an attempt to swing these governments to its side. Its side, however, could no longer be defined as that of Communism, if by Communism we mean either an ideology or a social system, whether of Marx, of Lenin, or even of the present-day Soviet Union. Rather, its side is now simply that of the Soviet Union in the international power conflict, in which the neutralist governments can lend support to the Soviet Union by denying to the United States and its allies military bases, raw materials, markets, and diplomatic support, and by extending similar advantages to the Soviet Union.

Soviet backing of neutralist regimes, therefore, is generally in no way dependent on the adoption by such regimes of policies favorable to the lower classes, such as land reform or support for trade unions, or even of policies favorable to the local Communist parties. Many nationalist movements do, for reasons of their own which we have discussed, pursue such policies, but regardless of that fact, there is today hardly a nationalist movement left anywhere, either in the government or in the opposition, with which Soviet foreign policymakers do not consider cooperation to be possible and profitable. Some of the few underdeveloped countries that are still so backward as to have virtually no movement of nationalist intellectuals—Ethiopia, Yemen, Afghanistan, and Nepal—are among the chief beneficiaries of Soviet foreign aid, again regardless of the fact that their governments are what traditional Communists would have considered the most reactionary regimes in the world today.*

The change in Soviet foreign policy deeply affected the role of the Communist parties in underdeveloped countries.[42] As the nationalist movements and governments changed, in the Soviet view, from stooges of Western imperialism to peace-loving defenders of national independence, Moscow expected the Communist parties to give up their opposition, which they had, with very few exceptions, maintained in the late

---

* [The government of Yemen was, after this was written, seized by some military "nationalist intellectuals" who have enjoyed Soviet support just like the government of the Imam they overthrew.]

[42] The changes in their strategy are clearly outlined against the background of the earlier neo-Maoist strategy by Bernard S. Morris, "Recent Shifts in Communist Strategy: India and South-East Asia," in Kautsky, ed., *op. cit.*, pp. 293–303. See also Bernard S. Morris, "Continuity of Communist Strategic Doctrine Since the Twentieth Party Congress," *The Annals of the American Academy of Political and Social Science,* vol. 317 (May 1958), 130–137.

1940's. At first, they were directed to support the foreign policies of the nationalists wherever these were anti-American in their implications. Soon, however, as the Soviet Union found the nationalist regimes of some underdeveloped countries useful for its now more limited purposes, Communist parties were pushed to give up their opposition to their governments' domestic policies as well. Particularly, as Soviet economic assistance to some underdeveloped countries expanded, the Communist parties were expected to support government policies in the area of economic development, a key issue in the politics of underdeveloped countries.

In countries where the Communists' appeal depends largely on discontent and particularly on the disillusionment that almost inevitably follows independence among some strata of the population, especially among some intellectuals, giving up their opposition role was likely to cost the Communists some strength, which might or might not be compensated for by increased prestige resulting from their association with the nationalist government. Some Communists in underdeveloped countries have certainly been most reluctant to praise the very movements and leaders that they had for so many years been denouncing as the representatives of capitalism, and, when that was no longer regarded as a proper enemy, of imperialism. The Communist Party of India, for instance, has followed Moscow's lead only slowly all through the 1950's, has been badly split during all this time over just how much support to lend to the Nehru government, and has sought to maintain its opposition to the Congress wherever this has been at all compatible with Moscow's directives, first in a shrinking area of foreign policy, then in a similarly shrinking area of domestic policy, and more recently still on some issues of local and regional government.[43]

Whether Soviet policies happen to strengthen or weaken Communist parties is probably of relatively little concern to the policy-makers in Moscow. Their main interest lies in strengthening their ties with the nationalist movements and governments of underdeveloped countries, which are generally far more powerful than the Communist parties, and can hence be far more useful for the accomplishment of Soviet foreign

[43] Kautsky, *Moscow and the Communist Party of India*, pp. 129–130, 133–134, 173–175; Marshall Windmiller, "Indian Communism and the New Soviet Line," *Pacific Affairs*, XXIX, No. 4 (December 1956), 347–366; Overstreet and Windmiller, *Communism in India*, pp. 304–323; and Gene D. Overstreet, "Soviet and Communist Policy in India," *The Journal of Politics*, XX, No. 1 (February 1958), 187–202, pp. 199–200.

policy objectives. The Communist parties are now only one tool, and generally one of decreasing importance, available to the Soviet government for influencing policy in underdeveloped countries. With the growing political and economic strength of the Soviet Union and the change in the character of its leadership, diplomatic pressures, economic aid, technical advice, and perhaps even cultural exchange programs are becoming the more important weapons of Soviet foreign policy. Khrushchev's visits to India and steel mills erected there by Soviet engineers are likely to be more significant in establishing Soviet influence in India than anything the Communist Party of India can do.[44] Similar efforts in Afghanistan could create a strong Soviet foothold there even in the absence of any Communist party. And in no case do such Soviet efforts have anything to do with the advancement of Communism if that term refers to a revolutionary social movement and ideology.

By 1956, Moscow began to hint that the Communist parties should take a further and even more startling step along their line of development from proletarianism to nationalism. It was now suggested that underdeveloped countries could evolve along "socialist" lines under the leadership of their bourgeoisie and that the Communist parties were to follow that leadership.[45] To Marx and even to Lenin such a view would have been utter nonsense—after all, it implies that the leadership in the class struggle be turned over to the enemy in that struggle—but, as we have seen, the class struggle has long been abandoned by the Communists, and if the term "socialism" is now devoid of any domestic-policy significance and merely means a government influenced or even dominated by the Soviet Union, the new view does make sense.

Of course, the Communist parties cannot be expected to take kindly

[44] For a summary of Soviet attempts in the late 1950s to influence Indian policy, see *ibid.*, pp. 194–199.

[45] See, for example, the quotation, *ibid.*, p. 193, from D. Degtiar, "Development of the National Economy of India," *Kommunist* (Moscow), March 1956, and the quotation in Overstreet and Windmiller, *Communism in India*, p. 326, from Modeste Rubinstein, "A Non-Capitalist Path for Underdeveloped Countries," *New Times* (Moscow), July–August 1956. Further references to more recent such Soviet statements, particularly with respect to Cuba (which is said to move toward socialism under the leadership of the petty bourgeoisie) and Africa (where leadership is to be left to the bourgeoisie) may be found in David T. Cattell, "Changes and Variations in Soviet Policies toward the Underdeveloped Areas," a paper presented to the annual meeting of the American Political Science Association, St. Louis, Mo., September 6–9, 1961, which discusses current Communist party and Soviet policy toward the nationalist movements in a manner extremely relevant to the analysis presented in this essay.

to the suggestion that they subordinate themselves to the non-Communist nationalist movements and give up the raison d'être they have always claimed, i.e., that they are the only ones capable of leading society to socialism (whatever that term may mean). However, Communist parties in non-Communist countries have historically almost never been in any position to resist Moscow's desires for long. More important than their opposition to the new view are the objections of the Chinese Communists. It would appear that, since about 1957, Peking would have preferred to revert to the neo-Maoist policy of "revolutionary" opposition—peaceful or violent—by a Communist-led front drawing followers from all social classes to the non-Communist nationalist movements and governments. Since the Communist parties in underdeveloped countries may also prefer an opposition role, it is not surprising that some of them have sided with the Chinese Communists in their controversies with the Soviet Communists. To be sure, the Chinese Communists have themselves not been entirely consistent on this issue; where non-Communist nationalist movements have been militantly "anti-imperialist," like the Algerian and Cuban ones, they have, if anything, been more eager than Moscow to support them.[46]

The split between Moscow and Peking over whether to support non-Communist nationalism and subordinate and possibly even sacrifice the Communist parties to it, or to support a rival Communist-led nationalist movement against non-Communist nationalism is part of the larger controversy over peaceful "co-existence" with the "capitalist" world, which had, by 1960, come out into the open.[47] It may be patched up again, but is likely to persist beneath the surface for some time, because it results not from different interpretations of the Marxist and Leninist classics, but from the different stages of economic development prevailing in the two countries at the present time, the different types of leader-

---

[46] The issues dividing the Soviet and Chinese Communists on the strategy to be followed in underdeveloped countries are well summarized and documented in Donald S. Zagoria, "Sino-Soviet Friction in Underdeveloped Areas," *Problems of Communism*, X, No. 2 (March–April 1961), 1–13. See also Thomas Perry Thornton, "Peking, Moscow, and the Underdeveloped Areas," *World Politics*, XIII, No. 4 (July 1961), 491–504.

[47] The controversy is analyzed by Richard Lowenthal and documented by a large collection of Soviet and Chinese statements in G. F. Hudson, Richard Lowenthal and Roderick MacFarquhar, *The Sino-Soviet Dispute* (New York: Frederick A. Praeger, 1961). [Since then, many more writings on the subject have appeared. For my own analysis, as of 1962, of the issues in the Sino-Soviet conflict most relevant there, see pp. 103–120 below.]

ship corresponding to each, and their different needs and views of the world.

The Chinese economy is not yet developed to the point of inspiring the Chinese Communists with confidence like that of the Soviet Communists in their ability to defeat the United States through economic competition and through economic aid to the so-called uncommited underdeveloped countries. Moreover, the views of the two Communist party elites as to what constitutes defeating the United States probably differ. Chinese society has not yet undergone the changes which, in Soviet society, produced the new leadership with its new attitudes that we have just mentioned. In China, the professional revolutionaries and agitators, rather than the managers and bureaucrats, are still in control. Such men are more likely to think of their mission in terms of social revolution and, in view of their specific background, of prolonged civil war, than in terms of diplomatic and economic conflict. "Revolution," however, as their early adoption of neo-Maoism indicates, does not mean to them class struggle or championship of lower class interests, but industrialization under the leadership of intellectuals, by totalitarian methods.[48]

The present Soviet policy of subordinating the Communist parties to the leadership of the nationalist movements in underdeveloped countries points, if carried to its logical conclusion, to the total abandonment of Communist parties as tools of Soviet foreign policy in favor of Soviet cooperation with the nationalists. In fact, such organizational liquidation, to follow the ideological one, is not likely to be carried out. To be sure, where the Communist party is weak and the nationalist movement is powerful and can serve Soviet ends, the Communists may be virtually, though perhaps only temporarily, abandoned and sacrificed by Moscow. Thus, the Egyptian Communist leadership was in jail, evidently with Khrushchev's approval, during the period of greatest friendship between Nasser and Moscow.[49] However, where Communist parties are fairly

---

[48] "Chinese communism has not fought anything resembling a class war. It has become instead a movement to discipline and regenerate the nation as a whole. The Chinese Communists . . . profess to lead 'the people' against 'the lackeys of imperialism,' whose status is defined not by their social standing but by their political attitude toward the Communist regime. . . . The real nature of the Communist movement must be understood on quite another basis than Marxism and the class struggle. This is particularly true of China. The equation of revolution and the class struggle is a Communist illusion." Robert Vincent Daniels, "The Chinese Revolution in Russian Perspective," *World Politics*, XIII, No. 2 (January 1961), 218.

[49] See the statement by an Iraqi Communist that "an anti-government conspiracy would be a crime in any Arab state struggling against imperialism, even if Com-

strong, as is the case in India and Indonesia and even more in Iraq and Cuba, they retain some usefulness to Moscow as instruments through which pressure can be brought on the nationalist movements to remain anti-American or become more so. Most Communist parties in underdeveloped countries thus have been assigned the rather unenviable function of making their domestic rival more, and themselves less, indispensable to the Soviet Union.

Organizationally, then, Communists retain their identity, and in terms of formal party membership it is still possible to distinguish between Commmunist and non-Communist nationalists. But in their policies, the Communist intellectuals, driving for industrialization and independence, and the non-Commnuist intellectuals, driving for industrialization and independence, have become virtually indistinguishable. The frequently asked question whether leaders like Touré in Guinea and Lumumba and Gizenga in the Congo and, above all, Castro in Cuba* were "genuine" nationalists or "really" Communists is hence meaningless; such nationalists came to be like Communists because Communists came to be like them. The identification of Communism with nationalism has gone farthest in Cuba where a non-Communist nationalist revolution in the short time of about two years turned the country into a self-proclaimed "socialist" one, following the present Communist party line—all without the Cuban Communist party, which had existed for years before the Cuban revolution, coming to power in the process, and with individual Communist leaders occupying top positions only in its later stages.

It is true that nationalist movements have advocated or pursued some

---

munism were persecuted," quoted from the Polish paper *Zycie Warszawy* of February 17, 1959, by Donald S. Zagoria, "Sino-Soviet Friction in Underdeveloped Areas," *Problems of Communism*, X, No. 2 (March–April 1961), 9. Even when Khrushchev, in his speech to the Twenty-first Party Congress, defended the Egyptian Communists against Nasser's attacks, he made it clear that first things come first: "We do not conceal that we and some leaders of the UAR have different views in the ideological field, but in questions of struggle against imperialism . . . our positions coincide. . . . Differences in ideological views must not hinder the development of friendly relations between our countries and the cause of the common struggle against imperialism." N. S. Khrushchev, "On the Middle East," in Alvin Z. Rubinstein, ed., *The Foreign Policy of the Soviet Union* (New York: Random House, 1960), p. 401. [In 1965, the Egyptian Communist Party dissolved itself. On this and similar cases of merger of Communist and non-Communist modernizing movements, see my article on "Soviet Policy in the Underdeveloped Countries," reprinted on pp. 145–162 below, which brings the present story further up to date.]
* [One could by now add revolutionaries in Zanzibar, Santo Domingo and Vietnam to a lengthening list.]

policies of nationalization of industry, of land reform, and generally of a redistribution of wealth to favor the poor, policies which are popularly associated with Communism and which may, indeed, be quite similar to those pursued by the Bolsheviks after their Revolution in Russia. If nationalists act in this fashion, it can be accounted for by their nationalism alone, however, and without reference to Communism. For nationalism in underdeveloped countries is, as we have seen, a movement directed against political and economic domination from abroad by colonialism and against domestic political and economic domination by the native aristocracy. Nor is it surprising that it may adopt policies similar to those of the Russian Revolution if we consider that Revolution itself as a nationalist movement in an underdeveloped country.

Individual nationalist intellectuals in underdeveloped countries have, to be sure, been influenced by Leninist thought, which, as we saw, adapts Marxism to the needs of such people.[50] In this sense, they may indeed be called Communists, but in this sense the Communists in Russia and in the Communist parties are not Communists any more. When nationalists today are expropriating and redistributing property, they may be influenced by Marx or Lenin, but they are not likely to be acting at the behest of Khrushchev and of local Communist parties. These domestic aspects of nationalism—the "class struggle"—are precisely the ones in which the Communists are least interested. To them, nationalism is chiefly useful as anti-Americanism, and hence changes in the property system matter to them only if the property involved happens to be American-owned, as was often the case in Cuba. On this point it is instructive to compare the non-Communist party member Castro's policies of far-reaching nationalization and land reform with the official Communist Party government in the Indian state of Kerala. The latter, the only Soviet-influenced Communist government to come to power since the present Communist attitude has matured, was far less radical on land reform than the Cuban government and no more so than the non-Communist Indian state governments. It took steps to attract private Indian capital to the state and did not even carry out its campaign promises to nationalize foreign-owned enterprises.[51]

[50] According to Adam B. Ulam, *The Unfinished Revolution,* every society undergoing industrialization passes through a "Marxist" stage, even if there is no Soviet or Communist influence whatever, because of Marxism's peculiar appeal to such societies. Cf. footnote 13, p. 73.
[51] Overstreet, "Soviet and Communist Policy in India," *The Journal of Politics,* XX, No. 1 (February 1958), 200–202.

Being largely interested in the foreign policy aspects of nationalism, the Communists, even more than the non-Communist nationalists, seek to maintain domestic unity cutting across all class lines. Since non-Communist nationalists may threaten this unity with their policies of expropriation of landed and sometimes of industrial and commercial proprietors, the Communists may be found to oppose such policies, as they apparently did in Iraq after Kassem's seizure of power. To the extent that they are ideologically distinguishable from the other nationalists at all, then, the Communists are likely to be found on the "right" and the others on the "left" on matters of domestic policy—that area of policy where the terms "right" and "left" have traditionally been used.

If Communism is defined not as some ideology of the past, whether Marx's or Lenin's, but as whatever movement abroad Moscow backs, then Communism has become more and more identical with nationalism in underdeveloped countries. It did not invent that nationalism any more than it had earlier invented proletarianism, but it is using it with vastly more success. Nothing said here implies that this nationalism can be used only by Communism. Its demands for rapid modernization and independence can perhaps also be met by the West, conceivably even better met. But it must be realized that in the past the Western powers have, by and large, been widely regarded as the enemies of independence and often also of modernization in the underdeveloped countries The Soviet Union, on the other hand, can claim never to have been colonialist and to have granted equality with the Russians to the subject peoples of the Tsarist empire. Soviet expansion both in Asia and in Eastern Europe has everywhere been accompanied by rapid industrialization and modernization. To the underdeveloped countries and particularly to their intellectuals, it is therefore anything but a relevant example of colonialism, no matter how much suffering and suppression it may have brought to many. Finally, the Soviet Union can claim a background similar to that of the underdeveloped countries and shares the enmity of many of their intellectual leaders towards the West, a situation of which the Communists have, if only in recent years, taken advantage by converting themselves into nationalists.

5. The Chinese and Soviet Views
of Communism in Underdeveloped Countries*

Introductory Note. When I wrote my "Essay in the Politics of Development" in 1960, the Sino-Soviet conflict had just become public, and I devoted only about one page to it. I noted even then that the conflict would persist, for I saw it as resulting from the very different levels of economic development of the two countries and the consequent differences between their elites and their policies. I explored this point a little further a year later in my article on "The Chinese and Soviet Views of Communism in Underdeveloped Countries." At a time when there was still widespread doubt as to the depth and even the reality of the Sino-Soviet conflict, I wanted particularly to document at some length what I had merely hinted at in my essay—that as Moscow moved to subordinate Communist parties to the leadership of non-Communist modernizing movements, Peking followed suit only part of the way and by the late 1950s tended to return to a policy of Communist party opposition to these movements. This divergence of the policies recommended to the Communist parties of underdeveloped countries by Moscow and Peking has since continued and has resulted in factionalism and even splits in these parties, notably in India, where separately organized Soviet- and Chinese-oriented Communist parties are now bitterly competing with each other.

However, while the Sino-Soviet conflict has grown in depth since my article was written in late 1961, the aspects with which I was concerned remain important elements in it. The article is therefore still of some interest in pointing to the beginnings of a major present-day development, particularly when it is read in the context of my general ideas on the development of Communist and Soviet policy on the one hand and on the different functions that Communist myths serve for the Soviet and Chinese Communists on the other. I touched on the latter subject in some of my later articles, particularly in "Myth, Self-Fulfilling Prophecy, and Symbolic Reassurance in the East-West Conflict" (reprinted on pp. 121–144).

* Reprinted, by permission, from *Survey* (London), No. 43 (August 1962), 119–129. Certain passages and footnotes eliminated from the original manuscript for publication have been restored here. So has the title which appeared in *Survey* as "Russia, China, and Nationalist Movements."

By 1949, as a result of the adoption of a new line by Moscow, the Soviet and the Chinese Communists had come to agree on the strategy to be followed by Communist parties in underdeveloped countries. Until about 1956, their views evolved in parallel fashion. In the next half decade, however, the Soviet view of the role Communist parties ought to play in such countries continued to develop, while the Chinese reverted to an earlier position vis-à-vis nationalist neutralist governments. The attitudes of the two governing Communist elites have thus increasingly diverged and come into conflict. In the following brief interpretive essay, an attempt is made to sketch the broad outlines of this development and to suggest some explanations for this important aspect of the current Sino-Soviet dispute.[1]

I

Within two or three years after the onset of the cold war between the United States and the Soviet Union, Communist parties the world over had begun to adjust to the new position of the Soviet Union in international politics. They did so by adopting—under Moscow's more or less efficient guidance and undergoing more or less painful internal upheavals—a new strategy. The prewar "popular front" and war-time "national front" had to be abandoned, for the Communists' allies under these policies—socialists, liberals, nationalists, etc.—had to be "unmasked" and fought as stooges of American "imperialism." The Soviet leaders now saw the world divided, as Andrei Zhdanov put it at the founding meeting of the Cominform in September 1947, into an imperialist, anti-democratic camp headed by the United States and an anti-imperialist, democratic camp headed by the Soviet Union.[2] All forces, including most nationalist movements in underdeveloped countries, that were not pro-Soviet were regarded as pro-American.

In an attempt to create as wide an anti-American front as possible, the popular and national front policies were not replaced by a return to Communism's earlier proletarian anti-capitalism. Rather, after some uncertainty prevailing on this point from 1947 to 1949, directives from Moscow made it quite clear that Communist parties were expected to

---

[1] For an excellent, well-documented analysis highly relevant to the present article, see Donald S. Zagoria, "Sino-Soviet Friction in Underdeveloped Areas," *Problems of Communism*, X, No. 2 (March–April 1961), 1–13.

[2] A. Zhdanov, "The International Situation," *For a Lasting Peace, for a People's Democracy!*, November 10, 1947, pp. 2–4.

appeal to and to claim to represent all individuals and groups, regardless of social class, who could be attracted by a program of opposition to American foreign policy objectives. Thus, a Communist leader like B. T. Ranadive, the General Secretary of the Indian Communist Party, who looked on the native bourgeoisie rather than foreign imperialism as the main enemy and, as late as 1949, attacked Mao Tse-tung's views on the bourgeoisie as "horrifying" and "reactionary and counterrevolutionary,"[3] had to be dismissed and his Party's line subjected to a sharp turn.[4]

The new strategy advocated by Moscow (which I have called the "neo-Maoist" one) was quite similar to the "four-class" appeal developed earlier by Mao, when he, too, sought to unite all strata of the population, including the "national bourgeoisie," against a foreign imperialist enemy (Japan) and could not do so through a united front with the major nationalist movement (the Kuomintang). By 1949, then, the strategies recommended to the Communist parties of underdeveloped countries by the Soviet and by the Chinese Communists had come to coincide. This was made public to all the world when Moscow chose Peking as the locale and leading Chinese Communists as the main speakers for the conference of its World Federation of Trade Unions held in November of that year. It was there that, with evident Soviet approval, Liu Shao-chi declared the "Chinese path" to be obligatory for the Communist parties of all underdeveloped countries and defined it primarily as one in which "the working class must unite with all the other classes, political parties and groups, organizations and individuals who are willing to oppose the oppression of imperialism and its lackeys."[5]

Under neo-Maoism as it was adopted in 1949, both the Soviet and the Chinese Communists regarded most of the nationalist movements in underdeveloped countries and the governments they formed in newly independent states as not "truly" nationalist or independent but as servants of American "imperialism." They did not, however, view all native capitalists or even what they call "feudal" forces in this light. Hence both stood for a nationwide anti-imperialist movement which had to

[3] "Struggle for People's Democracy and Socialism," *Communist* (Bombay), II, No. 4 (June–July 1949), 78–79.
[4] See particularly the editorial in the Cominform journal, "Mighty Advance of the National Liberation Movement in the Colonial and Dependent Countries," *For a Lasting Peace, for a People's Democracy!*, January 27, 1950, p. 1.
[5] *World Trade Union Movement*, No. 8 (December 1949), p. 14.

be led by the Communist party. Liu's statement, just cited, stressed this point:

This nationwide united front must be led by the working class and its party, the Communist Party . . . and must be built around the working class and the Communist Party as its center. It must not be led by the wavering and compromising national bourgeoisie or petty bourgeoisie and their parties.

For three decades, Communist parties in underdeveloped countries had, generally with disastrous results to themselves, insisted on their proletarian character. Now these parties, always led and often largely composed of intellectuals, were to appeal to all classes with an anti-imperialist policy of opposition to the United States abroad and of rapid industrialization at home. They were thus to be turned into parties very similar, both in their social composition and their appeals, to the major non-Communist nationalist movements—but were to be strongly opposed to these movements.

II

Soon after its adoption, the neo-Maoist policy of nationalist opposition to nationalist movements as recommended to the Communist parties by the Soviet and Chinese Communists began to be modified. The Soviet leaders evidently gave up or postponed for the time being the hope of Communist parties coming to power and accepted, instead, the stability, at least for some time to come, of the nationalist regimes. And, most important, they recognized that such regimes, even if they would not turn Communist, need not be and in fact were not entirely pro-American and could become anti-American.

This change in Soviet attitude is generally ascribed to the post-Stalin period, when, indeed, it became more and more obvious. There is evidence, however, that its beginnings must be looked for some time before Stalin's death. As early as December 1950, the Indian Communists, who, like the Soviet Communists, had been denouncing Nehru for his subservience to Anglo-American imperialism, were told that "indications of a divergence, even though still hesitant and limited, of Premier Nehru . . . from the reckless aggressive war policy . . . are a very important development."[6]

Since then Soviet diplomacy and propaganda have more and more

[6] "Palme Dutt Answers Questions on India," *Cross Roads* (Bombay), January 19, 1951, p. 7.

emphasized the role of the Soviet Union as the champion of the neutralist nations. Communist parties could consequently no longer be permitted indiscriminately to denounce the governments of such nations. They were now being urged by Moscow to recognize the independence from Western influence of their erstwhile nationalist enemies and to give support to their foreign policies. While they were still adapting themselves to their new role, the Soviet Union began to provide increasing amounts of economic and technical aid to certain neutralist countries, notably India. Thus committed to support of their domestic policies of economic development as well, Moscow had to push the Communist parties further away from their attitude of opposition to the nationalist regimes. R. Palme Dutt, serving as Moscow's voice guiding the Communist Party of India, in a significant article in October 1954 implied that Communist Party support for Nehru's government was really inseparable from support for his foreign policies.[7] And just before an important electoral contest in the Indian Communists' stronghold in Andhra between the CPI and Nehru's Congress Party, *Pravda,* on January 26, 1955, published an editorial praising the Nehru government not only for its foreign but also its domestic policy.[8]

Moscow's transition from the neo-Maoist strategy of opposition to nationalist regimes in underdeveloped countries to a policy of support for such regimes (which, however, retained the key feature of neo-Maoism—the Communists' appeal to all classes) was completed by the mid-fifties. In June 1955, Nehru was being given a tremendous reception in Moscow, where, only five or six years earlier, he had been regarded as a hireling of Anglo-American imperialism. At the end of the same year, Khrushchev and Bulganin made their famous visit to India (as well as Burma and Afghanistan) offering friendship and economic aid to Nehru's neutralist government. Finally, Zhdanov's two-camp concept was officially buried, when, at the 20th Party Congress in February 1956, Khrushchev recognized "the emergence in the world arena of a group of peace-loving European and Asian states which have proclaimed non-participation in blocs as a principle of their foreign policy," and

---

[7] "New Features in National Liberation Struggle of Colonial and Dependent Peoples," *For a Lasting Peace, for a People's Democracy!,* October 8, 1954, p. 6.
[8] *Current Digest of the Soviet Press,* VII, No. 4 (March 9, 1955), 33. A well-documented account of the CPI's slow and reluctant adjustment to the Soviet policy changes outlined here appears in Marshall Windmiller, "Indian Communism and the New Soviet Line," *Pacific Affairs,* XXIX, No. 4 (December 1956), 347–366.

included these, along with the Communist countries in "a vast 'peace zone.' "[9]

During the first half of the fifties, the attitude of the Chinese Communists toward the nationalist governments of neutralist countries paralleled that of the Soviet Communists. The position of these governments, particularly Nehru's, on the Korean war convinced the Chinese, too, that these were not mere puppets of American imperialism. Chou En-lai's visit to New Delhi in June 1954, where he and Nehru agreed to the Five Principles of peaceful co-existence, and the moderate role he played at the Bandung Conference in April 1955 made it amply clear that at that time the Chinese Communists supported the neutralist governments of Afro-Asian countries. Their policy, like that of the Soviet Union, implied that the Communist parties of these countries should not oppose their governments. They should, under Communist leadership, form united fronts of all anti-imperialist forces regardless of their class character and lend support to their governments' anti-imperialist policies.

III

At the 20th Party Congress of 1956, Khrushchev asserted that "in all the forms of transition to socialism, an absolute and decisive requirement is political leadership of the working class, headed by its vanguard. The transition to socialism is impossible without this."[10] However, in the very same year, this old established Communist doctrine, which provides much of the *raison d'être* of Communist parties, was beginning to be modified in Moscow with respect to underdeveloped countries.

The doctrine of proletarian leadership and—what amounts to the same thing in Communist thinking—Communist party leadership in all conflicts in which Communists have been engaged has occupied such a central place in Communist ideology that it has not been openly thrown overboard all at once. Soviet leaders and writers keep repeating it, as Khrushchev did at the 20th Congress, to provide symbolic reassurance

---

[9] N. S. Khrushchev, "The Central Committee Report," in Leo Gruliow, ed., *Current Soviet Policies—II: The Documentary Record of the 20th Party Congress and its Aftermath* (New York: Frederick A. Praeger, 1957), p. 33. The new program of the CPSU also speaks of the newly independent states as not belonging "either to the system of imperialist states or to the system of Socialist states," but as "a revolutionary force destroying imperialism." "The New Program of the Communist Party of the Soviet Union," in Arthur P. Mendel, ed., *Essential Works of Marxism* (New York: Bantam Books, 1961), pp. 371–486, at p. 405.

[10] N. S. Khrushchev, *op. cit.*, p. 38.

to their followers. They may continue to do so also in response to the pressure of the Chinese Communists to whom, for reasons to be indicated, insistence on Communist party leadership is a matter of great importance. The Communist parties all over the world, too, frequently cling to the concept, motivated not merely by doctrinal orthodoxy and habit but, more obviously, by the desire for self-preservation.

The repetition of old formulae cannot conceal the marked shift in Soviet behavior, however. It is most clearly visible in the changing foreign policies of the Soviet Union during the 1950's which increasingly rely on the non-Communist nationalist leaders and movements more heavily than on the Communist parties to support the Soviet Union in its conflict with the United States, i.e., to assume the leadership in the "struggle against imperialism."

The same Soviet approach of putting nationalist movements ahead of Communist ones may be seen reflected in the less well-known area of international trade union politics. Not only have Communist-dominated trade unions in underdeveloped countries, like the Communist parties themselves, been directed to make no trouble for nationalist governments, but, beginning in 1956, a number of them, frequently in the face of local Communist resistance, were dissolved and merged with their rival trade union organizations dominated by the nationalist movements. This happened in Tunisia, in Algeria, and in the former French West African colonies, and pressure in the same direction was apparently exerted by Moscow in India as well. Equally significant is the support extended by the Communist WFTU to the establishment of the nationalist-neutralist International Confederation of Arab Trade Unions (ICATU), created by Nasser in 1956, and All-African Trade Union Federation (AATUF), founded in Casablanca in 1961.[11] While all these maneuvers probably weakened the local Communist leaders and organizations, they no doubt strengthened the Soviet Union in the underdeveloped countries involved through its improved cooperation with their nationalist movements.

Though still relatively rare, statements more or less openly recognizing the leading position of the non-Communist nationalist movement and suggesting the subordination to it of local Communists have appeared in Communist writings of the past few years. Some Soviet statements

[11] A well-documented account of these events may be found in George E. Lichtblau, "The Communist Labor Offensive in Former Colonial Countries," *Industrial and Labor Relations Review*, XV, No. 3 (April 1962), 376–401.

on Africa contain no class analysis or any claim to the existence of Communist parties at all, but speak merely of conflict between "the people" and "imperialism," thus implying Soviet support of and reliance on non-Communist nationalism. Where class analysis is provided, the bourgeoisie seems to be expected to be more effective in that conflict than the proletariat. Thus, one article, after ritually stating that "The working class is the most active and consistent force in the national liberation struggle" immediately admits that that class accounts for only 1.5 to 5 per cent of the population in the African countries it mentions and proceeds to speak of the national bourgeoisie as a "progressive factor" in the struggle against colonialism and as a class "expressing at a definite stage the interests of the patriotic forces of the nation." "Patriotic tribal chiefs" are also mentioned as participating in the national liberation movements, which are characterized as democratic, anti-imperialist and anti-colonialist but not socialist.[12] Similarly, another article admits that "most African countries as yet have no parties of the working class which would be able to formulate the national tasks at the various stages of the liberation movement," but states that "in a number of countries that have won political independence genuinely national leaders have come to the fore and are leading the struggle for the achievement of complete independence, both political and economic."[13]

Blas Roca, the General Secretary of the Cuban Popular Socialist (Communist) Party stated quite frankly that the Cuban Revolution was not led by the Communists:

> The armed struggle was initiated by the petty bourgeoisie. The working-class action could not be the decisive factor of the revolution. . . . The revolution marched triumphantly from the countryside to the towns, from the provinces to the capital. The political leadership of the armed struggle was in the hands of the petty bourgeoisie while the rebel army consisted mainly of poor peasants and farm laborers.[14]

This admission cannot be undone by Castro's later retroactive claim that he had himself been a "Marxist-Leninist."

[12] A. Iskenderov, "A Continent in Ferment," *World Marxist Review*, III, No. 1 (January 1960), 42–46.
[13] I. Plyshevsky, "Some Problems of the Independence Struggle in Africa," *World Marxist Review*, IV, No. 7 (July 1961), 32–39.
[14] Blas Roca, "The Cuban Revolution in Action," *World Marxist Review*, II, No. 8 (August 1959), 16–22, p. 18.

With respect to India, Soviet statements have gone from finding Nehru's role a "progressive" one, as they had by 1955, to references to Nehru's "socialism" by 1956. Thus, speaking of the second Indian five-year plan, an article in *Kommunist* appearing at the time of the 20th Party Congress, says: "This aspiration toward socialism, concerning which Nehru has spoken so often, is heartily supported by the progressive circles of India . . . ," though it adds that Nehru's socialism "differs from our Marxist-Leninist understanding."[15] A few months later, another Soviet article praised the Indian Congress Party's commitment to a socialist goal and concluded that "given close cooperation by all the progressive forces of the country, there is the possibility for India to develop along socialist lines."[16]

That the bourgeoisie is leading the way to socialism, as this passage implies, is not, or certainly not yet, the general theme of Soviet analysis of present political trends in underdeveloped countries. More often it is credited with developing "state capitalism." which "plays a progressive role."[17] But frequently the attainment of socialism in underdeveloped countries is simply not dealt with at all or is, by implication, postponed to a sufficiently far-off future so as not to affect present-day Communist policy. The emphasis is invariably placed on the goal not of social revolution but of national independence, on conflict not with capitalism but with imperialism, i.e., American foreign policy—and there the bourgeoisie is seen as capable of playing a "progressive" role.

The Soviet Union's present policy of reliance on the nationalist movements was strongly defended by E. Zhukov, a leading Soviet expert on underdeveloped countries, in an important article in August 1960:

It is known that at the head of the majority of new national states of Asia and Africa stand bourgeois political leaders who usually take a position

[15] D. Degtiar, "Development of the National Economy of India," *Kommunist*, XXXII (March 1956), 72–87, quoted in Gene D. Overstreet, " Soviet and Communist Policy in India," *The Journal of Politics*, XX, No. 1 (February 1958), 193.

[16] Modeste Rubinstein, "A Non-Capitalist Path for Underdeveloped Countries," *New Times*, July and August 1956, quoted in Gene D. Overstreet and Marshall Windmiller, *Communism in India* (Berkeley and Los Angeles: University of California Press, 1959), p. 326, which also quotes from the Indian Communists' furious reply to this "astounding" suggestion from Moscow.

[17] *Fundamentals of Marxism-Leninism.* (Moscow: Foreign Languages Publishing House, 1963), p. 419. ". . . in the countries of Asia and Africa state capitalism in its present form . . . was called into existence in the endeavour to find a defence against the attack of the capitalist monopolies of the West and is objectively aimed against their expansion." *Ibid.*

under a nationalistic flag. However, this cannot belittle the progressive historical importance of the breakthrough that has taken place on the imperialist front. The working class is the most consistent enemy of imperialism. Nevertheless Lenin considered it natural that *at the beginning* of any national movement the bourgeoisie plays the role of its hegemonic force (leader) and urged that in the struggle for the self-determination of nations support be given to the most revolutionary elements of the bourgeois-democratic national-liberation movements. . . . An arrogant slighting of anti-imperialist actions when in certain historical conditions nonproletarian elements appear on the forestage, is a most dangerous form of sectarianism that leads to self-isolation.[18]

To be sure, both to maintain their own claims to orthodoxy and as a reaction to Chinese pressure, Soviet Communists acknowledge leadership by the national bourgeoisie only "at the beginning" or "in the present stage" of the national liberation movement. They even invented a new name for this stage, that of "national democracy," which is regarded as a transition to the ultimate attainment of "socialism."[19] That ultimate goal of socialism, however, is in their view too distant to influence Soviet policy decisions in the present, and it is thus the "transitional" stage that is decisive.[20]

The important innovation in the policy recommended to the Communist parties of underdeveloped countries by the Soviet Union since 1956 is the willingness to put the nationalist movements (labelled "bourgeois" or, in Cuba, "petty-bourgeois") in the position of leaders and the Communist parties in that of followers, whether it be in the march toward

---

[18] Ye. Zhukov, "Significant Factor of Our Times. On Some Questions of the Present-Day National-Liberation Movement," *Pravda*, August 26, 1960, pp. 3–4; condensed translation in *The Current Digest of the Soviet Press*, XII, No. 34 (September 21, 1960), 18–19. Italics in the original.

[19] "Declaration of Representatives of the Eighty-one Communist Parties, Meeting in Moscow, November–December 1960," Dan N. Jacobs, ed., *The New Communist Manifesto* (Evanston, Illinois: Row, Peterson, 1961), pp. 33–34. See also W. Z. Laqueur, "Towards National Democracy: Soviet Doctrine and the New Countries," *Survey*, No. 37 (July–September 1961), 3–11, and Zagoria, *op. cit.*, p. 5.

[20] As Zhukov wrote: "For many lagging countries of Asia, and especially Africa, . . . the central task . . . remains for a *comparatively long period* of time that of 'struggle not against capital but against survivals of the Middle Ages.' From this stems the possibility of the cooperation *over a long period* of the workers, peasants and intelligentsia . . . with that part of the national bourgeoisie which is interested in independent political and economic development of its country and is ready to defend its independence against any encroachments by the imperialist powers." Zhukov, *op. cit.* Italics added.

"socialism" or the march toward "national liberation" (a distinction which is in any case probably becoming more and more shadowy in the minds of Soviet leaders). That the idea of the bourgeoisie leading the proletariat toward socialism is a startlingly new one by all traditional Communist standards needs no emphasis or elucidation. However, the acceptance of the bourgeoisie in the leading role of the "national liberation" movement, too, is a decisive break with the policy advocated by Communists until the mid-fifties. To see this we need merely compare recent Soviet statements on the subject with Liu's insistence on Communist party leadership in his authoritative 1949 definition of neo-Maoism quoted above.

IV

The arrogant sectarians whom Zhukov attacked—or counterattacked—are the Chinese Communists. In cooperating with the nationalist governments of some underdeveloped countries, they had never gone as far as Moscow has since 1956 to subordinate the Communist parties to the nationalists, and beginning about 1957 or 1958 they returned more and more to the original neo-Maoist strategy of opposition to the nationalist governments.

Whatever the reasons for the reversal of the Chinese attitude toward the nationalist-neutralist governments, the divergence of Chinese from Soviet policy on this point is clear. However, just as the Soviet Communists' repetition of the doctrine of proletarian leadership obscures their actual policies, so the constant use by the Chinese Communists of the Marxian symbols of the class struggle and the dictatorship of the proletariat serves to distort the actual issues in the conflict between Moscow and Peking. That conflict does not turn on the relationship between the proletariat as a class and the bourgeoisie as a class.[21] Both sides are quite agreed on the necessity of Communist cooperation with the national bourgeoisie in the conflict with "imperialism"—though it now suits Peking more than Moscow to stress the vacillating character of the bourgeoisie in its alliance with the proletariat. The difference lies elsewhere: The Chinese Communists want Communist parties in underdeveloped countries to cooperate with the bourgeoisie *against* the na-

[21] That the Chinese Communists' revolution had even less to do with the "class struggle" than the Russian Communists' is well pointed out by Robert Vincent Daniels, "The Chinese Revolution in Russian Perspective," *World Politics*, XIII, No. 2 (January 1961), 210–230, particularly p. 218.

tionalist governments and even encourage Communist-led "armed struggle" against them, while the Soviet Communists want Communist parties to cooperate *with* these nationalist governments (whom they identify with the national bourgeoisie). What is at stake, then, is the relationship between the Communist parties (often labelled "the proletariat") and the nationalist governments.

The Chinese Communists evidently no longer trust the anti-imperialism of these governments.

. . . these states can never expect to effect the transition to socialism, nor indeed can they thoroughly fulfill the task of the nationalist, democratic revolution. It should be added that even the national independence they have won is by no means secure. . . . [The bourgeois nationalists] may even pave the way for the emergence of bureaucratic capitalism, which is an ally of imperialism and feudalism. . . . In the final analysis, they can never escape from the control and bondage of imperialism.[22]

To be sure, where the "anti-imperialist" character of a nationalist movement was beyond doubt, because it was in open conflict with one of the Western powers, the Chinese Communists have supported it, sometimes sooner and more vigorously than the Soviet Communists, as when they recognized the FLN as the government of Algeria at a time when Khrushchev still hoped for improved relations with de Gaulle.[23]

Generally, however, the Chinese Communists insist that the Communist parties in underdeveloped countries must remain independent of the nationalist movements, must lead their own united front against these movements, and must themselves eventually seize power—and they imply strongly that this can ordinarily be done only by means of "armed struggle." As against Soviet suggestions that Communist parties follow the leadership of non-Communist nationalists, Liu Shaochi, in 1959 insisted—as he had a decade earlier when he spoke for

[22] Wang Chia-hsiang in *Red Flag* on the 10th (1959) anniversary of the People's Republic, as quoted in Zagoria, *op. cit.*, p. 8.
[23] See Donald S. Zagoria, "Strains in the Sino-Soviet Alliance," *Problems of Communism*, IX, No. 3 (May–June 1960), 9–10. See also Yu Chao-li, "The Great Significance of Cuba's Victory," *Peking Review*, IV, No. 20 (May 19, 1961), 10–15; "Anti-Imperialist Struggle in Angola," *Peking Review*, IV, No. 19 (May 12, 1961), 11; and "1961 Sees Africa Freedom Strides," Peking NCNA in English to Asia, December 28, 1961, as three examples of Chinese statements supporting the "people" in their struggle against "imperialism" without any mention of classes or the Communist party.

both the Chinese and the Soviet Communists—on "the firm grasping of hegemony in the democratic revolution by the proletariat through the Communist party."[24] The Chinese continue to summarize "the experience gained and the road taken by the Chinese revolution" as "under the leadership of the working class (through the Communist Party) and based upon the alliance of the workers and peasants, to unite all the forces that can be united, wage armed struggles and establish the people's democratic dictatorship; then to achieve socialism and communism."[25] And as against Soviet emphasis on the nationalist movements, the Chinese emphasize the importance of the Party: "Lenin considered it of prime importance for the proletariat to establish its own genuinely revolutionary political party which completely breaks with opportunism, that is, a Communist Party, if the proletarian revolution is to be carried through and the proletarian dictatorship established and consolidated."[26]

To Moscow's suggestion that the non-Communist nationalist movements may be leading the way to socialism, Peking replies sharply: "The modern revisionists and certain representatives of the bourgeoisie try to make people believe that it is possible to achieve socialism without a revolutionary party of the proletariat and without the . . . correct [united front] policies of the revolutionary party of the proletariat. . . . This is sheer nonsense and pure deception." And in answer to Moscow's praise of Nehru's socialism, Peking sneeringly says that a "motley variety of so-called 'socialisms' have emerged from among the exploiting classes in certain countries. . . . They only put up the signboard of 'socialism' but actually practice capitalism."[27]

[24] Liu Shao-chi, *The Victory of Marxism-Leninism in China* (Peking: Foreign Languages Press, 1959), quoted in Zagoria, "Sino-Soviet Friction in Underdeveloped Areas," *op. cit.*, p. 4.

[25] Li Wei-han, "The United front—A Magic Weapon of the Chinese People for Winning Victory, *Peking Review*, IV, No. 23 (June 9, 1961), 13–16, and No. 24 (June 16, 1961), 17–21, at p. 21. For a Chinese statement heavily emphasizing the importance of "armed struggle" and directed against the Soviet position on the subject, see Kuo Chi-chou, "Acclaiming the Great Victories of the National Liberation Movement," in the New Year (1962) issue of *Red Flag*, summarized by Peking NCNA in English to Asia, January 1, 1962.

[26] "Long Live Leninism," *Red Flag*, No. 8 (April 16, 1960), reprinted in G. F. Hudson, Richard Lowenthal and Roderick MacFarquhar, *The Sino-Soviet Dispute* (New York: Frederick A. Praeger, 1961), pp. 82–112, at p. 84.

[27] *Ibid.*, p. 109. Also, while Moscow praises his anti-imperialism, Peking denounces "Jawaharlal Nehru and his ilk" for disseminating "absurdities . . . in the service of imperialism." Quoted from a *Ta Kung Pao* commentator by Peking NCNA in English to Asia, December 31, 1961.

V

The reasons for the different policies advocated by the two Communist elites are to be sought in the different attitudes and needs of these elites and the means available to them. It would, indeed, be surprising to find the leaderships of two societies in as different economic stages of development as the Soviet Union and China to have the same interests. The expectation of some analysts that Khrushchev and Mao would always agree and the insistence of some observers that, in fact, they still do, simply because both are Communists, rests on a misunderstanding of the role of Communist ideology and on acceptance at face value of the Communists' own assertion of Communism's monolithic and unchanging character.

The prime interest underlying the policies of both the Soviet and the Chinese Communist leaders may safely be assumed to be the consolidation and expansion of their respective power. Furthermore, they are in agreement that these interests must be realized by means of rapid industrialization at home and the reduction of American power and influence abroad. It is this similarity which permits both the Soviet and the Chinese Communists to use the same Marxian concepts and words, for terms like "socialism" and "communism"—as they have been modified since 1917 and so far as they now have any meaning at all—stand for the transformation of an underdeveloped country into an advanced industrial one and "anti-imperialism" means opposition to the Western powers and, above all, the United States.

Use of the same words, however, can no longer hide the fact that, as the result of the different levels of economic development of the two countries, the similarities of both means and ends are only superficial. "Industrialization" in China still means creating the bases of an industrial economy with consequent emphasis on the construction of heavy industry. In the Soviet Union it means more and more the satisfaction of the long pent-up demand for consumer goods, particularly the demands of the new managerial-bureaucratic upper class which is growing both in numbers and in power. This difference may well underlie the different attitudes of the two regimes toward Stalin and the methods of government he represents, for these were associated with the build-up of heavy industry.

More important in our context are the differences between the approaches taken by the two Communist regimes to the reduction of

American influence abroad. The present generation of Soviet leaders inherited a powerful governmental and economic apparatus, reasonably secure from internal and external threats. To them the achievements of the Revolution are to be preserved by their present beneficiaries; "the Revolution" has become a symbol of conservatism. The present Chinese Communist leaders, on the other hand, have spent most of their lives fighting to establish, maintain and expand their power, often by armed force, and much of the time against what they consider "imperialist" external enemies—first Japan and then, in Korea and Formosa, the United States. To them, "the Revolution"—meaning not the overthrow of the rule of one class by another, but consolidation of Communist party power—is still in progress and is likely to be thought of in terms of armed conflict. No wonder that when the Communist leaders in Moscow think of expanding their power abroad and reducing that of the United States, they think primarily of relations with established governments; when the Communist leaders in Peking pursue the same general goal, they think rather of overthrowing established governments.

In this difference in attitudes may lie one of the roots of the Sino-Soviet controversy on the role to be played by Communist parties in underdeveloped countries. But however that may be,[28] the means available to the two regimes in their opposition to American foreign policies compel them to assign different roles to these parties. To both the Soviet and the Chinese governments, foreign Communist parties appear as only one tool of foreign policy. Both also rely on "cultural" contacts, i.e., propaganda, in foreign countries and on economic aid to such countries, and on diplomatic and military pressure. It is the degree to which these various instruments can be effective and hence the relative importance of each in the foreign policy arsenal of Moscow and Peking that makes for the difference between the two.

A Soviet article is most revealing in this connection. It states:

The force of the influence of the world socialist system on the liberation struggle does not at all lie in "spurring" revolutions, but in something different.

First of all, under the influence of the successes of the socialist countries *socialism is becoming increasingly attractive to all the peoples of the world.* Capitalism cannot withstand peaceful competition with socialism because of

---

[28] R. V. Daniels, *op. cit.*, provides some cogent arguments against the view that the Chinese, unlike the Soviet, Communists are still in their "revolutionary" phase, emphasizing that, unlike the Bolsheviks in 1917, they had years of governmental experience by 1949.

the immeasurably greater opportunities which the socialist system has opened up for the growth of production forces and culture. . . . In the near future, the Soviet Union will have the highest standard of living in the world and the shortest working day.[29]

The Chinese Communists, facing the prospect of a low standard of living and a long working day for some time to come, may well be less sanguine about the attractiveness of their propaganda.[30] Similarly, with regard to foreign economic aid and technical assistance programs, the Soviet leaders are optimistic. The passage just cited continues: "In the transition to socialism each country can now rely . . . *on the economic assistance of the socialist countries, on close cooperation with them.*"[31] Without much capital or industrial expertise to export, the Chinese Communists cannot hope to hold out such a promise and to make the governments of underdeveloped countries dependent on them by this means.

Finally, in the diplomatic and military arena, too, China is not the equal of the Soviet Union—though this is likely to become less true as time goes on. She has fewer diplomatic contacts, in part as a result of her exclusion from the United Nations, and, as long as she is without nuclear weapons and long-range rockets, she can only put her immediate neighbors in the long arc from Korea to India under direct military pressure. Of this, too, the Soviet leaders are very much aware when they remind the Chinese that "changes have taken place in the world which no one can today ignore." "The fundamental changes in the correlation of forces in the international arena in favor of socialism have created a historically new situation . . . : The socialist countries, with the active support of the progressive forces of the whole world, have *a real possibility of paralyzing the interference of international reaction in the affairs of a country carrying out a revolution.*"[32] And they not

---

[29] A. Belyakov and F. Burlatsky, "The Leninist Theory of Socialist Revolution and our Times," *Kommunist*, No. 13 (September 1960), 10–27, translated in *The Current Digest of the Soviet Press*, XII, No. 39 (October 26, 1960), 3–10 and 20, at p. 4. Italics in this and the following quotations are in the original.

[30] It is conceivable, however, that as the emphasis in the Soviet Union shifts from production to consumption, its example will appear increasingly irrelevant—and hence unattractive, as does that of the United States with its economy of abundance—to the intellectuals in underdeveloped countries who must still solve the problem of industrialization.

[31] Belyakov and Burlatsky, *op. cit.*, *The Current Digest of the Soviet Press*, XII, No. 39 (October 26, 1960), 4.

[32] *Ibid.*, p. 5.

only take credit for the victory of the revolution in China, because they claim that their power prevented American intervention—a direct slap at their opponents in Peking—but they point specifically to their possession of atomic weapons and their ability to paralyze "imperialist intervention" in Suez and Cuba—the kind of successes far from their borders which the Chinese Communists cannot claim.

Given their outlook as conditioned by their own experience and, above all, given the relative weakness of their other foreign policy tools, the Chinese Communists, like the Soviet Communists in the early years of their power, think chiefly of the foreign Communist parties when they think of expanding their power abroad. If underdeveloped countries are to be brought under Chinese Communist domination, then their present governments must eventually be overthrown and replaced by Communist parties looking to Peking for leadership. Hence they want these parties now to oppose the nationalist governments, who, not being subject to direct Chinese influence, appear to them shaky in their anti-imperialism if not subordinate to imperialism. They may well remember the disaster that befell their own Party in 1927 as a result of cooperation with a nationalist regime.

The Soviet Union, on the other hand, has sufficient strength to orient the non-Communist governments of some underdeveloped countries toward Moscow even now and expects to have more strength soon. Why, then, rely on the uncertain success of Communist parties in the relatively distant future when non-Communist leaders already in control of their governments can be dominated now or in the much nearer future? Why risk the establishment of more troublesome Communist governments that cannot be rigidly controlled from Moscow, like the Yugoslav and the Chinese ones, when non-Communist nationalist governments are quite adequate means of serving the Soviet foreign policy purpose of reducing American influence? That, rather than the establishment of socialism abroad, is the operative goal of the Soviet Union or, rather, "socialism" has been redefined to mean no more than dependence on the Soviet Union—as the above-cited article proclaims with a frankness that would have startled earlier Marxists preoccupied with the problems of the prerequisites of socialism and stages of history: *"Relying on the economic and political support of the socialist system, any country of the world has the possibility of making the transition to socialism, regardless of its level of development."*[33]

[33] *Ibid.*

In the Soviet scheme of things, Communist parties in underdeveloped countries, then, occupy a far less important role than in the Chinese one. They are to cooperate with the nationalist governments, follow their leadership, and, if necessary or convenient, they can be sacrificed to them. They may be useful means of pressure on these governments, but they are not to take power in the foreseeable future. No wonder that local Communists in many underdeveloped countries—including Ranadive who so vigorously denounced Mao in 1949—prefer the Peking to the Moscow line. It allots to them the role of leading a broad neo-Maoist united front against the nationalist governments rather than playing second fiddle to them.

6. Myth, Self-Fulfilling Prophecy, and Symbolic Reassurance in the East-West Conflict*

Introductory Note. In an article, entitled "The Western Word and the Non-Western World,"[1] I gave vent to my frustration at the inadequacy of our Western political vocabulary for the purpose of analyzing the politics of underdeveloped countries. Among other points, I stressed that the connotations, both empirical and normative, of terms like "Left" and "Right," "nationalism" and "militarism," "Fascism" and "socialism" were Western in origin, hence inappropriate to underdeveloped countries where the group or interest content of movements denoted by them was quite different. But then I noted that such inappropriate terms were applied to the politics of underdeveloped countries not only by Western observers but also by their own Western-influenced intellectual elites. In their minds—as well as in those of others who ascribe the Western meaning to the concepts even after they have been transferred from their Western home to an underdeveloped environment—the concepts become myths. As such they do influence behavior, so that the inappropriate concepts are by no means irrelevant for an understanding of the politics of underdeveloped countries. Thus an African leader who thinks of himself as a "socialist," though he represents intellectuals aiming at rapid industrialization rather than workers aiming at improving their position in an already industrialized society, may in part pattern his behavior by what he learned of British or French socialism. And, what is more, Western European socialists or American businessmen, accepting the same myth of African "socialism," may react to this leader's movement as they would to socialism in Western Europe.

My prime example of the process by which Western concepts can, with reference to underdeveloped countries, become myths that are believed in the underdeveloped countries as well as the West and can thus condition political behavior, was Communism. In the article mentioned above I devoted only three paragraphs to the conversion of Marx-

* Reprinted, by permission, from *The Journal of Conflict Resolution,* IX, No. 1 (March 1965), 1–17.

[1] *The American Behavioral Scientist,* VII, No. 8 (April 1964), 25–29.

121

ian concepts into Communist myths and their acceptance by Communists and non-Communists alike. I soon felt, however, that this process and especially its complex policy consequences should be further explored and I dealt with some of its aspects in my article on "Myth, Self-Fulfilling Prophecy, and Symbolic Reassurance in the East-West Conflict."

Read in conjunction with my writings reprinted above, this article helps explain why the vast changes in Soviet and Communist policy noted there have been so little recognized and, in particular, why both Communists and non-Communists tend to persist in the use of the language of "revolution" to describe a nonrevolutionary policy. It would seem that the kind of rapid and far-reaching change that Communism has undergone can take place only when it is masked by the verbal denial of change. This article may, then, throw some light on the peculiar fact that so many Communists and non-Communists, especially among the policy makers, insist that, in a rapidly changing world, Communism does not change—a view that is bound to affect their behavior and decisions and thus has significant policy consequences.

I might add that when this article was written in 1963–1964, I was perhaps somewhat more inclined than I am today to believe that, in the subtle interplay of myths and policies, the myth of World Communism might, under the impact of changing policies, be beginning to fade away. Now, in 1967, I might put a little more emphasis on my point stressing the opposite possibility that the myth can serve as a brake on the development of policies that reduce tensions and can even reverse such policies.

The myth must be judged as a means of acting on the present; any attempt to discuss how far it can be taken literally as future history is devoid of sense.

GEORGES SOREL

The self-fulfilling prophecy is, in the beginning, a false definition of the situation evoking a new behavior which makes the originally false conception come true. The specious validity of the self-fulfilling prophecy perpetuates a reign of error.

ROBERT K. MERTON

Emotional commitment to a symbol is associated with contentment and quiescence regarding problems that would otherwise arouse concern.

MURRAY EDELMAN

The purpose of this essay is to throw some new light on the well-known data of World Communism and the East–West conflict through the use of three interrelated concepts—Georges Sorel's "myth," Robert K. Merton's "self-fulfilling prophecy," and Murray Edelman's "symbolic reassurance." It is not meant to provide any new data on its subject or to present any full discussion of the three concepts or their complex relationships.

Sorel's myth was "a complex of remote goals, tense moral moods and expectations of apocalyptic success."[2] Guided and inspired by such a myth, individuals will behave as they would not in the absence of the myth. Hence the myth, however false, has real behavioral consequences. To Sorel, the myth was significant in accounting for the behavior and often the success of a single group vis-à-vis some opposition. In the following, we shall deal with a situation where the same myth has been accepted by two opposing groups, one regarding it positively, the other negatively. Each has acted on the basis of the myth and thereby reinforced it in the mind of the other.

It is here that Merton's concept of the self-fulfilling prophecy comes into play. But, like Sorel, Merton seems to be chiefly concerned with accounting for the behavior of single groups,[3] while our case is one of false beliefs held by two groups evoking behavior on the part of each which justifies and validates the originally false belief on the part of the other. Finally, our case will illustrate that one and the same myth can at various times and to various people be either an inspiration to action (as Sorel saw it) or serve as a reassuring symbol to induce political quiescence, a function brilliantly pointed out by Murray Edelman.[4]

In pointing to the mythical origins of at least some of the hostility prevailing between the Communist and the Western powers, we do

[2] Edward A. Shils, "Introduction to the American Edition," in Georges Sorel, *Reflections on Violence* (New York: Collier Books, 1961), p. 17.

[3] Robert K. Merton, *Social Theory and Social Structure*, rev. ed. (Glencoe, Ill.: The Free Press, 1957), pp. 421–436. Merton cites numerous examples, particularly of the behavior of ethnic ingroups toward ethnic outgroups being conditioned by self-fulfilling prophecies. He does also mention in passing that, actuated by the conviction "that war between two nations is inevitable . . . representatives of the two nations become progressively alienated, apprehensively countering each 'offensive' move of the other with a 'defensive' move of their own . . . and eventually the anticiptation of war helps create the actuality" (*ibid.*, p. 423).

[4] Murray Edelman, "Symbols and Political Quiescence," *The American Political Science Review*, LIV, No. 3 (September 1960), 695–704. Edelman applies his thesis specifically in the area of government regulation of the American economy. However, he states himself that ". . . the conditions in which myth and symbolic reassurance become key elements in the governmental process . . . are present in substantial degree in many policy areas other than business regulation. They may well be maximal in the foreign policy area, and a similar approach to the study of foreign policy formation would doubtless be revealing" (*ibid.*, p. 703).

not suggest that the conflict is not a "real" one. On the contrary, the point is that myths, no matter how untrue, do have very real consequences; that prophecies based on initially false perceptions can produce conditions which really exist (and thus fulfill the prophecy); that men react to symbols by real behavior, be it activity or quiescence. "If men define situations as real, they are real in their consequences."[5]

By now, it is of course these "real" consequences of the initial mutual Communist and Western hostility—for example, the creation of Soviet satellites and of NATO, armaments on both sides, etc.—that are the immediate and principal cause of present-day hostility. Recognizing this obvious fact, and granting also that there have been numerous causes of mutual hostility between the Soviet and Western governments which may have been little or even not at all conditioned by the factors we are stressing here, it may nevertheless be of interest to point to the role which these factors played in the early years of Soviet–Western relations and continue to play today. If the missiles begin to fly and the bombs begin to drop, it will be little consolation to know that it all began with a myth; but we must understand the myth as a myth if we are to explain the behavior of those who accept it. Such explanation is intrinsically worth while for the social scientist; it might also possibly help keep the missiles from flying and the bombs from dropping.

Western Ideologies as Myths in Underdeveloped Countries

Beginning about half a century ago in Mexico, China, Russia, and Turkey, revolutions—violent or peaceful, sudden or gradual—have by now swept much of the underdeveloped world. Though they have differed very widely in many respects, all of them have, more or less explicitly, aimed at the removal of the traditional order and, sooner or later, at its replacement by a modern industrialized society. If this goal is to be attained at all rapidly, it almost invariably requires strong emphasis on the initial construction of heavy industry, which, given the absence of much private capital, in turn involves an active role of the government in the process of industrialization. Secondly it requires some kind of land reform to weaken the resistance of traditional elements, particularly an aristocracy, and then, in turn, some government control of agricultural production to insure a flow of food for the growing population engaged in industry.

[5] W. I. Thomas quoted in Merton, *op. cit.*, p. 421.

While some aspects of such programs can appeal to the relatively small labor movements in underdeveloped countries and have in some instances mobilized considerable peasant support, they are the product of an experience not accessible to members of these strata with their narrow intellectual horizon. Rather, these programs are generally formulated by intellectuals, and it is generally intellectuals who assume the leadership of the movements for modernization in underdeveloped countries. These intellectuals are themselves a product of an education appropriate to—and often acquired in—an industrially advanced country. While the policies they pursue when they gain power, as indicated above, are their practical response to the problem of bringing modernization to their own backward countries, their inspiration to do so is derived from the Western ideologies they absorbed in the course of their education.

The ideologies of which elements have been transferred by intellectuals from Western to underdeveloped countries have varied from nineteenth-century liberalism and Marxism to twentieth-century American democracy and Western European social-democracy. Since all of these ideologies are themselves the product of advanced industrialized societies and therefore presuppose a high degree of industrialization for the attainment of their goals, they are *ipso facto* irrelevant to the policies intellectuals must pursue to industrialize their backward societies. Thus Western ideologies, which in their own environment can have at least some realistic programmatic content, become myths in the Sorelian sense in their new underdeveloped environment; these myths inspire the intellectuals and their followers to act but cannot "be taken literally as future history."[6]

Naturally, a movement using certain symbols in an underdeveloped country is likely to gain the sympathy of those in advanced countries who are attached to these same symbols. Thus the Kuomintang and the Indian Congress were widely hailed in the West because they stood for "democracy" and "independence," for "liberty" and "justice." There was much applause in the United States for the Indonesian revolution, when it was found that slogans from the Declaration of Independence were painted on Indonesian walls. Similarly, in the early stages of the Cuban revolution, Castro was widely regarded as a fighter for "democracy" against "tyranny." As long as the revolutionary movement in the

---

[6] Sorel, *op. cit.*, p. 126.

underdeveloped country adheres to the same myth and continues to use the same symbols (which Castro did not), it can manage to retain the sympathy of the followers of its ideology in advanced countries. Except for the relatively few who suffer directly from the revolutionary policies, like investors in expropriated enterprises, much of the so-called informed public in advanced countries may maintain its positive attitude even as the policies of the revolutionary movement, in response to the environment it confronts, come into conflict with the professed ideology—as when such a movement adopts measures of repression and regimentation in order to advance rapid industrialization and to impose the sacrifices required by it on apathetic and increasingly hostile groups in the population.

Not only do professions of democratic ideology and use of democratic symbols by the modernizing revolutionaries in underdeveloped countries arouse widespread sympathy in Western countries, but they do not inhibit—even if, by themselves, they may not produce—friendly relations between their governments. The revolutionaries are usually, by their ideology, committed to anti-colonial policies, that is, to a set of relatively limited and attainable goals directed at certain interests in the West. Even with these goals there is widespread sympathy in the West. The revolutionaries are, however, in no way committed to the overthrow of the governments of Western countries or a revolutionary transformation of Western societies. Since they do not claim to be, they cause no such fears in the West. Thus the Indian Congress was pledged to get rid of British colonialism in India, but far from aiming at the overthrow of British institutions in Britain, it desired the introduction of some of them, like parliamentarism, in India.

Marxism in Russia: The Myth of the Proletarian Revolution

The Russian Revolution was one of the major modernizing revolutions in an underdeveloped country. Like the many others since then, it was led by intellectuals who had absorbed various Western ideologies. When some of these intellectuals, adhering to Western liberal, democratic, and social-democratic ideas, overthrew the old regime in March 1917, the event was greeted with enthusiasm or at least sympathy by most politically conscious groups in the West. But, as is not unusual in modernizing revolutions in underdeveloped countries, a rival group of intellectuals replaced the first group in November 1917. This second group, the Bolsheviks, were also committed to the overthrow of the old regime and to rapid modernization and they, too, acted in the name of a Western ideology.

Like all the ideologies of advanced countries, Marxism was irrelevant to the problems confronted by those in underdeveloped countries who professed to accept it. To be sure, it was a "revolutionary" ideology, which is why some of the Russian revolutionary intelligentsia had been attracted to it; but it assumed that the revolution it promised could come only as a consequence of far-reaching industrialization, and could certainly not precede and in turn produce industrialization. Hence all the principal concepts and symbols of Marxism—capitalism and the bourgeoisie, the proletariat, class-consciousness and the class struggle, the proletarian revolution, the dictatorship of the proletariat, socialism, and communism—made little or no sense in Russia.

The point here is not the oft-repeated one that the Bolsheviks put new content into old words and thus perverted Marxism; that the proletarian revolution became a revolution of intellectuals and the dictatorship of the proletariat the dictatorship of the Communist Party; that the goal of socialism came to mean industrialization; that, in short, the Bolsheviks made a revolution of intellectuals committed to the modernization of an underdeveloped country in the name of proletarian revolution committed to the socialization of an already existing industrial system. What needs to be stressed in our context is, rather, that the Marxian categories, which are clearly misapplied to the Bolsheviks' actions as explanatory or descriptive concepts, became myths that have affected behavior. The Communists' broad program of industrialization as actually followed, especially by Stalin, would quite probably have been pursued by other modernizing revolutionary intellectuals, even if they had never heard of Marx. But, obviously, the belief that they were proletarian socialists did affect the Communists' actions as well as their words in both domestic and foreign affairs. Here we are particularly interested in the foreign policy aspects of the matter.

As it developed in the mid-nineteenth century, Marxism regarded the existing governments and ruling classes of Western countries with hatred and was regarded as a menace by them. By the turn of the century, Marxist-inspired labor movements, notably in Germany, were in fact well on their way to becoming integrated into the political systems of their countries, and the question confronting their leaders was only whether to acknowledge this openly and abandon the myth of revolution (as the Revisionists proposed) or to continue the use of Marxian symbols of irreconcilable conflict as a better means of recruiting and holding together a mass following (as the "orthodox" Marxists advocated). Since the Bolsheviks in Russia were in total opposition to the old regime—as intellectuals in underdeveloped countries usually are to their traditional governments—they, too, clung to the old symbols of Marxism (and in the Revisionist controversy sided with the "orthodox" Marxists).

Unlike the Indian Congress or the Kerensky provisional government, then, the Bolsheviks were not committed to an ideology and symbols accepted by and popular with the governments and dominant groups in the West. They were not merely anti-colonialist and did not merely demand "democracy," "freedom," and "independence" for their own country. Rather, they were committed to the mid-nineteenth century Marxian ideology and its symbols demanding the overthrow not only of the traditional-aristocratic regime in Russia but also of the "bourgeois" governments in the West. This outlook of the new rulers of a large country aroused the fear and opposition of all those in the West benefiting from established institutions, that is, groups ranging from the remnants of the old aristocracy to the trade unions. On the other hand, the Bolsheviks' commitment to what was practically an unattainable goal produced frustration, aggressive behavior, and in turn also fear on their part. There thus developed a degree of long-lasting mutual hostility unparalleled in the relations between modernizing revolutionaries in underdeveloped countries and the dominant groups in advanced countries. Let us now have a somewhat closer look at this development.

The Self-Fulfilling Prophecy of East–West Conflict

As self-professed Marxists, the Bolsheviks considered themselves part of an international proletarian movement. When, at the beginning of World War I, the Second International broke up, Lenin could not admit to himself that there was in fact no international proletarian movement or that what proletarian movements there were had interests quite different from those he stood for. Instead, he asserted that he represented the "true" proletarian movement and that those socialist and labor organizations that opposed him were traitors to the working class.

When Lenin's group of intellectuals captured power in Russia with the aid of some proletarian elements and retained it in the civil war largely with the aid of peasants, he insisted that he had made a proletarian revolution. But unable to free himself completely from the elementary Marxian doctrine that the proletarian revolution must first come in advanced countries and overwhelmed by the problems of "building socialism" in backward Russia, he relied heavily on the expectation of proletarian revolutions in the West. While he paid more attention to the revolutionary potential of nationalism in underdeveloped countries than most Western Marxists, it was in Europe and especially in Germany that Lenin expected the fate of his own revolution to be settled. He anxiously looked for support from the Western European proletariat and sought to mobilize such support by means of propaganda and "technical assistance" in revolution-making. Thus Marxian concepts, in Russia, became myths that stimulated action—action that no revolutionary intellectual in an underdeveloped country holding some Western ideology other than Marxism would have taken.

Lenin and the Bolsheviks were not the only ones to be misled by their own use of Marxian symbols to believe that the Russian Revolution was a proletarian one and a victory for socialism. Many socialists in the West believed it, too, and became Communists in order to support the revolution in Russia. Their behavior, too, was conditioned by a myth. But only in France and Italy was Communism destined to become and to remain to the present a major proletarian movement, replacing not the socialist movement but the anarcho-syndicalist one of alienated labor in half-industrialized countries where the majority of the population was nonproletarian and governments anti-proletarian, and where the longing for "apocalyptic success" was hence strong among workers.

In spite of the Marxist symbols which they shared with Bolshevism, most socialists in advanced countries who had turned Communist became aware in one way or another of the differences between their values and policies and those pursued by the Soviet Communists. Within a decade or so after 1917, in the midst of interminable debates over the "true" meaning of Marxian concepts, most of them left Communist parties to return to socialist parties or to form various sects and splinter groups. What was now left in the Communist parties of advanced countries were only small groups,[7] often made up largely of personally maladjusted members of the middle class (and, in the United States, of poorly acculturated ones of certain ethnic groups), with little political power and few links with the working class. Yet, to justify their existence, they had to hold on to the myth that they were the vanguard of a

[7] Except in Weimar Germany, where the Party remained quite powerful and increased its strength in the pre-Hitler depression years of the early nineteen-thirties.

revolutionary proletariat, and the Soviet Communists, given their need to assert that they led a worldwide proletarian movement, had to maintain the same myth.

By and large, the Right in advanced countries proved to be more permanently deceived by the Communists' use of Marxist symbols than was the Left, or found them to be more congenial or satisfactory to its needs. Like the Bolsheviks, propertied and conservative groups in Europe and the United States believed that the Russian Revolution was a proletarian one. The Bolsheviks' incessant claims to that effect did nothing to dispel the belief of these groups that they were threatened by that revolution and its potential repercussions in their own countries and by their local Communist parties. When the Bolsheviks hailed and actively supported some minor revolutionary attempts in Central Europe, there was tangible evidence for that belief.[8]

It must not be forgotten that in the 1920s the threat of a revolutionary labor movement was still taken very seriously by conservative and propertied groups in the West. They had been affected by the Marxian myth of the socialist revolution (and also by the anarcho-syndicalist one) long before the Bolsheviks began to spread it. This was obviously true in Italy, Germany, Austria, and France, where, in the nineteen-twenties and thirties, some of these groups turned to Fascism in order to crush what they considered the threat of revolutionary socialism. It was even true in Britain and the United States, where this was the period of the Zinoviev letter and the general strike of 1926, of the Palmer raids and the application of criminal syndicalism and similar statutes. No wonder, then, that the Western governments, dominated by conservative parties almost throughout the 1920s, reciprocated Soviet support for local Communist efforts at subversion by adopting anti-Soviet policies.

These Western policies in turn confirmed the belief of the Bolsheviks that they were threatened by the "capitalist" powers. They had held this belief from the beginning of their revolution, for they regarded Soviet territory as the base for worldwide anti-capitalist action and expected everyone else to view it similarly, a belief soon reinforced by the Allied intervention during the Russian civil war.

[8] The Russian Revolution of 1917 was widely interpreted as an event that, like the French ones of 1789 and 1848, would set off sympathetic revolutionary reactions in other countries. Nor was this a quite incorrect interpretation. But just as the French revolutions appealed to those strata in other countries, notably in Central Europe, who corresponded to the ones who made the revolutions in France, so the Russian Revolution has had its appeal among corresponding groups—intellectuals in underdeveloped countries—and has failed among the workers of advanced countries.

In the early years of the Soviet Republic, that country was weak by all the traditional standards of international relations. Its economy was in chaos, its military strength not comparable to that of a major power, and no foreign government was allied to it. Feeling threatened by foreign powers, the Bolsheviks therefore relied all the more heavily on Communist parties, especially in the Western countries, and supported their revolutionary attempts as one of the few ways available to them of changing an unfavorable international balance of power. Thus the weak power position of the early Soviet Republic and the Marxist myth of proletarian internationalism, reinforcing each other, led to emphasis on world revolution and World Communism as Soviet policy goals.

The mutual hostility between the Bolsheviks and the governments of the Western powers, then, nicely illustrates Merton's self-fulfilling prophecy. The initial misunderstanding by each side of the character of the Russian Revolution, as aiming at the overthrow of the "capitalist" governments of the West, made each react to the other in such a way as to justify the original misunderstanding as correct, after all. And this, as Merton says, perpetuated "a reign of error."[9] Obviously, there is no point in asking who started it all, for the mutual antagonism of those using Marxian symbols and those against whom they are directed antedates the Russian Revolution by some decades, and, by the time Lenin came to power, the stage was set for inevitable hostility for anyone using these symbols.

It would, of course, go much too far to argue that all Soviet–Western antagonism has been due to the use by the Bolsheviks of Marxian symbols, which were actually irrelevant to the situation they confronted. Thus, the early attitude of the Allied governments toward the Soviet government was strongly influenced by the fact that the latter took Russia out of the war against the Central Powers. There is no need here to multiply the examples of conflict between the Soviet and Western governments that did not arise out of ideological differences, not to cite instances of cooperation that have taken place in spite of such differences. The fact remains that the mutual fear, distrust, and dislike that have pervaded Soviet–Western relations ever since the Bolshevik Revolution have been at least strongly conditioned by the symbols accepted by the Communists and their opponents alike.

Merely to gain some appreciation of the power of symbols, we might imagine for a moment that a group of intellectuals had come to power

[9] Merton, *op. cit.,* p. 423.

in Russia in 1917 who pursued exactly the same policy of rapid industrialization and collectivization of agriculture that the Bolsheviks pursued. However, having picked up liberal rather than Marxist ideology
in the West, they did it all in the name of creating a new democratic
order of liberty, justice, and material abundance, "to catch up with
and overtake the United States." Never once did they think or say that
their program was proletarian or socialist or had any revolutionary implications for advanced industrialized countries. Is it not quite reasonable
to assume that dominant Western reaction to them would have been
more like that to Sun Yat-sen or Kemal or Cárdenas, or more recently,
to Nasser or Nkrumah or Sukarno?[10] Their policies and methods have
been variously disliked or admired in the West, but their movements
have never been considered a threat, because both they and everyone
else have recognized that what they were doing had relevance to underdeveloped but not to advanced countries; that they did not represent
a revolutionary group in any advanced country.

To be sure, one might expect that any revolutionary regime coming
to power in a country as large as Russia and as close to Europe would
upset ruling elites in the West more than similar revolutions in China
or Turkey, in Ghana or Indonesia. Still, the regime produced by the
Russian Revolution of March 1917 did not seem to do so. One may
reasonably conclude, therefore, that much of the fear and suspicion
the Bolshevik Revolution engendered has been due to the mistaken belief
on both sides that it was a revolution appropriate to an advanced country, a revolution of a proletariat against capitalism. At any rate, what
was feared for quite some time after the revolution was not the Red
Army but Soviet-sponsored domestic revolution, not the Soviet spy so
much as the revolutionary and subversive agent. Even in this day of
massive Soviet military power, there are those in the United States who
rate the internal threat of Communism greater than the external threat
from the Soviet Union.

The Decline of the Myth of Proletarian World Revolution

Myths can inspire action and, through the mechanism of the self-fulfilling prophecy, they can even make some of their elements come true,

[10] When Perón, whose program was substantially similar to those of other intellectual
modernizers in underdeveloped countries, used Fascist symbols and thus, like Lenin,
seemed to align himself against dominant groups in some advanced countries, he,
too, incurred much hostility in these Western countries.

but they cannot wholly realize themselves. Inspired by the belief in the general strike, Sorel's syndicalists engaged in many strikes and induced fear and the counteractions of their opponents, but they did not, in fact, make a general strike or reorganize society after shattering capitalism. Similarly, the Bolsheviks' belief in proletarian socialism could condition many of their foreign policies, but it could not lead to rule by the proletariat nor to the socialization of an industrial economy, simply because not enough of either a proletariat or an industrial economy existed in Russia.

The myth, then, can influence policies, but it does not determine all policy; policy must have some relation to the real world if it is not to lead to disaster for the policy-makers. Soviet policy has obviously been successful in maintaining and strengthening the Soviet regime in power as it could not have been had it not reacted to the actual problems facing the regime rather than to the problems it thought and said it faced. Internally, it said and no doubt thought that it built socialism, but in fact it built industry. And externally, it continued to speak of world revolution, but by Stalin's time it ceased to rely on the "world proletariat." Yet, though he was committed to building "socialism in one country," Stalin inherited Lenin's fear and distrust of the Western powers as well as their fear and distrust of the Soviet Union. Here the real effects of the myth lived on and tended to reinforce it.

Still, myths do decline in the face of an environment that changes to make them increasingly irrelevant. Eventually they even die, but the myth of the world revolution is not yet dead. Khrushchev continued to expect to bury capitalism; he still conceived of the world of the future as some kind of commonwealth of Communist countries. He said so, and there is no need to doubt that he believed it. The myth thus continues to serve a function (to be discussed below), but it no longer influences policy as it did under Lenin. Stalin, too, still showed some interest in the Western European proletariat and directed his attention chiefly to the West rather than to underdeveloped countries. In the calculations of Khrushchev and his successors, however, even the powerful Communist parties of France and Italy and certainly the "proletariat" in Britain and the United States seem to have played very little role indeed.

For over a decade now, Soviet attention has been directed to the underdeveloped countries. In the last few years before Stalin's death, the Communist parties of those countries were already beginning to appeal to the "national bourgeoisie," thus watering down their "proletarian" character, but in the forties they were still expected to work toward revolution against the new nationalist–neutralist governments. In the fifties, however, and especially under Khrushchev, Soviet policy shifted to the support—including in some cases significant material support—of these anti-colonialist modernizing regimes, not only where they were friendly to existing Communist parties, as in the cases of Sukarno and Castro, or where there were no Communist parties, as with Nkrumah and Touré, but even where they were hostile to their Communist parties, as were Nehru and Nasser.

As the Soviet Union has grown in military strength, so that she can now threaten major powers, and in economic strength, so that she can attract governments of underdeveloped countries with offers of foreign aid; as her successful industrialization has proved to be a powerful propaganda weapon among modernizing intellectuals in underdeveloped countries; and as she has acquired diplomatic strength and allies, the Soviet government can deal more successfully with non-Communist governments than in the past and probably expects to be still more successful in the future. This is especially true where such governments share some of the Soviet anti-Western attitudes, as is the case with many anti-colonialist movements in underdeveloped countries. No longer does the Soviet government have to look to the overthrow of non-Communist governments as the principal way to change the international balance of power. Hence foreign Communist parties, once a primary weapon of Soviet foreign policy, are of declining significance in the new, more diversified Soviet arsenal.

The myth of proletarian internationalism was strong when the Soviet Republic was weak. It had to be strong then to make up for the country's weakness in international affairs, both because it was to mobilize support for Soviet policies abroad and because it helped maintain the morale of both leaders and followers at home. With the growing strength of the Soviet Union, the myth of proletarian internationalism could decline. By now, even in underdeveloped countries where the Soviet government has of late looked for support (let alone in advanced countries), the goal of Soviet policy is not the rule of Communist parties. Rather, it has been defined as "national democracy," that is, as rule by the anti-colonial modernizing intellectuals of the present-day non-Communist nationalist movements. The realization of World Communism has been postponed to the dim future.

World Communism as a Symbol of Reassurance

These postwar changes in their policies do not mean that the Communists have abandoned World Communism as a goal. As both Communists and anti-Communists, reinforcing each other as they so often do, never tire of proclaiming, the "basic" or "ultimate" goal of the Soviet government remains what it has always been: World Communism. This is true in the same sense as that the basic mission of the Church has not changed in nearly 2,000 years of history, or that the basic aspirations of American governments have remained the same since the Declaration of Independence. It is obvious, however, that policy-makers having to deal with the Church have faced rather different problems in the days of St. Peter, of Innocent III, of Martin Luther, and of the Rev. Billy Graham. Similarly, American administrations, pursuing the same "basic" goals, have behaved quite differently and posed different problems to foreign governments from George Washington to Abraham Lincoln to Lyndon Johnson.

Like the Church and the United States, the Soviet Union has undergone some far-reaching changes in the shorter period since its foundation. What, then, is it that remains unchanged in the Soviet regime's goal of World Communism? That the method for the achievement of the goal has changed is by now widely admitted even by Communists themselves, especially since the Sino-Soviet conflict has forced the Soviet leaders not merely to practice but to preach "peaceful coexistence."

However, it is often asserted by Communists and anti-Communists alike that while the methods may change, the ultimate goal remains unchanged. Will World Communism be the same under the present generation of Soviet rulers (if they see it realized) or their successors as it would have been had it been attained under Lenin? One could reason that a future world created in the image of a successful and powerful bureaucratic-technocratic elite is likely to differ widely from one that might have been shaped by a group of alienated revolutionary intellectuals, and that therefore the goal as well as the methods have changed. But to argue at all about what World Communism will be like, to take it literally as future history, is, as Sorel said, "devoid of sense." World Communism, like Sorel's general strike, is and always has been a myth. As Sorel also stated: "A knowledge of what the myths contain in the way of details which will actually form part of the history of the future is then of small importance; they are not astrological almanacs; it is even possible that nothing which they contain will ever come to pass—as was the case with the catastrophe expected by the first Christians.[11]

The significance of World Communism, then, lies in its function as a myth rather than in its eventual realization. However, a myth need not only serve, as Sorel thought, as "a means of *acting* in the present." No doubt World Communism has been and continues to be used in this fashion, to mobilize and inspire active support for Soviet policies. But as these policies have shifted away from the early ones of Soviet support for foreign Communist parties and their revolutionary goals, the myth of World Communism has more and more come to serve the function of what Murray Edelman has called "symbolic reassurance." He "distinguished between interests in resources (whether goods or freedoms to act) and interests in symbols connoting the suppression of threats to the group in question."[12] The continued use of the symbols "World Communism" and "revolution" satisfies the interest in symbols of those who desire whatever they think these symbols represent. It thus reassures them that their interests (presumably in radical change) are taken care of, and it may fill their needs as adequately as, or more so than, an actual realization of World Communism and the revolution could. The use of these symbols also reassures those who manipulate them that they remain orthodox and faithful to their heritage. One of the functions of symbolization, as Edelman notes, is "that it induces a feeling of well-being: the resolution of tension."[13] What sounds like a call to action—the demand that World Communism be realized and capitalism be buried—may well serve the purpose, or at any rate the function, of inducing quiescence.

Further applying Edelman's insights, we come to see that the more those who want World Communism—whatever they may mean by it—are reassured that the Soviet government is working for its attainment, the more is the Soviet government left free to pursue goals which can hardly be reconciled with any traditional conception of World Communism—for example, attacks on Communist governments like that of China and support for anti-Communist ones like that of India; support of a "neutralist" faction against a "Communist" one in the quarrel among Laotian princes; or agreement with the United States to withdraw mis-

[11] Sorel, *op. cit.*, p. 126.
[12] Edelman, *op. cit.*, p. 695.
[13] *Ibid.*, p. 702.

siles from Cuba. All such policies must be accompanied by vigorous declarations of the Soviet leaders' loyalty to the goal of World Communism.

One may expect that the more the Soviet government changes its policies from those that were once associated with the goal of World Communism, the less can it afford to stop insisting that it continues to stand for this goal. It is therefore unreasonable to expect a Soviet policy change to be initiated or accompanied by an open renunciation of the Soviet goals of burying capitalism and establishing World Communism. Such a renunciation can only be one of the last, rather than one of the first, concomitants of a policy change and will for a long time be as impossible psychologically and politically as a statement by an American president (no matter what his foreign policy) that he is no longer interested in fighting Communism. As Edelman points out, the policy can be changed to its opposite, but the "symbols must stand because they satisfy interests that are very strong indeed: interests that politicians fear will be expressed actively"[14] if their supporters, deprived of the reassuring symbols, feel threatened; for such active expression of these interests would then interfere with the pursuit of the politicians' policies.

It can hardly be expected that all the enemies of Communism will understand this subtle paradox. After all, to many of them, too, World Communism has become an important symbol, in their case a symbol of what they fear and hate (whatever that may be). They, too, have been reassured to remain politically quiescent, in this case by their leaders' promises of undying, unyielding opposition to World Communism. The same mechanism is at work on both sides: if the Soviet Union must continue its championship of World Communism, especially as it seeks an accommodation with the West, so Western governments, the more they pursue a similar policy vis-à-vis the Soviet Union, must continue their championship of anti-Communism. And Communists can no more be expected to understand the paradox than anti-Communists. As the latter feel threatened by the Communists' prophecy of World Communism and the revolution, so the Communists feel menaced by the anti-Communist posture of Western politicians.

Thus the power of symbols to maintain an established policy becomes clear. While abandonment of the old symbols would interfere with the

[14] *Ibid.*

adoption of a new policy, because those who would otherwise passively support the new policy might be aroused from their quiescence by the loss of the symbols, retention of the old symbols also tends to interfere with the new policy. These symbols are bound to act as a brake on the development of any policy seeking to reduce tensions. This is true not only because the policy-makers' freedom of action is more or less limited by the attitude of their supporters, but also because the policy-makers themselves are the victims as well as the manipulators of their symbols. The symbols may not only slow down, but they can even interrupt or conceivably reverse the policy trend before it has time finally to make the symbols so irrelevant that they die out.

Myths and Interests: Who Needs Symbolic Reassurance?

Can the cycle of symbols influencing policy and policy influencing symbols be broken, then? It can, because certain groups in each society are less attached than others to the old symbols of irreconcilable conflict. In some cases attachment may be due to a direct interest. Thus the military and groups allied to it, like the makers of the implements of war, in each society clearly have much to lose in power and prestige as well as material resources if symbols of conflict are replaced by those of cooperation. When a good part of a country's economy is directly or indirectly dependent on the military and on defense industry, as is true in both the United States and the Soviet Union, such interests can be very widespread. Whether people in this category are aware of the interest basis of their commitment or not, they are likely to cling quite stubbornly to the old symbols. This is probably even more true of a second category of people, individuals whose attachment to the symbols of irreconcilable conflict and the myth of "apocalyptic success" arise out of their personality needs.

Here we need not discuss specifically what interests and personality traits may be responsible for this kind of attachment. It is, in any case, clear that it is particularly these groups and individuals who need reassurance and therefore invite the continued use of the symbols. And the continued use of the symbols on one side of the international conflict in turn strengthens such groups and individuals on the other.

However, not all people cling so firmly to the old myths and symbols that they cannot be detached from them. The process of detachment can be eased where the leaders or the parties shifting to new symbols and policies have themselves become symbols of continuity and hence of reassurance. Thus Stalin could switch from the anti-Fascism of the Popular Front to the anti-Western imperialism of the Hitler–Stalin Pact period and back to the anti-Fascism of the World War II Soviet–Western alliance and, throughout, maintain the support of many Communists abroad who were under no external compulsion to follow him. To them, Stalin and the Communist Party of the Soviet Union were themselves symbols of continuity reassuring them that there could have been no "basic" change.

Similarly, President Eisenhower and the Republican administration could conclude an armistice in Korea and accept Communist regimes in North Korea and subsequently in North Vietnam, policies that President Truman and a Democratic administration might well have been unable to adopt. Eisenhower and the Republican Party themselves served as symbols reassuring those who would have accused Truman and the Democrats of appeasement that no "basic" change had taken place. Thus a politician identified with one policy may arouse less opposition when he pursues quite another policy than might a politician who is identified with the other policy.

To be sure, in each of the instances cited here, the major myth—the Soviet one of the realization of World Communism and the Western one of the utter defeat of Communism everywhere—was maintained intact (thus illustrating further that major policy changes can be made without changing the myth). However, there are clearly many people in the West, and presumably in the Soviet Union as well, whose interests and personalities do not require these myths and the symbols that accompany them at all. The history of changing attitudes in the West toward the Soviet Union demonstrates this. Some who looked on the Soviet Union with suspicion in the nineteen-twenties and early thirties regarded her with sympathy during the Popular Front period. Certainly during World War II, many who had responded to the symbols of anti-Communism earlier were now quite able and willing to see the Soviet Union as their brave ally in the fight for freedom and democracy. With the beginning of the Cold War, the overwhelming majority of the wartime admirers of the Soviet Union in the West (except in France and Italy, where the majority must have been smaller) had no difficulty in identifying her as the main enemy of freedom and democracy. Evidently a large sector of public opinion in the Western countries—and the same is no doubt true elsewhere, including the Soviet Union—is quite mobile in its attachment to certain symbols. In the West, the symbols of anti-

Fascism could serve as substitutes for those of anti-Communism, taking care of the interests and needs of individuals in this sector.

In evaluating the role of myths in politics, it would be a mistake to think of them as invariably and directly representing certain interests, each myth being used by a group more or less consciously to advance its interests. But it would be equally wrong to view myths as living independent lives of their own. Hence changes in interests, produced by new political situations, can and do affect the lives and even cause the deaths of myths. We already noted the decline of the myth of proletarianism in the face of the Soviet policy change toward the nationalist movements in underdeveloped countries; we shall return to the possibility of the death of the myth of World Communism in our final section.

The Sino-Soviet Conflict: One Myth Serving Different Functions

Though certain types of political behavior—both activity and quiescence—cannot be explained without regard to the myths that inspire them, behavior and myths must, for analytical purposes, be sharply distinguished, for the simple reason that the behavior does take place, while the myth of the "final goal," to which the behavior is directed, will never be realized. Those who do not distinguish between behavior and myth, and especially those who concentrate their attention on the myth of the final goal at the expense of current policies, are themselves victims of the myth.

This has been strikingly true in recent years of analysts of the Sino-Soviet conflict who regard it as "merely" one over strategy, since both sides are committed to the same goal of World Communism and the burial of capitalism. Some have even reasoned that, since both sides are Communist, the conflict is not "real" at all, thus denying reality to what is in fact happening and ascribing it only to the myth. For what the Soviet and Chinese Communists share is no more—and no less—than a common myth. A common myth can be a powerful bond, and World Communism served as such as long as it performed the same function for all its adherents. But this is no longer the case.

Like the early Soviet Republic, Communist China lacks the military force and the allies, the economic power and the propaganda strength derived from successful industrialization to influence strongly the policies of other governments (except those of a few of her immediate neighbors). Like Lenin, the Chinese Communist leaders therefore have to look to Communist parties, which they *can* hope to influence, to capture control of the governments of their countries. Hence to the Chinese Communist leaders, who have themselves spent the better part of their lives in a revolutionary struggle for power, World Communism remains a myth calling for action.

The present Soviet leaders, on the other hand, grew up within a functioning system rather than having to capture it from the outside; their attitudes are therefore conservative rather than revolutionary. Furthermore they now have, as we noted, means far more effective than Communist parties to influence foreign governments. To them the myth of World Communism now serves the function of a reassuring symbol.

The Chinese and the Soviet Communists appeal to the same myth of the ultimate triumph of World Communism and they use the same elaborate vocabulary of Marxism–Leninism in doing so. This gives the impression to non-Communists and probably even to the Communists themselves on both sides that they really are in agreement on fundamentals and that their differences are only superficial. The common myth, however, serves quite different functions in the two cases and thus is meant to mobilize support for sometimes diametrically opposed policies.

Failure in the West to recognize the Sino-Soviet conflict as such illustrates a familiar myth pattern which we might call that of the single enemy. It appears to be one form of the use of symbols noted by Edelman,[15] whereby a group confronted by a complex situation and unable to analyze it rationally adjusts to it by stereotypization and oversimplification. To the Nazis all domestic opposition, no matter what its source, and all their foreign enemies, Western and Soviet, were "really" Jewish in character. To Stalin, "left-wing" and "right-wing" deviationists at home and opposition from democratic and Fascist powers abroad were all "basically" a manifestation of capitalist hostility to the Soviet Union. To the "Radical Right" in this country, everything from the United Nations to the fluoridation of drinking water, from events in the Congo to the income tax, not to mention Soviet and Chinese policies, is the result of a single Communist conspiracy. And today, while some still see the Soviet Union and China as "basically" united, the Chinese Communists have discovered that all their enemies are "really" one, that the Soviet Union has become an ally of the "imperialist" powers by signing the nuclear test ban treaty, and the Soviet Communists now say that the Chinese have joined the imperialist camp by refusing to

[15] *Ibid.,* p. 703.

sign the treaty. In this peculiar triangular relationship each side denies that there can be more than one other side.

Toward the End of the Myth of World Communism?

In the turn of Soviet foreign policy toward the underdeveloped countries, the reality of Soviet experience as one of the first and certainly so far the most successful revolution by intellectuals in an underdeveloped country for industrialization is beginning to assert itself as against the myth of the Russian Revolution as the first Western socialist proletarian revolution. A third of a century after their revolution, it began to dawn on the Soviet leaders that the main relevance and hence the main appeal of that revolution lay in the underdeveloped countries and not the advanced countries of the West. It seems not unlikely that the more this dim realization is translated into policy decisions, those in the West who felt threatened by the Soviet Union's presumed character as a bastion of world revolution should be gradually reassured.

Just as, during most of the first four decades after the Russian Revolution, the various actions and counteractions of the Soviet and Western governments tended to reinforce the myth on which initial mutual hostility was based, so it is conceivable that in the next few years and decades, actions and counteractions will gradually tend to break down the myth and thus reduce hostility. Whether this will in fact happen and, if so, how smoothly and at what rate of speed, will depend in large part on domestic political developments on each side. These will determine the relative power within each society of the groups and factions deeply attached to the old symbols and myths and those more capable of introducing "a new definition of the situation."[16]

But can the myth of the world-revolutionary nature of Communism disappear in the West, even if the Soviet Union uses it merely as a reassuring symbol to induce quiescence? After all, it remains, for reasons indicated, a call to action to the Chinese Communists, and perhaps for similar reasons also the Cuban ones, and to other Communist parties in underdeveloped countries who have in effect been deprived of Soviet

---

[16] ". . . the tragic, often vicious, circle of self-fulfilling prophecies can be broken. The initial definition of the situation which has set the circle in motion must be abandoned. Only when the original assumption is questioned and a new definition of the situation introduced, does the consequent flow of events give the lie to the assumption. Only then does the belief no longer father the reality." (Merton, *op. cit.*, p. 424.)

support as Moscow has shifted its backing to the governments of their "national bourgeoisie." It would seem that the myth as wielded by Communist parties in underdeveloped countries, including China and Cuba, will not set in motion the mechanism of the self-fulfilling prophecy through mutual fear and hositility in quite the same way as did the myth of the Russian Revolution as a proletarian revolution.

It is less likely that the myth of revolutionary Communism emanating from underdeveloped countries now will appear as threatening to wide strata in the West as it did when the Bolsheviks used it after their revolution to suggest that Western institutions would soon by toppling under the onslaught of the proletariat. Unlike then, very few people in the United States, Britain, and Germany, and no doubt a rapidly declining number in France and Italy, can take the prospect of a revolution by the working class of their countries seriously. Furthermore, the myth that Communism stands for a *proletarian* world revolution has been growing threadbare for a long time, even though the vaguer myth of world revolution has persisted.[17] Perhaps the total absence of evidence that the Soviet Union has in fact been a base of working class revolutions has had some effect.[18] In the meantime, the Communist myth, as it has travelled to China and Cuba and other underdeveloped countries,

---

[17] While the political scientist cannot confront a political movement, including a revolutionary one, without asking what groups it represents, many others can evidently visualize revolutions representing nobody in particular and can hence take the spectre of world revolution seriously.

[18] Communists talked and no doubt plotted workers' revolutions for years, but their record is not impressive. They attempted some minor uprisings (of the "Putsch" type) in Central Europe after World War I, but these involved at most a tiny fraction of the working class and all failed. Armed resistance to Fascism in Austria and Spain in the thirties and in much of Europe during World War II was not initiated by the Communists and nowhere brought Communist regimes to power. In fact, Communist regimes have come to power only (1) through Soviet military occupation or the threat thereof (Eastern Europe and North Korea); (2) exceptionally and temporarily, through elections and parliamentary alliances (San Marino and Kerala—two minor underdeveloped areas); (3) evidently with little Soviet support, through guerrilla warfare (Yugoslavia, China, North Vietnam)—a method which, given its reliance on a discontented peasantry, is available only in underdeveloped countries and is hence quite "unproletarian;" and (4) through alliance and eventual merger with a successful nationalist movement (so far practiced only in Cuba, though partial attempts in the same direction were made in Iran under Mossadeq and in Guatemala under Arbenz, and perhaps in Indonesia under Sukarno)—again a method practicable only in underdeveloped countries where the goals of nationalist and Communist movements—rapid industrialization and anti-Westernism—and the strata from which they draw support often coincide.

has been largely transmuted from one promising the final liberation of an industrial proletariat from capitalism to one pledging liberation of colonial people, regardless of class, from imperialism.

Thus, while Marx's century-old Western European symbols are still being employed, in Soviet usage they have become reassuring symbols and in Chinese usage they have come to stand for myths rather different even from the Communist one in Lenin's day. At the same time, the Western societies from which the symbols originally sprang have changed so much that the irrelevance to them of the myths expressed by the symbols has become quite apparent. Under these circumstances, the day may yet come when statements from Moscow and Peking announcing the forthcoming burial of capitalism and the advent of proletarian rule will arouse as much fright in the West as do Labor Party predictions of the socialist commonwealth among British Tories; and when calls from Washington and Bonn for the triumphant march of Western democracy into the Communist lands and the liberation of their people will worry Moscow and Peking as much as the British Labor Party worries about a return to free enterprise capitalism. Old myths and symbols may, like old soldiers, never die; they just fade away. In the meantime, as the British example illustrates, they can remain useful to political leaders for long periods in producing both the support and the quiescence of their followers; yet they no longer arouse the fear and hostility of the opposition and thus do not set in motion the chain reaction of the self-fulfilling prophecy.

7. Soviet Policy in the Underdeveloped Countries: Changing Behavior and Persistent Symbols*

Introductory Note. In a lecture at Carleton University, Ottawa, in February 1966 on Soviet policy in the underdeveloped countries in the 1960s, I summarized my thoughts on the convergence of Communist and non-Communist modernizing movements, as I had developed them earlier, particularly in my "Essay on the Politics of Development," excerpted above, and especially to bring these up to date with references to more recent manifestations of the trend of convergence. Above all, however, I was here concerned with explaining this trend and with building some of my explanations on the concepts of myths and symbols as I had used them in the preceding article. In a sense, then, the lecture reprinted here represents a brief summary of some of my main ideas on Communism in underdeveloped countries introduced earlier, though they are here presented primarily with reference to Soviet policy in the 1960s.

> *. . . as in private life one distinguishes between what a man thinks and says of himself and what he really is and does, still more in historical struggles must one distinguish the phrases and fancies of the parties from their real organism . . . , their conception of themselves from their reality.* KARL MARX, The Eighteenth Brumaire of Louis Bonaparte.

The decade of the nineteen-sixties opened with what seemed to some observers to be renewed Soviet concern for Communist party strength, leadership, and ultimately control in underdeveloped countries. There was discussion in Soviet and Soviet-sponsored journals and meetings of the relation of the working class (virtually a synonym for the Communist party) to the national bourgeoisie, of the leading role of the working class, of a "non-capitalist" path of development and the

* Reprinted, by permission of Carleton University and Frederick A. Praeger, Inc., from Adam Bromke and Philip E. Uren, *The Communist States and the West* (New York: Frederick A. Praeger, 1967), pp. 198–217.

future transition to socialism.[1] All this culminated in the doctrine of "national democracy," as formulated in the Moscow Declaration of December 1960 of the Conference of Eighty-one Communist Parties[2] and embodied in the Program of the Communist Party of the Soviet Union of 1961.[3]

However, if we distinguish between what the Soviet government says and what it does, between its symbols and its behavior, we find that in fact no major change in Soviet policy toward the underdeveloped countries took place in the early 1960s. There may, indeed, have been renewed emphasis on some of the more traditional symbols of Communism in response perhaps to domestic developments and probably to Chinese Communist pressure,[4] but the trend, initiated a decade earlier, toward Soviet support for non-Communist neutralist regimes in underdeveloped countries and toward the convergence of Communist parties with modernizing nationalist movements in these countries has, apart from mostly verbal zigs and zags, been continuing down to the present.[5]

[1] See excerpts from an international seminar held in Leipzig in May 1959 on "The National Bourgeoisie and the Liberation Movement," in *World Marxist Review*, II, No. 8 (August 1959), 61–81, and No. 9 (September 1959), 66–81; Walter Z. Laqueur, "Communism and Nationalism in Tropical Africa," *Foreign Affairs*, XXXIX, No. 4 (July 1961), 610–621, which reprints a few excerpts from *The African Communist*, a journal founded in London in the fall of 1959, evidently to stimulate the organization of Communist parties in Africa; and *World Trade Union Movement*, No. 7 (1960), reprinting a resolution of the General Council of the WFTU of June 1960 on the "Struggle Against Colonialism."

[2] Reprinted in Dan N. Jacobs, ed., *The New Communist Manifesto and Related Documents* (Evanston, Ill.: Row, Peterson & Co., 1961); see particularly pp. 31–33. For comments and references to Soviet elaborations, see Walter Z. Laqueur, "Towards National Democracy: Soviet Doctrine and the New Countries," *Survey*, No. 37 (July–September 1961), 3–11, and William T. Shinn, Jr., "The 'National Democratic State': A Communist Program for Less-Developed Areas," *World Politics*, XV, No. 3 (April 1963), 377–389. For a discussion of "national democracy" in the general context of Soviet policy in underdeveloped countries, see Richard Lowenthal, " 'National Democracy' and the Post-Colonial Revolution," in Kurt London ed., *New Nations in a Divided World* (New York: Frederick A. Praeger, 1963), pp. 56–74. The same article, slightly changed and abbreviated, appeared as "On 'National Democracy': I. Its Function in Communist Policy," *Survey*, No. 47 (April 1963), 119–133.

[3] Reprinted in Jan F. Triska, ed., *Soviet Communism: Programs and Rules* (San Francisco: Chandler Publishing Co., 1962); see especially p. 58.

[4] The Conference of Eighty-one Parties was, after all, called to reconcile differences between Moscow and Peking. It may be noted, however, that the Chinese Communists never accepted the concept of national democracy, preferring their own formula of "new democracy." The difference is not merely verbal, for the former involves rule by the "national bourgeoisie," the latter rule by the Communist party.

[5] I have tried to place this trend in a broader perspective of the politics of underde-

This trend cannot be fully understood unless it is traced from its beginnings in the post-World War II period, but rather than to repeat this oft-told story[6] here, I will summarize it only briefly. I will then offer some possible explanations for the departure of Soviet policy from what is still commonly thought of as Communist policy. And, finally, I will suggest why Soviet and Communist statements do not reflect this departure.

I

In the late 1940s, with the onset of the cold war between the Soviet Union and the United States, the Soviet government, for the first time, ceased to claim that it represented exclusively an anti-capitalist proletarian or at least lower-class movement. Even in the popular and national

---

veloped countries and an interpretation of the Russian Revolution as a movement in one such country in my "Essay in the Politics of Development," excerpts of which are reprinted on pages 56–102 above. For an excellent critique of this essay, see Richard Lowenthal, "Communism and Nationalism," *Problems of Communism*, XI, No. 6 (November–December 1962), 37–44. On the point most relevant here, Professor Lowenthal wrote that, far from marking the ". . . assimilation of the Communists in underdeveloped countries to other movements of the nationalist intelligentsia, as Professor Kautsky assumes, the new strategy of 'national democracy' heralds a renewed Communist bid for leadership of the national fronts in rivalry to the established nationalist movements" (*ibid.*, p. 40). However, by 1965, Professor Lowenthal thought that "the new strategy" had been abandoned as a failure in the summer of 1963 and been replaced by "nothing less than the deliberate renunciation of independent communist parties, publicly acting as such, in a number of countries." Richard Lowenthal, "Russia, the One-Party System, and the Third World," *Survey*, No. 58 (January 1966), 43–58, p. 43. I prefer to think of the changes between 1959 and 1963 as merely verbal, since in fact there was continuing Soviet aid to the non-Communist governments in question and Communist parties did not challenge these governments, but admittedly the line between "words" and "facts" is never too clear, for policy often consists as much of the former as of the latter.

[6] Among numerous contributions on the subject, the following are particularly relevant here: Bernard S. Morris and Morris Watnick, "Current Communist Strategy in Non-Industrialized Countries," and Bernard S. Morris, "Recent Shifts in Communist Strategy," two articles reprinted in my *Political Change in Underdeveloped Countries, op. cit.*, pp. 282–303; Hugh Seton-Watson, "The Communist Powers and Afro-Asian Nationalism," in Kurt London, ed., *Unity and Contradiction* (New York: Frederick A. Praeger, 1962), pp. 187–206; and Donald S. Carlisle, "The Changing Soviet Perception of the Development Process in the Afro-Asian World," *Midwest Journal of Political Science*, VIII, No. 4 (November 1964), 385–407. I traced the early phases of the change in Soviet policy in some detail in my *Moscow and the Communist Party of India, op. cit.*, and indicated some later ones in "The Chinese and Soviet Views of Communism in Underdeveloped Countries," reprinted on pp. 103–120 above.

fronts of the late 1930s and early 1940s, Communists had only sought alliances with the bourgeoisie but never claimed to represent it. But now, in a search for anti-American allies, Communist parties, following instructions from Moscow, began to declare that they represented interests of all classes, quite explicitly including the "national bourgeoisie," that is, the capitalists, and not just the interests of the so-called exploited. The enemy now became, not capitalism, but imperialism, that is, American foreign policy. This was the beginning of the end of the class struggle and of proletarianism in Communist mythology.

In their attempt to unite all classes under the leadership of some intellectuals against foreign imperialism and also in favor of rapid industrialization, Communist parties in underdeveloped countries became quite similar to the non-Communist nationalist movements in terms of the support they solicited, the social background of their leadership, and the character of their program. At that time, though, they were still strenuously opposed to such movements and denounced them and their policy of neutralism as serving the interests of imperialism.

In the early 1950s, however, and especially after Stalin's death in 1953, the Soviet government evidently recognized that neutralist nationalists in underdeveloped countries could be genuinely anti-Western. Communist parties were therefore pushed by Moscow to support the foreign policies of their "bourgeois" governments. Then the Soviet Union began to provide substantial aid to the industrialization efforts of some of these governments, and Communist parties were now expected to support their domestic development policies as well. Gradually, by the late 1950s, they were urged more and more by Moscow to give up their independent role and follow the lead of the non-Communist nationalist movements.

During the very period when these major changes in Soviet policy took place, Soviet leaders and writers frequently repeated the old doctrines from which Soviet policy was now in fact departing. To cite only one instance, at the Twentieth Congress in 1956, Khrushchev asserted that, "In all the forms of transition to socialism, an absolute and decisive requirement is political leadership of the working class, headed by its vanguard. The transition to socialism is impossible without this."[7] Authoritative Soviet commentaries on the doctrine of national democracy

[7] N. S. Khrushchev, "The Central Committee Report," Leo Gruliow, ed., *Current Soviet Policies—II: The Documentary Record of the 20th Party Congress and its Aftermath* (New York: Frederick A. Praeger, 1957), p. 38.

of the early 1960s, too, dealt with this newly-invented stage of history as a transitional one leading ultimately to "socialism," that is, rule by the Communist party. In fact, however, the doctrine had been evolved in order to account for the new situation in which the so-called bourgeoisie in underdeveloped countries pursued Moscow-approved anti-imperialist policies. The definition of a national democracy in the Moscow Declaration of the Eighty-one Parties makes very clear that to qualify for inclusion in this category, a country must, above all, pursue, "anti-imperialist," that is, anti-Western policies. National democracies are explicitly recognized to be under the rule of "bourgeois," that is, non-Communist, nationalists and not to be attempting the construction of so-called socialism. Indeed, in three of the four countries described[8] as approximating national democracies—Guinea, Ghana, Mali (the fourth one is Indonesia)—there are no Communist parties. Nevertheless this stage is characterized by Soviet theoreticians as both a long lasting one[9] and a highly desirable one from the Soviet point of view.

In recent years, Soviet writers have also spoken with approval of the "socialism" of non-Communist nationalist movements in underdeveloped countries. To be sure, on this point, too, there have also been reassertions of the old doctrine associating the building of socialism solely with the Communist party. Still, it has now been recognized by Soviet writers that the old Marxist category of the bourgeoisie is inapplicable to the present leaders of nationalist movements and that these are, rather, intellectuals.[10] This, in turn, makes it easier for Moscow to proclaim that the present non-Communist regimes of certain underdeveloped countries are bringing about the transformation to socialism, that is, that they are doing what according to one of the firmest Leninist articles of faith could only be done under the leadership of the Communist party.[11]

[8] B. N. Ponomarev, "On the National Democratic State," *Kommunist*, No. 8 (May 1961), 33–48; condensed translation in *The Current Digest of the Soviet Press*, XIII, No. 22 (June 28, 1961), 3–7. Ponomarev, who specifically rejects as "schematic and harmful" classifying states as belonging or not belonging to the category of national democracy, also mentions Cuba, but it was soon promoted to the status of a country building socialism. See Shinn, *op. cit.*, pp. 383–384.

[9] See footnote 20 quoting E. Zhukov on p. 112 above.

[10] Cf. Carlisle, *op. cit.*, pp. 401–403, and the Soviet sources cited there.

[11] For a well-documented discussion of statements by Khrushchev and some Soviet writers in 1963 and 1964 that certain non-Communist-ruled countries, especially Algeria and Egypt, were "embarked upon the road of socialist development" and of opposition to this thesis by other Soviet figures and by Arab Communists, espe-

By now it is clear, then, that the doctrine of national democracy was but another step in the subordination of Communists to the leadership of non-Communist nationalist movements rather than a new strategy aiming at Communist leadership. In the three African countries once named as approaching the state of national democracy, there was no working-class leadership and no Communist party was permitted, but the Soviet Union, far from seeking to organize such parties, supported the existing regimes[12] and designated their single parties as "national democratic parties." In Indonesia, the large Communist party has been brutally suppressed, but Soviet relations with the Indonesian government do not appear to have deteriorated. Other governments of underdeveloped countries never recognized as national democracies, too, have continued to receive Soviet support and economic and military aid though they opposed or even banned and suppressed their local Communist parties. This has been the story in India ever since the 1950s and was true in Iraq under Kassem in the early 1960s.[13] Ben Bella was made

---

cially the anti-Nasserite Syrian Khaled Bagdash, see Uri Ra'anan, "Moscow and the 'Third World'" *Problems of Communism*, XIV, No. 1 (January–February 1965), 22–31. Georgi Mirsky, "The Proletariat and National Liberation," *New Times* (Moscow), No. 18 (May 1, 1964), 6–9, states very bluntly that "if the conditions for proletarian leadership have not yet matured, the historic mission of breaking with capitalism can be carried out by elements close to the working class. Nature abhors a vacuum." The vacuum is filled, on the one hand, by the "revolutionary-democratic leaders," with Ben Bella given as an example, and, on the other hand, by the Soviet Union, for "the socialist world system is performing the functions of proletarian vanguard in relation to imperialist-oppressed nations." *Ibid.*, pp. 8–9. For a recent Soviet statement sharply characterizing as "absurd" suggestions that Marxists-Leninists "deny the socialist aspiration of national-democratic parties," see A. Iskenderov, "The Developing Nations and Socialism," *Pravda*, June 4, 1965, p. 3; excerpt translated in *The Current Digest of the Soviet Press*, XVII, No. 22 (June 23, 1965), 16–17.

[12] In late 1961, Sékou Touré accused alleged Communists in the Guinea Teachers' Union of planning to overthrow his government and implied that they were in contact with the Soviet Embassy. It is not clear whether the accusations were justified, but the Soviet ambassador was replaced with an expert specializing in foreign trade, early in 1962 Anastas Mikoyan visited Conakry to stress Soviet promises of non-interference, and Soviet and East European aid and trade have continued to flow to Guinea. See Alexander Dallin, "The Soviet Union: Political Activity," in Zbigniew Brzezinski, ed., *Africa and the Communist World* (Stanford, Calif.: Stanford University Press, 1963), pp. 33–35, and Alexander Erlich and Christian R. Sonne, "The Soviet Union: Economic Activity," *ibid.*, pp. 72–73.

[13] On this period in Iraq, see Manfred Halpern, "The Middle East and North Africa," in Cyril E. Black and Thomas P. Thornton, eds., *Communism and Revolution* (Princeton, N.J.: Princeton University Press, 1964), pp. 304–311. In his excellent

a Hero of the Soviet Union by Khrushchev while the Communist party
was outlawed in Algeria. Nasser was closest to Moscow while the Egyptian Communists were in jail,[14] and even when Khrushchev voiced his
disapproval of the suppression of the Egyptian and Syrian Communists,
Soviet aid continued. As Khrushchev said at the Twenty-first Party Congress, putting first things first: "We do not conceal the fact that we
and some leaders of the UAR have different views in the ideological
field, but in questions of struggle against imperialism . . . our positions
coincide. . . . Differences in ideological views must not hinder the development of friendly relations between our countries and the cause
of the common struggle against imperialism."[15] Since then, Nasser, too,
has become a Hero of the Soviet Union who is traveling the road of
non-capitalist and/or socialist development.[16]

---

conclusions on Communism in the Middle East in general, Halpern finds that "the
USSR, through the requirements of its foreign policy, has become a major brake
on Communist revolutions in the Middle East and North Africa" and that "it
can cement government-to-government relations in this highly nationalist region
only at the cost of minimizing its support and encouragement for the Communist
party." *Ibid.*, pp. 324 and 326. See also the rather desperate attack by an Iranian
Communist leader on "the verbal subterfuge according to which an improvement
in relations between Iran and the Soviet Union can only prejudice the revolutionary
movement.' I. Eskandari, "Iran: Present Situation and Perspective," *World Marxist
Review*, VIII, May 1965, 68–76, at p. 75. The author rejects not only this Chinese
view but also, much more briefly and weakly, turns against the Soviet position
of making "the class struggle . . . dependent on peaceful coexistence with the
socialist countries" so that "the party of the working class would be a passive
factor waiting to see how world events develop before deciding on its own policy."
Ibid., p. 76.
[14] A recent Soviet article devoted mainly to Egypt, after noting "a phase of worsened
relations with the Soviet Union" during the period of the Syrian-Egyptian union
(1958–61), proudly states that "economic co-operation between the Soviet Union
and the United Arab Republic developed continuously, and the agreement on Soviet
economic and technical assistance in building the first stage of the High Aswan
Dam was signed at a time when the strain caused by political divergences was
at its highest (December 1958)." K. Ivanov, "National-Liberation Movement and
Non-Capitalist Path of Development," *International Affairs* (Moscow), No. 5 (May
1965), 56–66, p. 64.
[15] N. S. Khrushchev, "On the Middle East," in Alvin Z. Rubinstein, ed., *The Foreign
Policy of the Soviet Union* (New York: Random House, 1960), p. 401. Cf. also
the Soviet explanation that their aid was being granted "to the former colonies
on an inter-governmental basis rendering it to nations and not to some classes
within them" since they were engaged not chiefly in an internal class struggle
but a common struggle against imperialism. L. Stepanov, "Soviet Aid—and Its
'Critics'" *International Affairs* (Moscow), No. 6 (June 1960), 20–26.
[16] Ra'anan, *op. cit.* Khaled Bagdash, "Some Problems of the National-Liberation

II

How is one to explain the evolution of Soviet and Communist policy in the course of less than two decades from Communist parties serving as indispensable instruments both of Soviet foreign policy and domestic revolution to the virtual abandonment by Soviet foreign policy of both revolution and of the Communist parties?

This change is really startling only if we assume, like many people, including Communists themselves, that Communism is an unchanging and unchangeable phenomenon, that, for instance, one can learn about its present problems and policies by reading Lenin or even Marx. Once we recall the tremendous changes the world—and particularly the Soviet Union—has undergone in the last few decades, it would be far more startling if Communism had remained the same since the 1920s and 1930s.

Communist parties and the myth of the proletarian world revolution were important instruments of Soviet foreign policy when it had few other instruments. The early Soviet republic was weak militarily as compared to other European powers; it was isolated diplomatically, having no allies and not even membership in the League of Nations; it was certainly weak economically and could not offer any foreign aid to anyone, nor did it have the propaganda strength the Soviet Union could later derive from its successful industrialization. No wonder the Soviet government concentrated on one asset it did have in international affairs: the support of some disciplined followers of the Communist parties throughout the world who looked to Moscow for leadership and dreamed of overthrowing the many regimes hostile to the Soviet Union. Being unable to deal with existing foreign governments to its satisfaction, the Soviet government looked forward to their overthrow by Communist parties and hence emphasized the goal of world revolution.

All this is now changed. In the past decade or two, the Soviet power position in world affairs has become an utterly different one from that

Movement," *World Marxist Review*, VII, No. 8 (August 1964), 50–58, in what amounts to a weak defense of Communist party interests against Soviet policy, reluctantly admits that "there is no denying . . . that a number of progressive steps" had been taken by Nasser (*ibid.*, p. 53), but decries a "tendency to belittle the role of the working class both at the present stage of the national-liberation movement and in the future, and to exaggerate the role of the intelligentsia, the officers and other members of the petty-bourgeoisie who profess to be for socialism" (*ibid.*, p. 55).

of the 1920s and 1930s. Today the Soviet Union can powerfully influence non-Communist governments by means of military pressure or offers of military aid. It has allies and governments in sympathy with it and is a strong member of the United Nations. It can give substantial amounts of foreign aid to developing countries and has in some cases provided more aid than the United States. The success of its own program of industrialization, which turned a backward country into one of the most powerful and advanced ones, provides it with great propaganda appeal to intellectuals in underdeveloped countries, who are now in leading positions and are committed to similar programs.

As these military, economic, diplomatic, and propaganda weapons became available to her foreign policy, the Soviet Union could more and more influence non-Communist governments, and the more this became true, the less was the Soviet government interested in replacing such governments with Communist ones. Why bother to wait till established non-Communist governments can be overthrown when they can be influenced in the present? Why, for instance, wait for the weak Egyptian or even the stronger Indian Communist parties to grow strong enough to capture their governments, when their present non-Communist governments can be induced to serve some Soviet purposes by grants of military aid and by massive economic and technical assistance? To be sure, if Moscow followed such a policy it could then not expect to control these governments, but, after all, Moscow has not been able to control Communist governments either, particularly if they came to power without the aid of the Soviet army, like those of Yugoslavia, China, North Vietnam, and Cuba. Soviet support thus shifted from the Communist parties in underdeveloped countries to their non-Communist and often anti-Communists governments, and it is for this reason that the Communist parties were, as we noted, instructed to support these governments.

Communist parties can continue to serve a useful function for the Soviet government, on the one hand, by putting pressure on their own governments on behalf of pro-Soviet policies and, on the other, by keeping quiescent—in a manner to be discussed below—people who might otherwise cause trouble for governments cooperating with the Soviet government and by absorbing at least some of the support that might otherwise go to a party sympathetic to the Chinese Communists. If they fail to do so, if they, either independently or at the behest of the Chinese Communists, turn against the non-Communist nationalists, then, from the Soviet point of view, they become a nuisance interfering with good relationships on the governmental level.

The logical end of the development traced here might well be the dissolution of those Communist parties that the Soviet Union can control and their merger with the non-Communist nationalist movements.[17] It may not come to this in many countries for quite some time, but it is worthwhile to note that in a few places this has in fact occurred and that it may be the beginning of a trend.

In Cuba, this development has been obscured, because the non-Communist nationalist movement itself was declared to be Communist, but the fact remains that the official pre-Castro Communist party (the PSP—Popular Socialist Party) merged with that movement and is not, as such, in power today.[18] In Algeria, the leaders of the outlawed Communist party have cooperated with the government of the FLN and have merged their newspaper, the most widely-read paper in the country, with that of this single party. [19] In Ghana, Guinea and Mali, there were no Communist parties to merge but, as we noted, none has been created, and the official single parties were, in some ways, treated as substitutes for them. Thus, their delegates attended the Twenty-second Soviet Party Congress in October 1961. The most striking case is that of Egypt, where the Communist Party officially dissolved itself in April 1965 with a statement declaring that Nasser's single party was the only organization capable of carrying on the revolution.[20] Nothing could be more indicative of the trend under discussion than Communists stating that only their jailers can carry on their revolution.

It is evident, then, that ever since the 1950s, the Soviet government has come to feel that its goals could be pursued more effectively through cooperation with nationalist governments of underdeveloped countries than through their overthrow and replacement by Communist parties.

[17] Lowenthal, "Russia, the One-Party System, and the Third World," *op. cit.,* pp. 50–58, believes that the Communists are pursuing a policy of "licensed infiltration" vis-à-vis one-party regimes in underdeveloped countries and he recognizes that the main advantage of this policy for the Soviet Union is the "reduction of the grounds for possible diplomatic friction" (*ibid.,* p. 57) with the one-party states rather than any accretion to Soviet strength through a growth of Communist party strength.

[18] For a careful analysis of Castroite-Communist relations, see Theodore Draper, *Castroism: Theory and Practice* (New York: Frederick A. Praeger, 1965), pp. 3–56.

[19] "Red Paper to Join With Ben Bella's," *The New York Times,* June 6, 1965, p. 28.

[20] "Party Dissolved by Reds in Cairo," *The New York Times,* April 26, 1965, p. 16.

This change of attitude really involves an imperceptible change in the goals of Soviet foreign policy themselves. It has been a change from Communist revolution as a rather immediate policy objective—whether it was regarded as desirable in itself or for the protection of the Soviet Union—to the postponement of revolution to the indefinite, far-off future in favor of more immediate measures to strengthen the Soviet Union. This, in turn, in the period of the Cold War, meant also a weakening of the United States, and, for that purpose, cooperation with non-Communist nationalist movements and governments of many underdeveloped countries whose anti-colonialism predisposed them against the Western powers, quite apart from any Soviet influence, proved more fruitful than the old pro-Communist policies.

This change of attitude toward the world revolution resulted from a development parallel and related to the changing power position of the Soviet Union, which we just discussed, namely the evolution of Soviet society and leadership. The people who came to power in Russia in 1917 were revolutionary intellectuals. They had spent their lives dreaming, plotting, and making the revolution and they were not going to stop being revolutionaries simply because they had succeeded. As is the case with all revolutionaries, to them the revolution had to go on, and world revolution was hence an important policy to them. This generation of revolutionary intellectuals was replaced during the Stalinist period of industrialization by technically trained bureaucratic and managerial intellectuals.

Today, the party is neither the Leninist one of professional revolutionaries nor the Stalinist one enforcing immense sacrifices to achieve rapid industrialization. The new intelligentsia has become a new upper class demanding more consumer goods. They inherited the benefits of the revolution, and hence the revolution lies for them in the past, not in the present or the future. Thus, the 1961 Program of the Communist Party of the Soviet Union proclaims the final victory of socialism and the end of the class struggle in the Soviet Union.[21] To the new Soviet elite, the word "revolution" has become a symbol of conservatism, like the term "American Revolution" to the Daughters of the American Revolution. Soviet leaders have hence lost interest in the revolution abroad and sympathy with revolutionary groups abroad and have shifted their interests to developing the Soviet system of production. Indeed, the

[21] Triska, *op. cit.*, pp. 24 and 31–32.

1961 Party Program characterizes this concern with Soviet domestic de-development as "the Soviet people's great *internationalist* task."[22]

If the foregoing analysis is valid, Soviet policy in the underdeveloped countries should, in the future, have little to do with the advancement of Communism. This has, of course, been true for quite some time, concealed only by the constant repetition of old myths both in the East and the West. The Soviet Union has supported some Communist parties and has sacrificed others (and ignored many); her allies and friends include Communist governments as well as anti-Communists ones, both of the traditional variety, as in Afghanistan and Ethiopia, and of the modernist variety, as in Egypt and India; and she has among her enemies both anti-Communist governments and Communist ones, especially China. In the period of governmental instability that lies ahead for much of the underdeveloped world, Soviet policy will no doubt seek to gain or maintain its influence with those in power regardless of their attitude toward the domestic Communist party. Thus, in the Algerian coup of June 1965, Moscow was quick to cooperate with Boumedienne who had eliminated its erstwhile friend Ben Bella, and, as already noted, a similar development occurred in the anti-Communist upheaval in Indonesia beginning in October 1965. The Soviet government, after some grumbling in its press, has also tried to maintain friendly relations with the government of Ghana that overthrew the Convention People's Party, even though Moscow had recognized the latter as a kind of surrogate Communist party.

More and more, it becomes necessary for an understanding of Soviet policy to distinguish between the fate of the Soviet Union and that of Communist parties abroad. Just as Communist party defeats, like those in Egypt, Iraq, and Indonesia, have not necessarily been Soviet setbacks, so Soviet advances are not necessarily Communist advances. Thus, the growth of Soviet power in Asia, as demonstrated in Moscow's role as peace-maker in the Indian-Pakistani dispute and potential role as a peace-maker in Vietnam, rests on Soviet economic, diplomatic and military strength rather than on Communist party strength. Far

---

[22] *Ibid.*, p. 25, italics added. The same point was more recently made in *Pravda:* "The Socialist countries' course of building socialism and communism, far from retarding the revolutionary initiative of the working people of the capitalist countries, is the most effective means for its all-round development." "The Supreme Internationalist Duty of the Socialist Country," *Pravda,* October 27, 1965; translated in *The Current Digest of the Soviet Press,* XVII, No. 43 (November 17, 1965), p. 8.

from relying on the Communist parties in the areas concerned or advancing their cause, Soviet policy may well tend to weaken them.

Soviet success on the governmental level may, then, be accompanied by a loss of Soviet influence over Communist parties. Though this is not necessarily tantamount to a gain in Chinese influence—for there is also the third possibility of a growing independence of Communist parties—the long-range trend with respect to influence on parties may well be in favor of the Chinese. Communist parties in underdeveloped countries may feel resentful of Moscow as Soviet policy has more and more supported their non-Communist governments and thus effectively helped keep them out of power. Initially, Soviet cooperation with non-Communist governments was anti-American. Now that the Soviet Union would seem to seek stabilization and even some accommodation with the West, it may find it even harder to compete for the allegiance of Communist parties and even non-Communist nationalist movements with China whose strident anti-Westernism appeals to many nationalist intellectuals of underdeveloped countries. More generally, the Soviet Union may gradually lose out to China in its attempts to continue to identify itself with aspirations of the revolutionary intelligentsia in underdeveloped countries. The very success of Soviet industrialization, which once made her so attractive to this intelligentsia, may now have gone so far as to make the Soviet model with its shift from producers goods to consumer goods and its declining growth rate less relevant to their needs than the Chinese one with its emphasis on heavy industry.

III

In effect, just as the class struggle was given up by Communist parties in the late 1940s, when they began to claim to represent the national bourgeoisie, so world revolution, too, has now been dropped as an objective of Soviet policy. But why, then, the continued use by the Communists of not only class struggle or "proletarian" terminology, but also of world-revolutionary verbiage?

Terms like "the proletarian revolution," "socialism," and the very word "Communism" itself have never, in Communist usage, meant what they seemed to suggest. Some have been myths all along from their Marxian and pre-Marxian beginnings, but all of them functioned as myths when transferred from their Western European origins to underdeveloped Russia and subsequently to other underdeveloped countries where the Marxian vision of an advanced industrial proletariat converting highly developed private capitalism into socialism and Communism simply did not apply.[23] This does not mean the Communist words are meaningless, but that they have been meaningful not as predictions but as myths. What has happened over the years, then, is not that they have lost their meaning, but that the function these myths have served has changed.

At one time, the Communist myths, like those of class struggle and world revolution, were calls to action; they urged those to whom they were addressed to rise up and change the status quo. In recent years, their function has become one of inducing not action but quiescence. They now serve to reassure those who are attracted to the old symbols, who have an interest in radical change, that their interests will be taken care of.[24] The more the Chinese Communist revolutionary intellectuals still use the same myths as calls to action and the more Communist parties are attracted to them, the more must Soviet voices, in order to prevent or delay this process, appeal to these myths that suggest that the Soviet government is still centrally concerned with Communist party strength, leadership, and ultimate victory.

However, this is not to imply that the Soviet leaders consciously use Communist symbols and myths as myths, that is, as lies. Rather, the leaders themselves believe in the myths, though to what extent is impossible to establish and no doubt varies among individuals. They cannot dispense with the revolutionary mythology—or even with their belief in it—for they derive their legitimacy from a revolutionary tradition. Their symbols reassure them that they remain faithful to this tradition.*

[23] I have dealt with the phenomenon of Western analytical concepts becoming myths in underdeveloped countries in "The Western Word and the Non-Western World," *The American Behavioral Scientist,* VII (April 1964), 25–29, and have tried to analyze its complex results with respect to Communism in "Myths, Self-Fulfilling Prophecy, and Symbolic Reassurance in the East-West Conflict," reprinted on pp. 121–144 above.

[24] On the concept of symbolic reassurance, see Murray Edelman, *The Symbolic Uses of Politics* (Urbana, Ill.: University of Illinois Press, 1964), especially Ch. 2.

* [Since even the revolutionary intellectuals, like Lenin and Trotsky, who fashioned the myth of revolution, always regarded industrialization as a goal of the revolution, the mangerial intellectuals, like Brezhnev and Kosygin, who succeeded them and have reached this goal, have no difficulty in seeing themselves as executors of the revolutionary program, i.e., as "revolutionaries." In fact, however, industrialization was merely a symbol of reassurance to the revolutionaries and became a call to action to the managers; revolution, on the other hand, was a call to action for the revolutionaries and became a symbol of reassurance to the managers. This point is placed in the broader context of the politics of these two types of intellectual elites in my paper on "Patterns of Elite Succession in the Process of Development," excerpts of which are reprinted on pp. 163–171 below.]

Thus symbols assure everyone that there has been no change—no so-called basic or fundamental change—and paradoxically thus leave the policy-makers free in fact to change their policies. Soviet leaders could not have maintained themselves in power nor could they have kept their consciences quiet as they supported anti-Communist governments in a number of countries even against Communist parties and also as they withdrew missiles from Cuba, sent war planes to India to be used against Communist China, backed, for quite some time, a neutralist against a Communist faction in Laos, and signed the test ban treaty with the United States if they had announced that they were abandoning the goal of world revolution. They are free to *do* all these new things only because they *say* that they continue to pursue the old policy.[25]

The Sino-Soviet conflict is, of course, an integral part of the story of Soviet policy in underdeveloped countries. To be sure, it could be argued that it has chiefly served to reinforce tendencies that can be explained from changes in the internal and international position of the Soviet Union, both the tendency to cooperate with non-Communist governments in underdeveloped countries and the tendency to continue to describe these new policies in terms of the old symbols of Communism. In any case, there is no need here to deal at any length with the Sino-Soviet conflict as such, but some light can perhaps be thrown on it in the present context.

Unlike the present Soviet leaders, the Chinese Communist leaders are not conservatives, for they do not have much to conserve yet, they are not the heirs of a successful revolution, they *are* the revolutionaries themselves and, like all revolutionaries, they regard their revolution as still unfinished.[26] Not only are their experiences and quite possibly their

[25] That words remain the same while policies change, probably because old words provide symbolic reassurance, that . . . "environmental stimuli and even the substantive content of one's world view may vary more than his verbal output: policy changes more dramatically than prayers or vocabularies" is interestingly demonstrated by William John Hanna, "Environmental Change and Verbal Stability," *The Journal of Communication*, XV, No. 3 (September 1965), 136–148, p. 136, who subjected Soviet delegates' speeches to the UN Security Council from 1946 to 1960 to a thematic intensity content analysis and found that ". . . the Soviet delegates' formal political communications did not basically change during the years 1946–1960 . . ." in spite of major changes in the domestic and international environments of the Soviet elite and probable changes in its world view. *Ibid.*, p. 147.

[26] On the differences between Chinese and Soviet societies and the attitudes of their leaders contributing to the Sino-Soviet conflict, see J. H. Rigby, "The Embourgeoisement of the Soviet Union and the Proletarianization of Communist China," in London, ed., *Unity and Contradiction, op. cit.*, pp. 19–36.

personality needs different from those of the present Soviet leaders, but the power position of their country is very different from that of the Soviet Union, too. Much like Lenin's and unlike Khrushchev's and Brezhnev's Russia, China has few allies and no representation in international bodies and only enough military strength to threaten her own immediate neighbors, no economic strength to provide any substantial foreign aid to developing countries and no obvious success of her industrialization program to use as propaganda appeal.[27] The Chinese Communists, then, like the early Soviet government, cannot hope to influence many non-Communist governments, though in a very different world situation, they have been trying to do so with some limited success, not only around the Chinese borders but also in Africa.[28] As compared to Khrushchev and Brezhnev, however, Mao, like Lenin and Stalin, still relies heavily on foreign Communist parties and hopes that they will capture power.[29] Hence the sometimes diametrically opposite policies that the Soviet and Chinese Communists urge on the Communist parties in underdeveloped countries and the consequent splits of Communist parties in a number of countries, notably in India where the Chinese Communists want Communists to oppose and eventually replace the

---

[27] However, as has been noted, the unsolved problem—though not the failure—of Chinese industrialization may be more appealing to some intellectuals in underdeveloped countries than the success of Soviet industrialization.

[28] See Richard Lowenthal, "China," in Brzezinski, ed., *Africa and the Communist World, op. cit.,* pp. 142–203, and William E. Griffith, "Africa," in "International Communism: The End of an Epoch," *Survey,* No. 54 (January 1965), 185–187.

[29] In practice the distinction is not so sharp, because it is becoming more and more difficult to define what constitutes a Communist party, especially from the Chinese point of view. Where Communist parties are non-existent, as in much of Africa, or are under Soviet domination, as in Northern Africa, the Chinese have sought contacts with non-Communist anti-imperialist groups, whether in power or not, including some of the governments whom the Soviet Communists also cultivate, like Ben Bella's and by late 1963 even Nasser's. They have even suggested that any group or leader, for example Ben Bella, regardless of class and regardless of party, can, like Castro, by self-declaration become "Marxist-Leninist." As Chou En-lai remarked in 1963: "Marxism-Leninism cannot be the monopoly of the Communist Party." Quoted by Benjamin Schwartz, "The Polemics Seen by a Non-Polemicist," *Problems of Communism,* XII, No. 2 (March–April 1964), 106, who excellently sums up this remarkable stretching of Communist dogma, which the Soviet Communists had, in effect, accepted earlier in the Cuban case, as follows: "Thus, the essence of the true proletarian class nature is now not only detached from the industrial proletariat, it is even detachable from constituted Communist parties. It is now a completely free-floating fluid which may find its embodiment where it listeth."

very government that the Soviet Union wants Communists to support.[30] Chinese and Soviet Communists use the same symbols, and this gives the superficial appearance of agreement which has deceived both people in the West and the Communists themselves. Yet words that are calls to action for one side are calls to quiescence for the other.[31]

It should be made clear that the development analyzed here is merely a tendency. Since myths can, to some extent, be self-fulfilling prophecies and can therefore have concrete consequences and since the symbols producing quiescence are difficult to distinguish from those calling for action, this development evolves in the form of a zig-zag line rather than a straight one.

It should also be added that the argument presented here is such that it cannot be satisfactorily proved by quotations from Soviet statements. Such statements sometimes hint at the change, but they cannot fully admit it. It is in the nature of a myth that it is never described as such by those who believe in it, and it is in the nature of symbols leading to quiescence and inaction that they sound as if they were calls to action. This is unfortunate, because both academic experts on the Soviet Union and also, paradoxically, those anti-Communists who insist that the Communists' words cannot be trusted have a long tradition of relying on these very words, sometimes including the ancient ones of Lenin and even Marx, to prove their points about Soviet policy. The Communists' words can, indeed, not be trusted, and the Communists do deceive others—but they also deceive themselves, for their calls to revolutionary action are really symbols of reassurance. If policy speaks louder than words, if one considers what the Soviet government and Communist parties, insofar as they follow Soviet policy, do and not what they say, it becomes clear that their policy has not for a long time been one of either class struggle or world revolution. It has, in short, not been the policy which we have for half a century been accustomed to calling "Communism."

---

[30] For the positions of the two Indian Communist parties, as outlined from a pro-Soviet point of view after the split, see G. Adhikari, "The Problems of the Non-Capitalist Path of Development in India and the State of National Democracy," *World Marxist Review*, VII, No. 11 (November 1964), 35–42.

[31] For an excellent brief analysis of the different Soviet and Chinese attitudes toward the underdeveloped countries as a function of "different needs of Communist parties ruling societies in different stages of economic and social development," see Richard Lowenthal, "Preface to the American Edition," *World Communism: The Disintegration of a Secular Faith* (New York: Oxford University Press, 1964), pp. ix–xv.

What, then, is Communism in underdeveloped countries today as distinguished from the intellectual-led nationalist and modernizing movements in these countries? The answer, difficult as it is to accept for those who cling to the old meaning of the word Communism, is simply that Communism *cannot* be sharply distinguished from them, as Soviet policy has sought to identify Communism more and more with these movements. Indeed, it can be argued that Communism itself has all along been a modernizing movement in underdeveloped countries, including Russia,[32] though its use of Western proletarian symbols concealed that character from Communists and non-Communists alike.

The difficulty of drawing the distinction between Communist and non-Communist modernizing movements is well illustrated by recurring debates in the West over whether certain nationalist-modernizing movements are Communist or not. Castro conveniently, but not really satisfactorily, resolved this question when he himself declared that he was a Marxist-Leninist. But were Lumumba and Gizenga Communists? What about Sékou Touré and Jomo Kenyatta and even Sukarno? Were the revolution of 1964 in Zanzibar and the uprising in 1965 in Santo Domingo Communist or not? To what degree are the Viet Cong Communist? Such questions have been debated time and again, and similar ones are bound to arise in the future as modernizing nationalists in underdeveloped countries employ symbols similar to the traditional Communist ones and receive the support, verbal and even material, of the Soviet government.

Both sides to these questions can always produce evidence, yet neither can prove its case, because the debates themselves rest on the false assumption that any man or any movement or revolution must either be Communist or non-Communist.[33] In fact, the Communists have come to support the non-Communists or, to put it even more paradoxically, Communists have gone non-Communist. Clearly, the very concept of Communism has become a source of confusion. It is hence useless for analytical purposes, useful as it remains as a myth to both those who support and those who oppose whatever they choose to regard as Communism.

[32] Cf. Theodore H. von Laue, *Why Lenin? Why Stalin? A Reappraisal of the Russian Revolution, 1900–1930* (Philadelphia: Lippincott, 1964).

[33] On the use of nationalist-modernist symbols by Communists and the role of the concept of national democracy in this connection, see Justus van der Kroef, "The Vocabulary of Indonesian Communism," *Problems of Communism*, XIV, No. 3 (May–June 1965), 1–9.

8. *Patterns of Elite Succession in the Process of Development**

Introductory Note. In several of the foregoing articles I indicated that changes in Soviet leadership are one important variable that accounts for change in Communist policy in underdeveloped countries and particularly for the trend toward the convergence of Communist and non-Communist modernizing movements. I did not, however, deal with these changes in Soviet leadership at any length.

In a paper I presented in Brazil to an international seminar on political development, I was concerned with "Patterns of Elite Succession in the Process of Development." This paper did not focus specifically on the Soviet Union or on Communism, but it reflected my conviction that these can, for my purposes, be analyzed in a larger framework of the politics of development. I am reproducing here two excerpts from this paper which, dealing with patterns of elite succession that accompany the process of industrialization generally, may throw some light on this process—past, present, and future—in the Soviet Union and in other Communist-governed countries.

I discussed earlier, especially in my "Essay in the Politics of Development," excerpted above, how the Russian Revolution may be regarded as a revolution of modernizing intellectuals turning against the traditional order in an underdeveloped country. In my paper on "Patterns of Elite Succession" I pointed out, drawing on examples from all over the underdeveloped world, why and how such successful revolutions tend to be followed by a period of conflict among groups of revolutionary intellectuals. Unable to carry out their far-reaching promises of rapid modernization and of the quick elimination of powerful traditional institutions and strata, various factions within the revolutionary intelligentsia come to accuse each other of betraying the revolution, and, in the name of the revolution and its goals, they fight each other and replace each other in office.

The first two decades after the outbreak of the Revolution of 1917 can certainly be regarded as such a period of conflict among revolutionary intellectuals. From March to November 1917 various revolutionary

* Excerpted from a paper delivered to the International Seminar on Political Development, University of Minas Gerais, Belo Horizonte, M. G., Brazil, September 18–23, 1966. All footnotes irrelevant in the present context have been omitted.

163

parties and factions maneuvered and fought against one another. After Lenin's coup, the non-Bolshevik groups were reduced to impotence and, especially after Lenin's death, factions and individual leaders among the Bolsheviks opposed and eliminated one another. Out of this process, Stalin, himself a revolutionary intellectual, emerged triumphant. Under his rule, his rivals among the revolutionary intelligentsia were gradually replaced by a new generation of managerial intellectuals. The rise of this new elite, which has in the persons of Brezhnev and Kosygin at last reached the very top of the Soviet hierarchy, is a development concomitant with that of industrialization, each one requiring the other. The distinctions, conflicts and policy differences between revolutionary and managerial intellectuals are discussed in the first of the two excerpts reprinted here.

Further on in my paper, I sought to predict patterns of future political change in underdeveloped countries. After first casting grave doubts on the prospects of successful industrialization in many of these, I then distinguish between two broad patterns of political development that might emerge in countries that do advance industrially. In one, on the Mexican and Indian model, managerial intellectuals develop simultaneously and come to share power with other groups, like workers' and peasants' organizations, sometimes led by remnants of the revolutionary intelligentsia, as well as with developing business groups and also traditionally oriented ones that survived the revolution, like landed and religious groups. For the other pattern only the Soviet Union can so far serve as a prototype, though China, too, may now be entering on a similar development. In it, managerial intellectuals both maintain themselves in sole control of power against potential opposition and advance rapid industrialization. Both suppression and forced industrialization (which we associate with "Stalinism") can be accomplished by the use of terror, regimentation, and propaganda.

The second excerpt reproduced below analyzes this "Soviet-type" pattern of political development and also seeks to project some of the trends now visible in it into the future. It may thus serve in our present context to round out the picture of Soviet development that I began to draw with my references to the Russian Revolution as a modernizing one and to the subsequent emergence of a new managerial elite. Once again, however, the discussion is not specifically focused on the Soviet Union. It is deliberately couched in more general terms to point out that the Soviet pattern of change need not be unique to the Soviet Union or even to Communist countries, such as China, but may be relevant to the future of other underdeveloped countries as well. To show this, I sought to explain the pattern in terms of the politics of development, that is, of the group conflicts accompanying the process of industrialization, rather than, as is more common, merely in terms of ideology. That I do not regard ideology as irrelevant for such an explanation should be obvious from much of the foregoing material in this book. Rather,

I see it, including Communist ideology, itself as a crucial aspect of the politics of development, to be explained in part by the situation confronted by those active in politics and in part by the myths and symbols that they inherited from the past and from other countries.

I

We have, so far, spoken of "modernizing intellectuals," intellectuals committed to the goal of rapid industrialization. However, commitment to a goal is not tantamount to ability to reach it. The skills and talents and perhaps even the personality attributes of those who become successful revolutionary leaders are different from those of successful industrial organizers. It evidently takes one kind of intellectual to build a mass movement and quite another to build a factory. Revolutionary intellectuals are generally lawyers, journalists, and teachers, students of the humanities and social sciences, philosophers, novelists and poets, they are men with a vision of the future and men who speak and write well. Managerial intellectuals, on the other hand, are administrators, technicians, and scientists.

The nature of the revolutionary leadership that has come to power pledged to carry out a program of industrialization may, then, itself be an obstacle to the realization of that program. Successful industrialization, if it is possible at all, may require the replacement of the revolutionary leaders by a group of managerial intellectuals. The revolutionary intellectuals thus confront a serious dilemma. They are under considerable pressure, generated by their own ideological commitments and the beliefs they have helped instill in others, to industrialize. Since they can neither do the job themselves nor rely on specialists from advanced countries, they must foster the growth of a managerial intelligentsia to enlarge what relatively small one they may have inherited from the colonial economy. These managerial intellectuals, however, are bound to become impatient with the revolutionary intellectuals' slowness or failure to industrialize, they are bound to think that they could do a better job themselves, to become, in short, a threat to any regime of revolutionary intellectuals.

In the face of this threat, the response of the revolutionary intellectuals is to insist that they remain indispensable, that, even though they are in power, their specialty of revolution-making is still required. Like all revolutionaries, they feel that their revolution is as yet incomplete and must be carried on. They point to the remnants of their domestic enemies—the "bourgeoisie," the aristocracy, the Church, tribalism—and to their ideologies as continuing threats, and, above all, they claim that the revolution and the independence of the country are not secure from foreign enemies until the revolution is carried abroad. Lenin's and Trotsky's world revolution, Mao's and Castro's concepts of anti-imperialist "national liberation" throughout the underdeveloped world, Sukarno's fight against his three-in-one devil "necolim" (neo-colonialism, colonialism, imperialism), Nasser's pan-Arabism, Nkrumah's and Touré's pan-Africanism may all be seen as serving the function of justifying the rule of revolutionary intellectuals.

The attitudes of the revolutionary leaders have policy consequences. When, in search of an imperialist threat—and such prophesies may to some extent be self-fulfilling—a Sukarno concentrates the scarce resources and energies of his country on the struggle against the Dutch in Western New Guinea and, when that is no longer possible, against the British in Malaysia, when a Ben Bella sends aid to rebels in the Congo and Angola, when both make lavish preparations for Afro-Asian meetings, when a Nasser sends aid to the Congo and troops to Yemen, they all effectively delay industrialization—and thus maintain themselves in power as against the alternative of a regime of managerial intellectuals.*

Though the policy differences between the revolutionary and managerial intellectuals are clear enough, the two groups cannot easily be distinguished, because it is in the interest of both to obscure the differences between them. While pursuing different policies, they employ the same symbols to justify them. The revolutionary intellectuals advocate not only revolution, both before and after they come to power, but also industrialization which, with its promise of eventual abundance, serves to justify the revolution. The managerial intellectuals advocate not only industrialization, but also insist that they will carry on the revolution, for it is only from it that they derive their legitimacy. Thus, a Stalin, a Khrushchev, and even a Brezhnev claim to be merely Lenin's disciples and heirs and continue to employ revolutionary slogans. The symbols are used by both groups, but they serve different functions. To the revolutionary intellectuals, the revolutionary symbols are calls to action, those calling for industrialization are symbols of reassurance;

---

* [The same was true when a Lenin and a Trotsky devoted some of their energies to attempts at revolution in Germany and China.]

to the managerial intellectuals, the demands for industrialization are calls to action, but the revolutionary symbols are designed to induce political quiescence.

Since it is easier to distinguish managerial intellectuals from revolutionary ones by their deeds than by their words, we do not yet know whether the military men that have, in 1965 and 1966, replaced Ben Bella, Sukarno, and Nkrumah and those who have taken power in Dahomey, the Central African Republic, and Upper Volta can be better classified as belonging to or representing one grouping or the other. The matter is clearer in retrospect if we consider societies that have been under intellectual rule for something like half a century. The beginning of the first Five-Year Plan and the collectivization of agriculture indicated that Stalin represented a different brand of intellectual from Lenin and Trotsky, and, in the great purges of the thirties, the generation of revolutionary intellectuals was replaced with managerial ones. In the Chinese revolution, Sun Yat-sen was a revolutionary intellectual, Chiang Kai-shek eventually failed as such, and Mao again played that role. But, perhaps because, unlike Lenin,' he spent much of his life governing and not merely planning revolution, Mao has played the role of both Lenin and Stalin in China. Industrialization has been pushed forward under the rule of the revolutionary intelligentsia and, inevitably, a new managerial intelligentsia has grown up. For some time, the two have been in conflict, with the ruling revolutionaries insisting that the revolution must go on and its militant spirit be maintained and seeking to denigrate the managerial intellectuals as revisionists and careerists and to downgrade the technicians' concerns as of secondary importance. The distinctions are not so sharp and the lines of conflict not so clearly drawn in Mexico, but perhaps it is possible to designate Lázaro Cárdenas as the last of the revolutionary intellectuals. Similarly, in India the transition from Nehru to Shastri may have been that of revolutionary to managerial intellectual. Finally, in the case of Turkey, another country whose modernizing revolution lies some decades back, that transition may not have come at all yet.

II

In intra-intelligentsia conflicts, revolutionary intellectuals in power are likely, if they can, to use a measure of terror to intimidate their rivals and some mass propaganda to try to mobilize support of the lower classes for their own cause. These methods may find much more widespread use if and when managerial intellectuals come to control the government. These will not only confront the hostility of various groups of revolutionary intellectuals, but, if they succeed in advancing industrialization (which we now assume), they will also create and strengthen new groups, especially among industrial workers, that become organizable and could, at least potentially and at first perhaps under the leadership of some disgruntled revolutionary intellectuals, become a threat to the managerial intellectuals. The latter may respond with the use of mass terror, mass propaganda, and mass regimentation to intimidate, suppress, and persuade any potential opposition and to organize the population on behalf of the objectives of the regime. Since regimes of managerial intellectuals are interested in rapid industrialization, they use these methods for purposes not only of suppression but also of aiding industrialization.

Industrialization is always and everywhere a painful process, because it radically changes the lives of people, especially peasants, who are not prepared for change. The more rapidly the change occurs, the more painful it becomes. Intellectuals intent on pushing industrialization forward will, then, confront a good deal of passive and even some active resistance from already politicized peasants and those peasants who have already been turned into workers—the very groups that supported the intellectuals in their struggle against the traditional-colonial order— as well as indifference and apathy from those peasants not yet caught up in the process of change. Being fanatically convinced, on the basis of their understanding of Western history, that industrialization is the key to their country's domestic and international problems, that it will, indeed, eventually bring contentment to the very groups that oppose it, the intellectuals use their control of the government to compel workers and peasants to cooperate in the industrialization effort. As they see it, they know the "true interests" of workers and peasants and must hence force them and persuade them to take a course which they resist taking on their own.

Terror, regimentation, and propaganda can all be employed to solve problems which must be solved if rapid industrialization is to succeed. They can help mobilize and control a supply of labor for industry and elicit a flow of food and raw materials from the remaining peasants in the countryside, and the intellectual rulers can hope that both can be accomplished with less expenditure of scarce capital than incentive wages or payments might require. Some forms of forced labor and control of workers and of government organization of agriculture are likely to be employed by managerial intellectuals in power, then.

Terror, regimentation and propaganda can also serve to compel those whose expectations of abundance have been aroused by promises of industrialization to accept postponement of their fulfillment. Trade unions, which demand a larger share of the product of industry for consumption and thus tend to slow down the industrialization process by reducing capital left for investment, are suppressed and converted into government agencies seeking to make the worker work harder for less. Mass propaganda is employed to convince everyone, but especially those who cannot be made to work and accept deprivations by terror or regimentation, like professional and technical personnel, that industrialization will, indeed, bring abundance—but not for a while; in the meantime sacrifices are demanded. The ideology of managerial-intellectual regimes invariably combines the two elements of demands for present-day sacrifice and promises of future abundance.

If regimes of managerial intellectuals industrialize their societies, they thereby, whether they desire and know it or not, change themselves. Since managerial intellectuals are difficult to distinguish from the revolutionary intellectuals and may replace them only gradually, they come to power with the support of some workers and perhaps some peasants. Their symbols being the same as those of the revolutionary intellectuals, they continue to appear as champions of labor organizations and land reform and of the workers' and the peasants' right to their product. As managerial intellectuals turn to effective industrialization, however, it soon develops that strong trade unions and the individual peasant's control of his land and product are obstacles to rapid industrialization with scarce resources. The regime's policy toward workers and peasants changes, then, to one of regimentation and compulsion, though in form trade unions and peasant ownership, now called cooperative or collective, are maintained, for the managerial intellectuals even now continue to hold the ideology of their revolutionary predecessors which makes them appear to themselves as well as others as the representatives of the "masses."

In fact, if managerial intellectuals succeed in advancing industrialization, they lose the support of workers and peasants (as well as of the revolutionary intellectuals). However, in the very process of industrialization, they build up new bases of support. These are the rapidly growing governmental hierarchies—the government and party bureaucracies, the military and the police, and the managerial, technical, and scientific personnel directing industry—into which the multiplying managerial intellectuals now divide and into which some workers, peasants, and former revolutionary intellectuals are recruited. In pursuit of their diverse functions, these hierarchies and their subdivisions come into conflicts with each other, which constitute the politics of this type of society, but they all share an interest in maintaining the regime in power.

If and as industry advances further, the functions of the regime of managerial intellectuals and the relative strength of the various groups among them change. When opposing revolutionary intellectuals have been eliminated, by being either purged or absorbed into the managerial intelligentsia; when industry begins to produce consumer goods and the feverish pace of work begins to slacken so that worker and peasant discontent can be reduced; when, in time, mechanization and eventually automation shrink the numbers in these discontented strata and increase those in the white-collar and professional groups who tend to identify with the regime—then the threat of opposition to the government and of obstruction to industrialization decreases. Then, the suppressive functions of the governmental, party and military hierarchies decline and the police apparatus loses some of its power. On the other hand, those directly in charge of industry—the managers and engineers and scientists—grow in power, and the other bureaucracies come more to reflect their interests, such as those in greater autonomy of managerial and technical personnel and in regularized bureaucratic procedures to replace the arbitrariness associated both with the crash programs and the terror of the period of rapid industrialization. More generally, a consumer ethic comes to replace the producer ethic of the earlier period within the new upper class and eventually perhaps in the entire society.[1]

This process of change does not proceed in a straight line, for at each point there are groups within the regime that have an interest in the *status quo* and may even seek a return to the *status quo ante*. The process is also slowed by the persistence of the old ideology of the revolutionary intellectuals with its symbols of revolution and struggle

---

[1] The growth of bureaucracy and bureaucratic interests in the Soviet Union is stressed by Zbigniew Brzezinski, "The Soviet Political System: Transformation or Degeneration?" *Problems of Communism*, XV, No. 1 (Jan.–Feb. 1966), 1–15; for evidence pointing to the emergence of a consumer ethic even two decades ago, see Alex Inkeles and Raymond A. Bauer, *The Soviet Citizen: Daily Life in a Totalitarian Society* (Cambridge, Mass.: Harvard University Press, 1959).

against imperialism and its championship of the lower classes, an ideology from which the new upper classes still derive their legitimacy and some support at home and abroad. If the prophesies of the ideology are taken seriously by the regime and by its foreign enemies, they can become self-fulfilling and produce conflicts which are bound to slow and may even stop the development outlined here.

9. The Appeal of Communist Models
in Underdeveloped Countries*

Introductory Note. If, as the last excerpt suggests, the evolution of the
Soviet political system may constitute one type of political change accompanying industrialization, then the Soviet Union may be regarded
by those so inclined as a model to be followed by other underdeveloped
countries. In the paper that is here reproduced I tried to answer the
question why the Soviet Union and also China might be appealing
models to some intellectuals in underdeveloped countries. In doing so,
I was chiefly concerned with pulling together relevant concepts and
lines of thought developed more fully in my writings reprinted above
and to bring them to bear on this question.

L ike beauty, the relevance of models is in the eye of the beholder.
This paper will, therefore, not compare conditions in the early Soviet
Union and in present-day underdeveloped countries to establish whether
and to what extent the Communist development model seems to us
relevant to the future of underdeveloped countries. Rather, it will address itself to the question why the model does seem to be relevant
to people in underdeveloped countries regardless of whether it appears
to be relevant to us or not.

To approach that question, we must, first of all, seek to know to
whom in underdeveloped countries the appeal of Communist models
is directed. It is surely not directed, or at any rate not attractive, to
these countries or their societies or peoples in general, as it is often
put. The very nature of the Communist development model is such
that it could hardly be expected to appeal to the vast majority of people
in underdeveloped countries. To the traditional elites of these countries,

* A paper presented at the Conference on "The Dynamics of Development,"
Institute of World Affairs, University of Southern California, March 26–28, 1967.
Reprinted by permission of Willard A. Beling and George O. Totten. A bibliographi-
cal note has been omitted here.

often composed of aristocratic rulers, big landowners, and the clergy, who might have some understanding of the model, it promises only disaster and must appear repulsive. To the great mass of the population, made up principally of a mostly tradition-bound peasantry and also an urban petty bourgeoisie, and, in some countries, a more modern working class emerging from these two old strata, the model must be largely incomprehensible. The experience and the intellectual horizons of individuals in this great mass are too narrow to be able to encompass such concepts as rapid industrialization and to imagine any future benefits to be derived from it.

If the Communist development model cannot effectively appeal to either the masses or the traditional elites of underdeveloped countries, it can be attractive only to the modern elite, to people who can be loosely described as the intellectuals. What we know of the social background of those who look to this model indicates that they are, indeed, in large numbers such intellectuals. This is true not only of the leaders of Communist parties in underdeveloped countries who, without question, accept the Communist model, but also of the leadership of non-Communist, so-called nationalist movements who are attracted to the Communist development model in various degrees and often indicate this by referring to themselves and their ideologies and goals as "socialist."

To understand the appeal of the Communist model to intellectuals in underdeveloped countries we must further define this group in terms both of its origins and its goals. With respect to its social origins, the intelligentsia is not a homogeneous group, though most intellectuals are likely to have grown out of the upper classes of the old society. While the social groupings of the traditional society are largely determined by certain inherited characteristics, the intellectuals are people who have broken out of this framework and who are defined by certain common acquired characteristics. These include, above all, values they have taken over from foreign, industrially advanced societies and political interests and goals resulting from these values. To the extent that they have common interests, we are justified in calling them a group.

Among the values of industrialized societies absorbed by some natives of underdeveloped countries are the desirability of material progress and a greater and growing measure of wealth, social equality, education, and political participation or mobilization for the great mass of the population. Typically, such values are acquired in the course of a higher education, especially when it is obtained abroad in an industrialized society. More and more, though, modern education appropriate to industrialized societies is also available in universities in underdeveloped countries. It is because modern values are held so largely by university-educated natives of underdeveloped countries that we refer to the group characterized by these values as intellectuals. It should be noted, however, that similar values can also be acquired in modern institutions other than universities, such as armies, bureaucracies, and trade unions, both through formal indoctrination or training courses and through informal exposure.

The values we mentioned are commonly accepted in industrial societies, but in traditional societies they are highly subversive of the established order. For their realization, they require revolutionary changes, and intellectuals are therefore revolutionaries in traditional societies. Their commitment to material progress and greater wealth, equality, and participation generally leads them to adopt a program including the interrelated demands for rapid industrialization, for independence, and for the removal of the traditional ruling groups and their institutions from power, each of these being designed to reinforce the others.

Industrialization, if it is to be rapid and if it is to insure independence from already industrialized countries and eventually a position of power in international affairs, requires first the build-up of heavy industry and consequently the postponement of the fulfillment of consumer demands. Independence, in turn, is demanded to permit rapid industrialization. It is stressed as an objective not only in countries ruled outright by foreigners as colonies but also in legally sovereign nations which stand in a colonial relationship of economic dependence to industrialized countries, serving as suppliers of raw materials for them. Attacks on the traditional ruling groups, finally, are required because these groups are, as its eventual victims, likely to be opposed to industrialization and they are also frequently allied with colonial interests in a mutually supportive relationship. Such attacks may be directed at monarchical and at religious institutions and at the ideologies associated with them. Very commonly, they involve demands for land reform (or rent or tax reform) which not only represent intellectuals' hopes for greater wealth and equality for the peasants but also strike at the roots of the power of the traditional aristocracy, its control of the land and the peasants.

Intellectuals committed to the goals summarized here have by now come to power in most of the underdeveloped countries of the world.

However, in almost all cases, they have so far been able to make only relatively little progress toward the full achievement of their goals. At best, the beginnings of industrialization have been attained, and their countries remain overwhelmingly agrarian. Hence dependence on the colonial-industrial powers abroad and domination by traditional ruling groups at home have been removed only partially, though to a quite different extent in different countries. Material wealth, social equality, and education and political involvement for the great mass of the population still remain largely unfulfilled dreams. Indeed, to those intellectuals who have attained power, it must become painfully clear that the obstacles to the realization of these dreams are far greater than they had imagined in their early enthusiasm and impatience for rapid change.

If the values and goals of intellectuals are principally those indicated here, one might well assume that they would turn to the West for their development model. It is, after all, in the countries of Western Europe and in the United States that, in varying degrees, the greatest technological progress has been made and the greatest amount of wealth has been produced; that wealth has been most widely distributed and thus great strides have been made toward the abolition of mass poverty and the attainment of social equality; and that the highest proportion of the population is actively involved in the political process.

Indeed, for the societies that intellectuals in underdeveloped countries wish ultimately to attain, the Western countries have served as the primary models, especially Britain, France, and the United States, whose position has been such a dominant one in much of the underdeveloped world and where so many students from that world have received their education and their first powerful impression of the benefits of industrialization. The well-nigh universal use by intellectuals in underdeveloped countries of the Western concept "democracy" to describe the societies they hope to achieve testifies to the predominance of the Western model in their minds.

However, for the process of achieving these Western-type societies, the history of the Western countries seems far less relevant as a model to many intellectuals in underdeveloped countries than that of some Communist countries. In the Western countries, industrialism and its social and political concomitants evolved organically from within the native societies. This process was necessarily a gradual and slow one which makes it unattractive to many intellectuals in underdeveloped countries who, precisely because they have the Western model to catch up with, as the West did not, are impatient to see industrialization realized in the course of one generation rather than of centuries.

Furthermore, in the Western countries industrialization was carried through not by intellectuals, the group that will probably serve this function in underdeveloped countries, if it will be served at all, and in any case ought, from their own point of view, to serve it. Rather, it was achieved largely by an industrial bourgeoisie, a group that either has virtually no equivalent in underdeveloped countries or is too weak there to carry through a rapid and massive industrial build-up and that is often suspect in the eyes of intellectuals because of the association in their minds of private capitalism with colonialism.

Even Japan, which is often cited as a relevant development model for the underdeveloped countries, because it is, after all, an Asian country, and because its industrialization proceeded relatively rapidly, does not appear attractive to many intellectuals. Here, too, industrialization was not carried out by intellectuals and did not bring intellectuals to power. Rather, somewhat as in Germany, its development was sponsored by the traditional aristocratic regime itself (which was, of course, modified in the process) and for long remained compatible with aristocratic rule. To many intellectuals in underdeveloped countries, however, removal of such aristocratic rule and its replacement by the rule of intellectuals is quite as important a goal as industrialization and each is regarded as a means to the attainment of the other.

Since, as we saw, the goal of intellectuals in underdeveloped countries is not mere industrialization in any form but industrialization that must be rapid and anti-colonial (which is often interpreted by them to mean also anti-capitalist) as well as anti-traditional in character, neither Britain, France, and the United States nor Germany and Japan can serve as relevant development models to many of them. The Communist countries, on the other hand, notably the Soviet Union and China, may seem to them to fit their needs for a relevant model far better.

This is so, simply because Communist movements, in countries other than the Western ones, are or were at one time themselves intellectual-led movements for rapid industrialization and against traditional rule and Western colonialism. The Communists of underdeveloped countries, including Russia and China, have had the same ambiguous love-hate attitude toward the West, the same anti-Western Westernism that has characterized other intellectuals in underdeveloped countries and that, in its very nature cannot be duplicated in the West itself to make it an equally attractive development model.

Communist regimes, then, are similar to intellectual-led regimes in other underdeveloped countries to the extent that, when they came to power, they represented similar social strata, opposed similar enemies, and, in the name of a Western ideology, pursued similar goals. These similarities were long concealed from the Communists themselves, from their opponents and their observers in Western countries, and, most important in our context, from intellectuals in underdeveloped countries, because the particular Western ideology used by the Russian Communists to legitimize their course was Marxism. Entrapped in its categories, the Communists saw themselves as the representatives of an industrial proletariat struggling against capitalism at home and abroad in order to socialize an industrial economy rather than as intellectuals seeking to industrialize an underdeveloped country. Their use of the Marxian symbols of proletarianism thus deceived both Communists and non-Communists for decades and, to some extent, to this day and tended to make the Soviet model seem irrelevant in underdeveloped countries.

In the post-World War II period, however, a number of developments occurred which made the Soviet model seem far more relevant to the goals of intellectuals in underdeveloped countries. For one thing, the Soviet regime had by then become the one intellectual-led regime in an underdeveloped country that had strikingly succeeded in attaining the goals more or less aspired to by all such regimes. It had not only utterly wiped out the old aristocracy and removed or converted its institutions, but it had turned an agrarian into an industrial society and it had changed a weak and dependent country into a big power in international affairs. On the other hand, intellectual-led anti-colonial movements, still small and relatively rare at the time of the Russian Revolution, were rapidly growing throughout the underdeveloped world in the post-World War II period and were coming to power in country after country. Thus, both the appeal of the Soviet model and those to whom it appealed were developing in this period.

To be sure, the Communists' Marxian symbolism of proletarian revolution, so irrelevant in underdeveloped countries, still tended to weaken the appeal of the Soviet model in these countries. However, the post-World War II period also brought changes in the Communists' symbolism and even more in their policies which were, less than before the War, influenced by the old symbols. On the symbolic level, subtle changes of "capitalism" into "imperialism," of "the proletariat" into "the masses" and even "the people," of "the revolution" into "national liberation" took place. These were responses to and in turn facilitated changes in policy on the part of the Soviet government and of Communist parties which have by now outrun the symbolic changes. For while "revolution" and even "proletarian revolution" are still cherished Communist symbols, the policies of Communism in underdeveloped countries have become outright anti-revolutionary ones in everything but name.

These policy changes have taken place in response to changes in the nature of Soviet society and especially of the Soviet ruling elite, to be alluded to below, and to the growing military, economic and diplomatic strength of the Soviet Union in international affairs. It has permitted the Soviet government to deal effectively with non-Communist governments, which therefore need no longer, from the Soviet point of view, be overthrown and replaced by Communist ones. The difficulties the Soviet government has experienced in controlling Communist governments may well have further reduced its desire for Communist revolutions. Soviet and Communist policy changes have also been a reaction to the cold-war needs of the Soviet government and of Communist parties for new allies in the face of the loss of the old ones of the pre-War popular front and the War-time national front, who had become pro-American. Such allies appeared in the anti-colonial and hence anti-Western movements in underdeveloped countries. The changed character of the Soviet elite and its growing strength in international relations permitted the Soviet government, and, under its pressure, the Communist parties to shift, in the course of the 1950s, from a policy of complete opposition to the non-Communist anti-colonial movements to one of growing support for them. As a result, Communist and non-Communist anti-colonial movements have been converging in terms of their policies, to some extent of their ideologies, and in a few countries even in terms of their organizations.

Soviet experience from its beginnings, then, had sufficient similarities with the recent history of underdeveloped countries that it could appear as a relevant development model to intellectuals in these countries. Its appeal, however, was until fairly recently, greatly reduced by the Communists' adherence to the Marxian myth, which pictured them as proletarian revolutionaries, and to policies, which, corresponding to that myth, made them look to the industrial countries of the West both for proletarian supporters and for capitalist enemies. As this myth and these policies have been eroded by developments incompatible with them, the appeal of the Soviet model to intellectuals in underdeveloped countries has increased.

The story of what appeal the Soviet Union has had as a model in the West is just the opposite one—which may explain why it is so difficult for many in the West to understand the nature of its appeal in underdeveloped countries. In the West, it was precisely the Marxian myth rather than the reality of Soviet development that was appealing, and it was hence in the earlier years of the Soviet Republic that its appeal in the West was greatest. It was then still associated with anti-capitalism, with socialism and social progress, and a victorious industrial working class, all concepts that appeared relevant and attractive to some people in the West.

The Stalinist period of Soviet development with its rapid forced build-up of heavy industry made it clear that the Soviet model could be regarded as highly relevant in underdeveloped countries but was irrelevant in the already industrialized countries. The grave deprivations both of material well-being and of freedom of movement and expression imposed on vast masses of people in the Soviet Union could hardly appear attractive in the West, especially since they were designed to attain goals in the future—industrialization and a higher standard of living at home and power abroad—which had already been attained in the West in the past. No American or British worker will be attracted by the demands that he give up his steak dinner and his freedom to organize in return for promises of things that he already enjoys.

What appears as intolerable sacrifices in the West may not have the same implications in underdeveloped countries, however. The peasant has no steak dinner to give up, and freedom of movement and expression is meaningless to him. The promise of a higher standard of living in the future may well seem like a promise of something for nothing, then, while in the West it amounted to a promise of nothing for something.

Moreover, it must be recalled that the appeals of Communism are, in fact, directed at the intellecuals in underdeveloped countries rather than the peasants. Even if peasants opposed rapid industrialization by refusing to go to work in the factories and mines or to carry out the reorganization of agriculture that industrialization requires, intellectuals can, in their own minds, easily justify imposing the necessary measures and sacrifices on them by force, as happened in the Soviet Union under Stalin. Knowing the benefits of industrialization, they are, after all, convinced that they would be acting for the peasants' and workers' own good, even if the latter in their ignorance and short-sightedness fail to understand this.

In any case, intellectuals do not expect to bear the sacrifices entailed in the Soviet model themselves. Quite on the contrary, one reason why this model can be so appealing to some of them is that it promises positions of prestige and power and satisfying careers to intellectuals, people who are often frustrated by the lack of opportunities in their underdeveloped societies to practice their professional skills or to realize their values. Is it not intellectuals who occupy the positions of power in the Soviet Union, both the old positions taken over from the aristocracy and the innumerable new ones created by industrialization?

The answer to this last question is yes and no. Those in power in the Soviet Union are intellectuals, if we merely mean by that term natives of an underdeveloped society (or one that was until recently underdeveloped) who hold certain values appropriate to an industrialized society and pursue corresponding political goals. They are, however, quite different from most of the leaders of the anti-colonial movements in underdeveloped countries to whom their appeal is directed. These latter are what we might call revolutionary intellectuals, people who have dedicated themselves to bring about a new society and have spent most of their lives dreaming and theorizing about it and plotting and fighting for power, often underground or in prison or abroad in exile or as students. When such men come to power, they do not cease to be revolutionaries and hence they typically proclaim that their revolution is not yet finished. They profess, sometimes in self-fulfilling fashion, to see continuing threats from both their domestic and their foreign enemies and pursue policies, regarded by them as revolutionary, directed against remaining traditional elements at home and colonialism abroad. Committed as they are to the goal of a richer and more powerful society to be created by rapid industrialization (which makes the Soviet model so attractive to them), their policies may well run counter to that goal, as they involve expenditures of scarce resources on the support of revolutions abroad and on military adventures, on the building of magnificent conference halls and stadia, rather than on the construction of industry. Typically trained in the law or in journalism, in the humanities or the less practical of the social sciences, revolutionary intellectuals must do what they can do best—make or at least talk revolution—to justify holding on to positions of power. They cannot afford to proceed very far with industrialization without risking the loss of power, though they cannot afford either to admit this even to themselves.

Somewhat paradoxically, the phases of Soviet development that can be most attractive as a model to such revolutionary intellectuals in underdeveloped countries were not created by revolutionary intellectuals like them, by the Lenins and Trotskys, the Sinovievs and Bukharins. It is not the chaos of War Communism nor the compromises of the New Economic Policy that appeal to them but the rapid industrialization under Stalin's Five-Year Plans and the relative prosperity under Khrushchev and Brezhnev. The very success of Soviet industrialization, which revolutionary intellectuals in underdeveloped countries admire, had as one of its conditions the replacement of the revolutionary intellectuals in the Soviet Union by a new generation of what we might call managerial intellectuals, men who are not the makers but the beneficiaries of the revolution. This process of replacement began under Stalin, especially spectacularly in the great purges, and was brought to full fruition in the recent past when two managerial intellectuals—Brezhnev and Kosygin—reached the pinnacle of Soviet power.

Just as the revolutionary intellectuals, to justify their revolution, must promise and believe in industrialization, though their policies work against it, so the managerial intellectuals, typically trained as administrators, scientists, and especially engineers, must continue to believe in and profess to pursue the policies of the revolution from which they derive their legitimacy. The use by Soviet managerial intellectuals of revolutionary symbolism can appeal to revolutionary intellectuals in underdeveloped countries, while their actually quite non-revolutionary policies, mentioned above, do not threaten these revolutionary intellectuals, but in fact support them in power. Being already in power, they obviously prefer the symbols of revolution directed against some common enemy to the actuality of revolution directed against their own regimes.

Still, as the Soviet Union comes more visibly under the rule of bureaucrats and technocrats with their non-revolutionary values, as there emerge from zig-zagging policies gradual trends toward greater freedom of managers from central controls and toward emphasis on the production of consumer goods rather than on heavy industry, and as the growth rate of the Soviet economy declines, the Soviet development model should lose some of its glamor for revolutionary intellectuals in underdeveloped countries. In effect, Soviet industrialization has been too successful for them; Soviet society has entered a phase of development so far removed from those immediately aspired to by the revolutionary intellectuals for their own underdeveloped societies as to seem no longer relevant.

However, the rise of managerial intellectuals is not a phenomenon confined to the Soviet Union. Though they may become dangerous rivals to the revolutionary intellectuals, the latter cannot prevent a new generation of intellectuals, which takes the promises and prospects of industrialization seriously, from turning to fields like administration and engineering. Indeed, revolutionary intellectuals, in making these promises, often, whether intentionally or not, encourage the growth of a managerial intelligentsia. It may well be that as the Soviet model loses its appeal to the revolutionary intellectuals, it will become more attractive to the managerial intellectuals who may now be emerging in a number of underdeveloped countries.

So far, this tendency has been most apparent in China. There, unlike in the Soviet Union, the revolutionary intellectuals who brought the revolution to victory still occupy the top positions of power. However, industrialization under them has evidently progressed to a point where they feel gravely threatened by a rising managerial intelligentsia which they are now attacking for its lack of revolutionary spirit. While the revolutionary leaders of China idealize Lenin and—though they were in conflict with him in his lifetime—Stalin, they denounce the "revisionism" of Khrushchev and Brezhnev and accuse their own managerial intellectuals, probably quite rightly, of following similar "revisionist" tendencies. For revisionism, as the term has come to be used in the Chinese vocabulary, approximates the set of attitudes and policies associated with the managerial intelligentsia.

It is clear that the Sino-Soviet dispute is not only a major international conflict but also has grave domestic implications for each of the two regimes, but especially for the Chinese one. To the Chinese revolutionary regime, the Soviet regime represents the domestic challenge of the managerial intelligentsia, as it well might in the future for other regimes of revolutionary intellectuals in other underdeveloped countries. For the Soviet managerial regime, the Chinese regime is an embarrassing reminder of its own revolutionary heritage to which it remains tied by its own symbols and its need for legitimacy, but which has become increasingly irrelevant to its foreign and domestic policies. The more glaring the contrast between Communist symbols and Soviet policies becomes, the more embarrassing it is for the Soviet regime to have another Communist regime pursuing policies more in line with the common symbols and thus to serve as an effective rival development model for the revolutionary intellectuals of underdeveloped countries. As long as the regime of revolutionary intellectuals in China does in fact pursue revolutionary policies abroad as well as successful policies of industrialization at home, it may, indeed, replace the Soviet regime as the favorite development model for some revolutionary intellectuals in underdeveloped countries. One may predict, however, that such a combination of policies, if it is possible at all, cannot be maintained for very long. For either Chinese industrialization will fail, which ought to reduce the attractiveness of the model considerably, or it will succeed. In that case, the managerial intellectuals will replace the revolutionary ones, as they did in the Soviet Union, and the Chinese model, like the Soviet one would appeal more to managerial than to revolutionary intellectuals in underdeveloped countries.

10. Communism and Economic Development*

(CO-AUTHOR ROGER W. BENJAMIN)

Introductory Note. Much of the foregoing material suggests that Communist parties in underdeveloped countries are modernizing movements. Such movements are virtually nonexistent in the most backward countries and become stronger as economic development advances. One might expect, then, that by and large Communist party strength would increase with economic development. Since both Communist party strength and degrees of economic development are quantitatively measurable—however inadequate and unreliable some of the available data may be—Roger W. Benjamin, then a doctoral candidate in Political Science at Washington University, and I undertook, in 1965–1966, to test this hypothesis. Our argument and conclusions in the article that follows should be easily understood also by readers who are not familiar with the statistical techniques that are used.

In this article we were not concerned merely with Communism in underdeveloped countries. We reasoned not only that Communist party strength would increase with economic development in such countries, but that it would rise to a peak in those advanced countries where a substantial working class was still isolated and alienated and would plunge sharply downward in the most advanced industrialized countries. Our evidence shows that this hypothesized curvilinear relationship between economic development and Communist party strength does indeed exist.

Generally, our article is of some interest as a still all too rare attempt in the field of comparative politics to test a broad hypothesis by the use of quantitative data drawn from most countries of the world. In the context of this book, it is of significance, because it tends to confirm that, in underdeveloped countries, Communist parties are indeed modernizing movements, a point on which many arguments made in the foregoing articles rest.

* The authors are indebted to their colleague at Washington University, John Sprague, for advice on statistical matters. Financial support of the Washington University Computing Facilities through National Science Foundation Grant G-22296 is also gratefully acknowledged. I thank Roger W. Benjamin, University of Minnesota, for his agreement to the publication of this article in the present book. It is reprinted, by permission of the American Political Science Association, from *The American Political Science Review*, LXII, No. 1 (March 1968).

The peculiar relationship between economic development and Communist party strength suggests that Communist parties in different societies serve different functions, that they represent different interests. In the concluding section of our article we stress that Communist movements can then fruitfully be compared with non-Communist ones representing similar interests, that there is then no longer any excuse for maintaining as two separate areas of study the field of Communism and that of political development, a point also alluded to in the Introduction to this book. Indeed, if Communist parties aggregate different interests in different societies, grave doubt is cast on the very concept of Communism, which, after all, suggests that Communist parties are all alike or have some significant elements in common. I turn to this problem in my Conclusion to this book.

I

One of the major efforts of students of comparative politics in recent years has been directed at establishing, more or less systematically, relationships between economic development and political change. Much of the literature in this area, perhaps because of its stated or unstated value and policy orientation, has been concerned with the conditions and the prospects for democracy. In the present article, we attempt to correlate economic development with another phenomenon of political change, that of Communism and, more specifically, the strength of Communist parties.

We begin with the hypothesis that the relationship between economic development and Communist party strength is curvilinear.[1] In underdeveloped countries—and these included all Communist-ruled countries at the time the Communist party came to power except East Germany and the Czech sections of Czechoslovakia—Communist parties may be regarded as merely one variety of the modernizing movements that evolved in these countries in response to the impact of Western industrialism. Where no or virtually no modernizing movements have as yet developed, because there has been relatively little impact of Western

[1] The interesting research note by Robert M. Marsh and William L. Parish, "Modernization and Communism: A Re-Test of Lipset's Hypotheses," *American Sociological Review*, XXX, No. 6 (December 1965), 934–942, establishes that Communist party strength is not inversely related to economic development, as had been suggested by Seymour Martin Lipset, *Political Man: The Social Bases of Politics* (Garden City, N.Y.: Doubleday, 1960). Whereas Marsh and Parish attempt a critical evaluation of existing theoretical propositions, we are attempting to utilize evidence for the purpose of hypothesis corroboration.

industrialism and little economic development, there should, then, be no or practically no Communist parties. As economic development proceeds, modernizing movements, and hence also Communist parties, are composed largely of intellectuals and are therefore small. With the further progress of economic development and consequent social mobilization,[2] however, these movements may grow, sometimes to considerable size, as they attract support not only from more intellectuals, but also from incipient and growing labor movements, from urban middle strata, and, more rarely, from peasants.

In the now industrially more advanced countries, where economic development came from within rather than without, Communist parties historically grew out of anarcho-syndicalist or socialist movements representing some intellectuals and large numbers of workers more or less alienated from and hostile to their societies and governments. Where, in these countries, economic development is relatively backward (though more advanced than in any of the underdeveloped countries just mentioned) and workers find themselves in a minority in a largely anti-labor society, Communist parties can be expected to be strong. It is at this level of economic development that they reach their greatest strength, especially since they represent not only sizable labor movements and intellectuals in sympathy with them, but also draw support from small peasants and the middle strata of shopkeepers and artisans, still numerous, but feeling threatened by industrialization. As economic development proceeds, however, these latter groups are absorbed by the advanced industrial economy, either to disappear or to be converted into farmers or small businessmen, and workers become integrated into the society and are no longer alienated. With high economic development, then, Communist party strength may be expected to be very low.

In the interpretation of our findings we shall draw some further distinctions between types of societies at various levels of economic development and between Communist parties aggregating different interests in such societies, but the above suffices as a statement of our hypothesis.

II

Figure 1 presents graphically the relationship we predict between Communist party strength and level of economic development. We

[2] The concept of social mobilization ·is developed by Karl W. Deutsch, "Social Mobilization and Political Development," *American Political Science Review*, LV, No. 3 (September 1961), 493–514.

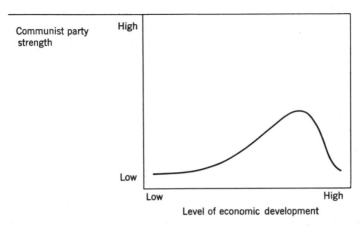

Figure 1. *Predicted relationship between level of economic development and Communist party strength.*

hypothesize that Communist party strength is lowest at the lowest stage of economic development, rises gradually with economic development, crests at a fairly high level of such development, and declines sharply with the highest level.

We have three potential measures of Communist party strength, our dependent variable: estimated membership of the Communist party, membership of the Communist party as a percentage of the working-age population, and per cent of total vote cast for the Communist party in national elections. There are difficulties with each of these, which finally limited our selection to principally one—estimated membership of the Communist party (see Appendix A).[3] To be sure, that measure

[3] Data on estimated membership of Communist parties and on Communist party percentage of total votes cast in national elections appear in U.S. Department of State, Bureau of Intelligence and Research, *World Strength of the Communist Party Organizations* (January 1965). See pp. 1–5 of this report for a discussion of the reliability of the data. It goes without saying that Communist party membership figures are likely, for most parties, to be neither precise nor reliable. The State Department report itself states (p. 4): "The reader is reminded . . . that although the best usable sources have been consulted, communist party membership figures are very difficult to obtain and are not subject to verification." Indeed, in the case of illegal Communist parties and especially of "fronts," "crypto-Communist" and divided parties, it may even be difficult to define "the" Communist party. We are, nevertheless using the State Department's 1965 estimates as the best membership figures available and feel that, for our purposes, they are adequate. Examination of the 1966 report, which became available only after our analysis was com-

does not show Communist membership as a percentage of the total population of the country, but the significance of that proportion is dubious, especially in traditional societies where modernization is just beginning and where the politically active strata of the society are small. We should really know what proportion of these active strata the Communist party membership constitutes, but no such data are available.

Per cent of the vote given to the Communist party in national elections might be superior to the other measures in some respects, but here also data limitations make use of this measure impractical. Above all, there are no national elections or only one-party elections in many countries, or Communist parties do not participate in elections, or published election results are unreliable or not subject to comparison. Membership of the Communist party as a percentage of the total working-age population (see Appendix A) removes some of the possible limitations found in the Communist party membership indicator. It is used only as a check on the latter measure to allow the amount of congruence between the two indicators to be computed. All that we are willing and able to assert is that our measures of Communist party membership provide at least strong partial indicators of Communist party strength.

On economic development, our independent variable, we took data and measures from Banks and Textor, *A Cross-Polity Survey*.[4] Six commonly used indices of economic development were selected from the Banks and Textor code (see Appendix B):

1. Level of urbanization
2. Agricultural population as a percentage of the total population
3. Gross national product
4. Per capita gross national product
5. Status of economic development
6. International financial status

Three screening procedures eliminated all but our sample of 91 countries (see Appendix A for the country listing). First, all countries were eliminated for which we had no estimates of Communist party member-

pleted, indicates relatively little change in State Department estimates of world Communist party membership. Membership figures for the Communist Party of the United States, which are not given by the State Department, were obtained from *The New York Times,* June 22, 1966, Section 3, p. 1.

[4] Arthus S. Banks and Robert B. Textor, *A Cross-Polity Survey* (Cambridge, Mass.: The M.I.T. Press, 1963).

ship. Secondly, since Communist strength is obviously affected by different factors in Communist-ruled countries than in non-Communist ones and is hence not comparable, we omitted all Communist-ruled countries from our sample. Thirdly, only countries on which *A Cross-Polity Survey* contains data were selected.

To test the hypothesized relationship between Communist party strength and level of economic development, contingency coefficients,[5] frequency distributions and percentages were computed comparing our measures of Communist party strength—party membership and party membership as a percentage of the working-age population—to the six measures of economic development presented above. If our hypothesis is correct, the countries should be spread along the predicted path, as in Figure 1 above, when the dependent variable, Communist party membership, is compared to the measures of economic development.

First, to view the reliability between the two measures of Communist party strength, the mean and range for the contingency coefficients relating the two Communist party strength indicators and the six economic development measures are presented. The mean contingency coefficient between Communist party membership and the economic development measures is .59, whereas it reaches .55 when Communist party membership as a percentage of the working-age population and the economic development measures are related. The range of the contingency coefficients between Communist party membership and the economic development measures is from .47 to .70, and .53 to .67 between the economic development measures and Communist party membership as a percentage of the working-age population.

Two representative measures of economic development, per capita gross national product (contingency coefficient .60) and agricultural population as per cent of total population (c.c. .51), were selected to present the results of the analysis. To put the data in convenient form, an index was constructed for the purpose of evaluating the shape of the plotted relationship between economic development measures and Communist party membership. Table 1 is an example of a raw table out of which the index was constructed.

The index for Communist party membership is simply a 9-point scale which corresponds to the coded categories for Communist party membership shown in Appendix B. The frequencies in each cell were multiplied

[5] The contingency coefficient is appropriate for tests of association for nominal and ordinal categories and non-linear relationships.

TABLE 1

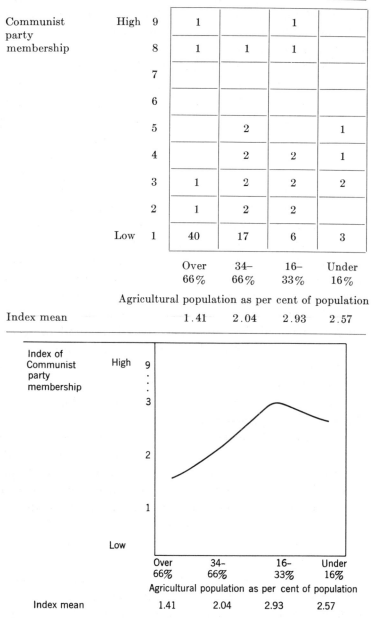

Communist party membership			Over 66%	34–66%	16–33%	Under 16%
	High	9	1		1	
		8	1	1	1	
		7				
		6				
		5		2		1
		4		2	2	1
		3	1	2	2	2
		2	1	2	2	
	Low	1	40	17	6	3

Agricultural population as per cent of population

Index mean	1.41	2.04	2.93	2.57

Index of Communist party membership — High 9 ... 3 ... 2 ... 1 ... Low

Over 66%   34–66%   16–33%   Under 16%

Agricultural population as per cent of population

Index mean   1.41   2.04   2.93   2.57

Figure 2. *Communist party membership and agricultural population as per cent of population.*

190

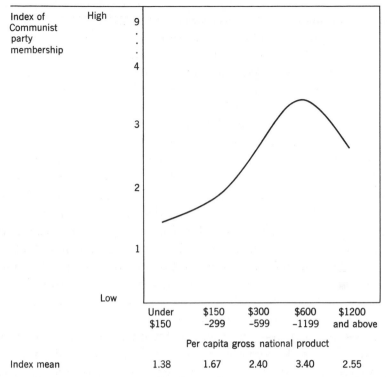

Figure 3. *Communist party membership and per capita gross national product.*

by the rank in the scale, and the mean for each total category was computed by dividing the result of the multiplication by the column frequency.

Figures 2 and 3 demonstrate the closeness with which the relationship of our economic development measures to Communist party membership agrees with our hypothesized relationship presented in Figure 1.

III

Our evidence shows, then, that a definite curvilinear relationship exists between degree of economic development and Communist party strength. A correlation, however, is not an explanation; rather, it requires one. Since our initial hypothesis has been corroborated, we may now present a somewhat more refined version of it as our explanation, or at least interpretation, of the relationship we established.

Even though all Communist parties profess to adhere to the same

well-codified ideology, to accept the same organizational model and to
pursue the same ultimate goal, and all have, until a few years ago,
looked for inspiration, guidance, and support to the Soviet government,
we suggest that Communist parties in different types of societies aggregate different interests.[6] We shall now briefly describe five roughly distinguishable types of societies and in each identify the major interests,
if any, aggregated by the Communist party.

As stated earlier, we regard Communist parties in underdeveloped
countries as modernizing movements. Both their elites and their mass
following, if any, are drawn from the same social strata as those of
non-Communist modernizing or so-called nationalist movements,[7] and
their goals are similar and may be summed up in the interrelated demands for political and economic independence from the West, rapid
industrialization, and land reform. Indeed, in the past two decades, many
policies of the two movements have become more and more alike, the
formerly sharp distinctions between Communist and non-Communist
modernizers with respect to the symbols they have employed have become more and more blurred, and in the last few years even the distinct
organizational character of Communist parties has been breaking down.

The anti-colonial and anti-traditional modernizing movements with
their characteristic love-hate attitude toward the West (which Communism shared with the others from its beginnings in Russia) are clearly
a response to the impact of Western industrialism on traditional societies.
The first type of society we must distinguish, then, is one in which
this impact has so far been so slight as to elicit little or no response
in the form of modernizing movements. Since the interests the Communist parties aggregate in underdeveloped countries are here virtually
or entirely nonexistent, it is not surprising that Communist party strength
in countries at the lowest level of economic development is, as we found
it to be, near or at zero. Among countries to be included in our Societal

[6] Our typology of Communist parties is not dissimilar from that developed by Almond, as expanded by Burks. Gabriel A. Almond, *The Appeals of Communism*
(Princeton, N.J.: Princeton University Press, 1954), distinguished between the sectarian or deviational parties of the advanced Western industrial countries and the
mass proletarian parties of France and Italy. R. V. Burks, *The Dynamics of Communism in Eastern Europe* (Princeton, N.J.: Princeton University Press, 1961),
adds a third category of national and anti-Western Communist parties to be found
in underdeveloped countries, including those of Eastern Europe.
[7] Cf. Robert C. North, *Kuomintang and Chinese Communist Elites* (Stanford, Calif.:
Stanford University Press, 1952).

Type I are Afghanistan, Saudi Arabia, Libya, Ethiopia, Liberia, and some of the most backward former French colonies in West and Equatorial Africa.

In societies in the early stages of economic development (Type II), modernizing movements are composed mainly of intellectuals, that is, of those relatively few natives who, usually in the course of acquiring an advanced education by Western standards, whether at home or abroad, have absorbed the Western-industrial values of the desirability of material progress and abundance, of growing social equality and political participation. In their industrially backward environments, they become anti-colonial revolutionaries favoring industrialization, and where applicable, land reform. Among these intellectuals may be those who think of themselves as Communists, whether they are organized in parties or not, and whatever relation of affiliation or rivalry to other modernizing movements they may have. Since modernizing movements are small in this type of society and Communists account generally for only a fraction of them, Communist parties, if they are organized at all, are very small at this level of economic development. Among countries included in Societal Type II are many in Africa and the Middle East not included in Type I as well as some of the least developed countries of Central and South America.

If economic development proceeds (in Societal Type III), at first under the influence of economic colonialism and then perhaps under regimes of revolutionary intellectuals, labor movements of plantation workers and miners, transportation and factory workers may emerge. They are led by intellectuals and furnish a more or less substantial mass base for their modernizing movements—Communist or non-Communist or both. Thus, in India, some trade unions are close to the Congress, others to the Communists; in Indonesia most unions were, until the coup of 1965, Communist-led; in Tunisia they are non-Communist "nationalist"; in Cuba, in pre-Castro days, some were Communist-controlled; in Argentina most have been Peronist.

Advancing economic development may also threaten the old urban middle class of artisans and shopkeepers who may then become politicized and provide some strength for the anti-colonial movement. And in some instances, where intellectuals are driven out of the cities, they may turn to the peasants, whose traditional village communities may be disintegrating under the impact of economic development, and may organize them to support the modernizing movement, again whether it be Communist or non-Communist. Thus, in China, peasant guerrilla warfare was Communist, in Algeria non-Communist "nationalist," in Vietnam it may be both.

Communist party strength varies widely in countries in Societal Type III. In some of them, where what mass movements have developed have come under the leadership of non-Communist intellectuals, the Communist party may be non-existent, as in Ghana and Guinea, or small, as in Egypt (where it dissolved itself in 1965) and in Turkey. In others, however, where the Communist party has organized mass support, especially among workers and peasants, as in India and, above all, until 1965, in Indonesia, it can become a very sizable party. Among underdeveloped countries (other than Communist-ruled ones) it is in those in Societal Type III, i.e., those with the relatively highest economic development, that Communist parties attain their greatest membership strength.

The modernizing movements, Communist or non-Communist, may or may not actually advance their society to the status of industrial ones. If they do, they in effect destroy themselves and are replaced in power either by a combination of other groups, e.g., labor and business groups, or by a technical-managerial intelligentsia. Such an intelligentsia may, then, constitute another type of Communist party that appears where an underdeveloped Communist-ruled country becomes rapidly industrialized. This has happened in Russia beginning under Stalin and is probably happening in Eastern Europe and possibly in China now. Since we are excluding Communist-ruled countries from our comparative survey, we mention this type of society here only parenthetically. There is no need to assume, however, that the replacement of revolutionary intellectuals by managerial-technical intellectuals cannot also take place in non-Communist underdeveloped countries, as may be the case in Mexico. One can assume that the Communist party in such countries should be weak, since a non-Communist one will perform its functions as the organization representing the technical-managerial intelligentsia.

Our first three societal types are found in countries to which economic development has come from without, under the impact of Western industrialism. They represent roughly three levels of economic development and, on the whole, one can expect that the greater the Western impact and economic development the more support there is for the anti-colonial modernizing movement and the better the chance for a big Communist party.

Countries where economic development took place indigenously, too, may be subdivided by the degree to which such development has progressed. In some of them (Type IV), as compared to the most advanced countries, industrialization came late and slowly and has still not penetrated the entire economy. In such societies, Communist parties express the protests of people drawn chiefly from three strata, two of them large enough to provide mass support for Communism. The principal one of these is industrial labor, a class that remains a minority in the population and whose trade unions are both numerically and organizationally weak as compared to their counterparts in more advanced countries. Confronting a seemingly permanent strong anti-labor majority of both industrial and preindustrial propertied groups, many workers are alienated, turn their backs on their society and political system, and look for some kind of radical change. This attitude was expressed in the anarcho-syndicalist tradition at the turn of the century, to which Communism has fallen heir.

The second major stratum consists of propertyless or propertied but relatively poor small peasants and of the old middle class of shopkeepers and artisans, groups still very numerous and in the non-industrialized regions of the country. They feel threatened by the advances of big industry and big commercial organizations and can thus be attracted by either the Fascists' or the Communists' anti-capitalist posture. Many are ideologically still preoccupied with their ancient fight against the Old Regime and its present-day remnants in the Church, the army, and the bureaucracy, and the old revolutionary tradition is hence still alive among them. Since the Communists have inherited much of this, too, such members of the peasantry and old middle class may support the Communist party.

The third stratum from which the Communists draw some strength are the intellectuals. They, too, are frequently deeply attached to the revolutionary tradition, whose ideology their predecessors did so much to fashion. Also, they tend ideologically to associate themselves, often due to a sense of guilt, with the underprivileged proletariat.

Since industrialization has progressed relatively slowly, at least until recently, the groups mentioned above and the social and economic order against which they protest have been subject to little change. Protest has become a permanent feature of the political landscape and so has the vehicle of that protest, the Communist party. The party is thus not only large but also very stable in the support it enjoys and in its organizational structure. It is deeply entrenched in the trade unions and in many social organizations as well as the organs of local government in both industrial and rural areas and thus, paradoxically, becomes a well established and, indeed, widely respected part of the society it professes to reject.

This description, obviously applies most nearly to France and Italy. In the underdeveloped southern regions of Italy, however, the Communist party may function in part as a modernizing movement, especially as the organizer of a peasantry demanding land reform. With advancing industrialization in Spain, it is conceivable that the formerly anarcho-syndicalist workers and poor peasants may turn to the Communist party there. And possibly the Communist parties of Greece and Finland, too, serve functions of interest aggregation similar to those of France and Italy. It is in countries of Societal Type IV, the "less developed advanced" countries of Europe, especially France and Italy, that Communist parties attain their greatest strength, because the interests they represent in these societies are numerically very large.

Quite a few now more advanced industrialized countries (Type V) share the traditional past of France of a feudal-aristocratic society. As industry grew in their hierarchical environments, workers reacted in large numbers by adhering to class-conscious socialist movements. Historically, the Communist parties of these countries originated from these movements and they have maintained some strength among radical workers and especially intellectuals in sympathy with them. However, unlike many workers of France and Italy, most of the workers in these advanced countries are not alienated. Through their economic and political power, they have become integrated into their societies and have come to share their growing wealth. As a result, workers, and intellectuals ideologically attached to the labor movement, have turned to socialist labor parties, leaving only insignificant Communist parties to exist on the fringe of the labor movement. As the socialist labor movement is now rapidly losing its radicalism and class consciousness and labor parties are making the corresponding political adjustments, a few workers and particularly some intellectuals deeply attached to the crusading socialist tradition, may yet move over to the Communist parties. Whatever slight gain may accrue to them from that source is likely to be more than offset, however, by losses due to death and defection among old-line adherents for whom the new society produces no replacements. Britain (and perhaps also Australia), Sweden and Denmark and probably Norway, Belgium and the Netherlands, Germany and Austria, and, to a large extent, Japan, all fit into this Societal Type V. In these highly industrialized countries,[8] then, Communist parties must be expected to be very weak.

Some other societies that developed advanced industry from within, but have no significant traditional aristocratic background, need not be sharply distinguished from the last-mentioned category for our purposes here. As industrial labor grew in them, it developed class consciousness or a socialist tradition only exceptionally among some groups of recent immigrants not yet fully adjusted to their new environment and especially among isolated groups of workers, like miners and lumbermen in syndicalist organizations.[9] It was from these sources that the Communists received some initial support in these societies, but they were destined to disappear by absorption. What little is left of Communist strength can hardly be explained in terms of any major social group or movement. It would seem to consist largely of individuals who joined the party in response to needs arising out of personal maladjustment. The United States and Canada are major examples of such societies, though Switzerland, too, and, to some extent, Australia and Norway would seem to fit into this category (which we include in Societal Type V).

IV

We have now interpreted the relationship between economic development and Communist party strength, which we demonstrated earlier, in terms of different functions performed by Communist parties in different types of societies. We have allocated each non-Communist-ruled country for which adequate data are available to one of our five societal types (See Appendix C). In applying the criteria of the five societal types outlined above, we have made frankly qualitative judgments. Since the criteria are by no means sharply defined, there are many borderline cases in which these judgments have, no doubt, been somewhat arbitrary and are subject to disagreement.

As a check on our allocation of countries to societal types and thus on our interpretation of the curvilinear relationship between economic development and Communist party strength, we related our five societal

[8] Agriculture is not necessarily insignificant in these countries, but their peasants—now more accurately described as farmers—are thoroughly integrated into the industrial system with respect both to what they produce and what they consume.
[9] On the relationship between labor radicalism and social isolation, see S. M. Lipset, *op. cit.*, pp. 232–236, 248–252.

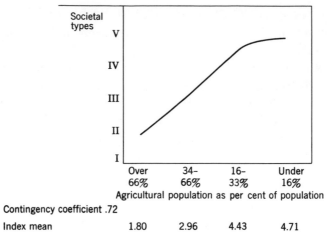

Contingency coefficient .72

Index mean	1.80	2.96	4.43	4.71

Figure 4. *The societal types and agricultural population as per cent of population.*

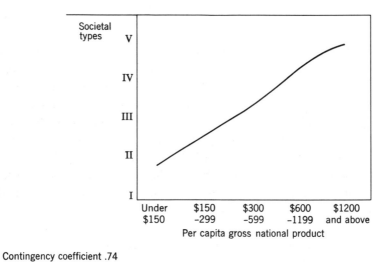

Contingency coefficient .74

Index mean	1.81	2.55	3.30	4.20	4.91

Figure 5. *The societal types and per capita gross national product.*

types both to economic development and to Communist party membership.

To establish whether our societal types measures are highly associated with Banks and Textor indicators of economic development, we computed a five-point index in a manner similar to that used in the index for Figures 2 and 3 above. Figures 4 and 5 report linear relationships and contingency coefficients at a level which allows us to assume close correspondence between our measures of economic development and our societal types.

Finally, Figure 6 relates the five societal types to Communist party

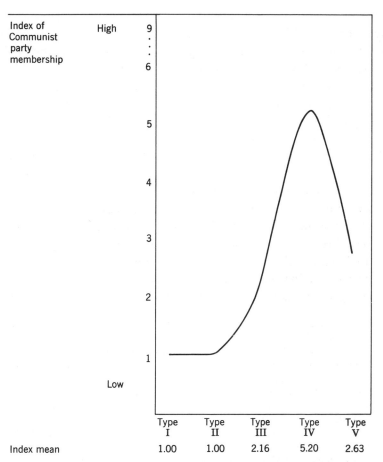

Figure 6. *Communist party membership and societal types.*

membership. The curve is closely congruent to those in Figures 2 and 3, above, which related Communist party membership to two different measures of economic development.

V

Our evidence shows that Communist party membership strength differs with different levels of economic development and our interpretation of this relationship suggests that Communist parties perform different functions, especially with respect to interest aggregation, in different types of societies. Though they have all borne the same name, Communist parties are not all alike. On the other hand, this also suggests that their Communist character, however it may be defined, does not make them unique but leaves them functionally comparable not so much with each other as with other parties and movements, especially those that perform similar functions in similar social and political environments.

It follows further that comparative analysis of Communist parties may best proceed within similar types of societies or societies grouped at similar stages of economic development. If Communist parties are to be compared using countries from different societal types or different levels of economic development, care has to be taken to provide control devices to hold the social and economic development factors constant so as to preclude actually comparing stages of economic development or modernization rather than Communist parties.

As the study of comparative politics has, in recent years, moved from the analysis of individual countries toward a truly comparative approach, there has been a growing awareness among political scientists of the need to integrate the analysis of the politics of the Soviet Union and of other Communist-ruled countries with the study of comparative politics.[10] Economists have for some time applied the same concepts regard-

[10] H. Gordon Skilling, "Soviet and Communist Politics: A Comparative Approach," *The Journal of Politics*, XXII, No. 2 (May 1960), 300–313; an unpublished address by Gabriel A. Almond to the Conference on Soviet and Communist Studies at the annual meeting of the American Political Science Association, September 10, 1964; H. Gordon Skilling, "Soviet and American Politics: The Dialectic of Opposites," *Canadian Journal of Economics and Political Science*, XXXI, No. 2 (May 1965), 273–280; H. Gordon Skilling, "Interest Groups and Communist Politics," *World Politics*, XVIII, No. 3 (April 1966), 435–451; Robert C. Tucker, "On the Comparative Study of Communism," *World Politics*, XIX, No. 2 (January 1967), 242–257; Alfred G. Meyer, "The Comparative Study of Communist Political Systems," *Slavic Review*, XXVI, No. 1 (March 1967), 3–12; John H. Kautsky, "Communism and the Comparative Study of Development," *ibid.*, pp. 13–17.

ing economic development to Communist and non-Communist societies, but it has been historians who have first pointed to some similarities in the political processes accompanying economic development in Communist and non-Communist countries,[11] while political scientists have been relatively slow to study Soviet and Communist politics as a form of the politics of development.[12]

As the Soviet Union has moved from the ill-defined status of a "developing" country to that of a developed one, efforts at comparison with other industrially advanced societies have been made. Economists have noted uniformities in the industrialization process with respect to managers and workers,[13] sociologists have pointed to the evolution of similar individual values, including a consumer ethic,[14] and more recently two political scientists have undertaken a bold pioneering effort to compare certain aspects of the political systems of the Soviet Union and the United States.[15]

Now that political systems ruled by Communist parties are beginning to be drawn into the purview of comparison both with underdeveloped and advanced non-Communist systems and it is thus being recognized that the element of Communism does not render these systems unique, the time may be ripe for a comparison of non-ruling Communist parties with non-Communist parties and movements. It is our hope that our research, reported here, may help open the way to such a further development of the study of comparative politics.

[11] For example, Hugh Seton-Watson, "Twentieth Century Revolutions," *The Political Quarterly*, XXII, No. 3 (July–September 1951), 251–265, and the same author's *Neither War Nor Peace* (New York: Frederick A. Praeger, 1960); Robert C. Daniels, *The Nature of Communism* (New York: Random House, 1962); Theodore von Laue, *Why Lenin? Why Stalin? A Reappraisal of the Russian Revolution, 1900–1930* (Philadelphia: Lippincott, 1964).

[12] For one of the present authors' attempt, see Kautsky, "An Essay in the Politics of Development," in Kautsky, ed., *Political Change in Underdeveloped Countries* (New York: John Wiley and Sons, 1962). Communist and nationalist single-party systems in underdeveloped countries are, along with Fascist ones, compared as "three species of a single political genus" by Robert C. Tucker, "Towards a Comparative Politics of Movement-Regimes," *The American Political Science Review*, LV, No. 2 (June 1961), 281–289.

[13] For example, Clark Kerr, John T. Dunlap, Frederick H. Harbison, and Charles Myers, *Industrialism and Industrial Man: The Problems of Labor and Management in Economic Growth* (Cambridge, Mass.: Harvard University Press, 1960).

[14] Especially Alex Inkeles and Raymond A. Bauer, *The Soviet Citizen: Daily Life in a Totalitarian Society* (Cambridge, Mass.: Harvard University Press, 1959).

[15] Zbigniew K. Brzezinski and Samuel P. Huntington, *Political Power: USA/USSR* (New York: Viking Press, 1964).

Appendix A

ALPHABETICAL LIST OF COUNTRIES AND THEIR COMMUNIST
PARTY MEMBERSHIP

COUNTRY	C.P. MEMBERSHIP[16]	C.P. MEMBERSHIP AS PER CENT OF WORKING-AGE POPULATION[17]
Afghanistan	No known members	.000
Australia	5,000	.078
Austria	35,000	.760
Belgium	11,000	.186
Bolivia	6,500	N.A.
Brazil	31,000	N.A.
Burma	5,000	N.A.
Burundi	Nil	.000
Cambodia	100	.004
Cameroun	Nil	.000
Canada	3,500	.033
Central African Republic	Nil	.000
Ceylon	1,900	.040
Chad	Nil	.000
Chile	27,500	.650
Colombia	13,000	N.A.
Congo (Brazzaville)	Nil	.000
Congo (Leopoldville)	Very small	N.A.
Costa Rica	300	.051
Cyprus	10,000	3.243
Dahomey	Nil	.000
Denmark	5,000	.170
Ecuador	2,500	N.A.
El Salvador	200	.023
Ethiopia	Nil	.000
Finland	40,000	1.441
France	260,000	.905
Gabon	Nil	.000
Germany, Federal Republic	50,000	.138
Ghana	Nil	.000
Greece	20,000	.366
Guatemala	1,300	N.A.
Guinea	Nil	.000
Honduras	2,400	.261
Iceland	1,000	.999
India	135,000	.055
Indonesia	2,000,000	3.800
Iran	1,500	.015
Iraq	15,000	.474

[16] Source: U.S. Department of State, *op. cit.*
[17] Calculated from working-age (15–64) population figures obtained from *United Nations Statistical Yearbook* (New York: United Nations Statistical Office, 1963).

COUNTRY	C.P. MEMBERSHIP[16]	C.P. MEMBERSHIP AS PER CENT OF WORKING-AGE POPULATION[17]
Ireland	100	.006
Israel	2,000	.156
Italy	1,350,000	4.190
Ivory Coast	Nil	.000
Jamaica	Nil	.000
Japan	120,000	.200
Jordan	500	N.A.
Laos	100	N.A.
Lebanon	3,000	N.A.
Liberia	Nil	.000
Libya	Nil	.000
Luxemburg	500	.221
Malaysia	2,000	.060
Mali	Nil	.000
Mauritania	Nil	.000
Mexico	50,000	.275
Morocco	1,250	.017
Nepal	3,500	N.A.
Netherlands	12,000	.169
New Zealand	500	.039
Nicaragua	250	.031
Niger	Nil	.000
Nigeria	Less than 100	N.A.
Norway	4,500	.199
Pakistan	3,000	.007
Panama	400	.070
Paraguay	5,000	.600
Peru	8,500	.180
Philippines	1,800	.013
Portugal	2,000	.035
Rwanda	Nil	.000
Saudi Arabia	Negligible	N.A.
Senegal	Nil	.000
Sierra Leone	Nil	.000
Somalia	Nil	.000
Spain	5,000	.025
Sudan	2,500	.382
Sweden	20,000	.402
Switzerland	Less than 6,000	.167
Syria	4,000	.190
Tanganyika	Nil	.000
Togo	Nil	.000
Trinidad	Very small	N.A.
Turkey	1,000	.007
Uganda	Nil	.000
United Arab Republic	1,000	N.A.
United Kingdom	34,372 (claimed)	.114
United States	12,000 (claimed)	.007

COUNTRY	C.P. MEMBERSHIP[16]	C.P. MEMBERSHIP AS PER CENT OF WORKING-AGE POPULATION[17]
Upper Volta	Nil	.000
Uruguay	10,000	.600
Venezuela	30,000	.760
Yemen	Negligible	N.A.

Appendix B

CODE

The following measures and categories were used in our research.[18]

(1) Membership of Communist parties:

1. 5,000 and below
2. 5,001–10,000
3. 10,001–20,000
4. 20,001–35,000
5. 35,001–50,000
6. 50,001–75,000
7. 75,001–100,000
8. 100,001–1,000,000
9. 1,000,001 and above
10. N.A.

(2) Membership of Communist party as per cent of working age population:

0. 0.25 and below
1. 0.26–0.50
2. 0.51–1.0
3. 1.1–5
4. N.A.

(3) Level of urbanization:

1. High (20% or more of population in cities of 20,000 or more and 12.5% or more of population in cities of 100,000 or more)
2. Low (less than 20% of population in cities of 20,000 or more and less than 12.5% of population in cities of 100,000 or more)
3. Ambiguous
9. Unascertained

(4) Agricultural population as per cent of total population:

1. High (over 66%)
2. Medium (34–66%)
3. Low (16–33%)

[18] The economic development measures are taken from Banks and Textor, *op. cit.*, where additional explanations of the measures are provided.

    4. Very low (under 16%)
    9. Unascertained

(5) Gross national product:

    1. Very high ($125 billion and above)
    2. High ($25–124.9 billion)
    3. Medium ($5–24.9 billion)
    4. Low ($1–4.9 billion)
    5. Very low (under $1 billion)

(6) Per capita gross national product:

    1. Very high ($1200 and above)
    2. High ($600–1199)
    3. Medium ($300–599)
    4. Low ($150–299)
    5. Very low (under $150)

(7) Status of economic development:

    1. Developed (self-sustaining economic growth; GNP per capita over $600)
    2. Intermediate (sustained and near self-sustaining economic growth)
    3. Underdeveloped (reasonable prospect of attaining sustained economic growth by the mid-1970's)
    4. Very underdeveloped (little or no prospect of attaining sustained economic growth within the foreseeable future)
    8. Ambiguous

(8) International financial status:

    1. Very high (UN assessment of 10% or above)
    2. High (UN assessment of 1.50–9.99%)
    3. Medium (UN assessment of 0.25–1.49%)
    4. Low (UN assessment of 0.05–0.24%)
    5. Very low (minimum UN assessment of 0.04%)
    9. Unascertained

Appendix C
Countries by Societal Types

Type I

Afghanistan
Burundi
Cambodia
Central African Republic
Chad
Dahomey
Ethiopia
Gabon
Laos
Liberia
Libya
Mali
Mauritania
Nicaragua
Niger
Ivory Coast
Saudi Arabia
Sierra Leone
Togo
Upper Volta

Type II

Cameroun
Congo (Brazzaville)
Congo (Leopoldville)
El Salvador

Honduras
Iran
Jordan
Malaysia
Nepal
Nigeria
Panama
Paraguay
Rwanda
Senegal
Somalia
Syria
Tanganyika
Uganda
Yemen

Type III

Bolivia
Brazil
Burma
Ceylon
Chile
Colombia
Costa Rica

Cyprus
Ecuador
Ghana
Guatemala
Guinea
India
Indonesia
Iraq
Ireland
Israel
Jamaica
Lebanon
Mexico
Morocco
Pakistan
Peru
Philippines
Portugal
Sudan
Trinidad
Turkey
United Arab Republic
Uruguay
Venezuela

Type IV

Finland
France
Greece
Italy
Spain

Type V

Australia
Austria
Belgium
Canada
Denmark
German Federal Republic
Iceland
Japan
Luxemburg
Netherlands
New Zealand
Norway
Sweden
Switzerland
United Kingdom
United States

Conclusion:
The Future of Communism

Since the preceding articles were not written to become parts of a book, each contains its own conclusions, and there is no need to summarize these here. Even to reemphasize the themes that recur in all or most of them and thus hold them together, such as the convergence of Communist and non-Communist modernizing movements and the changing role of the myths of Communism in that process, would merely involve needless repetition of points made earlier. In conclusion, it may not be inappropriate, however, by utilizing the concepts and the general approach developed in the articles, to project some of the trends that were noted and to speculate on the future of Communism—its future as a political movement, as a myth, and finally as an analytical concept.

Turning first to Communist parties in the industrially most advanced countries, a subject on which I touched only in the first and the last article, it is tempting to write them off by merely saying that they never did have a future and are not likely to acquire one in years to come. In an environment in which workers, by the time of the Russian Revolution, were no longer revolutionary (if they ever had been), the Communists' revolutionary myths could not be attractive to great masses, and in already industrialized countries the example of revolutionary intellectuals coming to power in an underdeveloped country and of their managerial successors industrializing it could not appeal to intellectuals or to any other stratum in significant numbers.

All this is likely to become even more true as industrialized countries advance further technologically, as materials well-being grows, and as the lower classes become even better integrated into their societies and political systems. The concomitant alienation of some intellectuals that finds expression in the New Left does share some of its vocabulary with the Communists, for the myths of "revolution" may appeal to it. But even the New Left can find little of relevance to its needs in the success story of Soviet Communism, either in its early Leninist "underdeveloped-revolutionary" phase or its later Stalinist "totalitarian-industrial-izing" one, or in Brezhnev's highly bureaucratized system now evolving.

It is, of course, conceivable that even in an advanced country some future development—perhaps a depression or involvement in a widely unpopular war—might provide existing Communist parties with new bases of support and thus give them a new lease on what little life is left in them. On the whole, however, they are likely to continue to vegetate merely as sects of a relatively few individuals that are peculiarly attached to outdated myths. As they become divorced organizationally and more and more also ideologically from the Soviet Union, they should eventually wither away altogether. The label "Communist," however, will continue to be used in the politics of advanced countries, for move-ments of that name will persist in other countries and, seeking simplicity in a complex world, some in the advanced countries will want to identify their domestic enemies with their real or imagined foreign ones.

In the less developed Western countries of France and Italy, Commu-nist parties became powerful and deeply rooted movements as repre-sentatives, above all, of an alienated working class. As with advancing industrialization its alienation decreases now, one might speculate, that the Communist parties would lose strength. It seems much more prob-able, however, that neither the loyalty of the workers to these parties nor their strong organizations would crumble very rapidly. In the mean-time, these two parties, responding to the changed attitudes of their constituencies and taking advantage of the freedom of movement that they gain from the dissolution of the ties of international Communism, can themselves become better integrated into the political systems of their countries.

In a sense, the French and Italian Communist parties may be repeating the history of the German Social-Democratic Party (a parallel not likely to appeal to the adherents of either side), for the social structure of Germany was, in some ways, similar to that of France and Italy, but Germany has been some decades ahead of France and Italy in economic development. As long as workers constituted a disadvantaged minority confronted by a strongly antilabor majority and government (in Germany until the turn of the century or the beginning of World War I; in France and Italy until quite recently), their parties represented their alienation through a policy of intransigent opposition clothed in the mythology of revolution. As labor becomes bigger, more strongly organized, and more prosperous, as its alienation declines, and as the lines between it and "bourgeois" society become blurred, its parties give up their relentless opposition role. While long retaining some of their revolutionary mythology, they become in effect participants in the process of negotiation and compromise with other parties representing other groups through which public policy in advanced industrialized countries is shaped.

The future of the French and Italian Communist parties, then, might lie in the direction of the present German Social-Democratic party and the British Labour Party, provided that industrialization continues rapidly in France and Italy and that their workers become more strongly organized. What effect such a development would have on the present Socialist parties of these two countries, insofar as they are still parties of labor rather than of the white-collar and professional middle class, need not concern us here. But it must be emphasized that any movement in this direction is likely to be slowed and can even be stopped by the persistence of the Communists' old myths both in their own minds and in those of their opponents. What I wrote in my article on "Myth, Self-Fulfilling Prophecy, and Symbolic Reassurance in the East-West Conflict," reprinted above, on the power of symbols to retard reduction of tensions is quite relevant here, too.

If France and Italy lag behind Germany and Britain in economic development, Spain and Greece are lagging behind France and Italy. One could argue, then, that the Spanish and Greek Communists still have a future as powerful representatives of an alienated working class—not to mention an even more distant future as labor parties that are integrated in their societies. Their suppression by military and/or Fascist regimes in both countries need not prevent such a development and might even advance it, as the French and Italian Communist parties emerged greatly strengthened from the Pétain and Mussolini regimes (though these two parties benefitted from their participation in an ultimately victorious resistance movement against a foreign enemy).

However, to predict the fairly distant future by means of such historical analogies is extremely risky. For one thing, industrialization in the future, if it does advance very far in countries like Spain and Greece, may, given modern technology, not involve the growth of a large working class at all. For another thing, even if the economic, social, and political development of labor in Spain and Greece should parallel that in France and Italy, one cannot assume that it would be Communist parties that would come to represent labor. Other parties, which would quite probably use the other time-honored laborite label of "Socialist," may well play that role. That they would, indeed, play the same role as "Communist" parties merely supports the point I made in the preceding article and am driving at here, too: the functions performed by Communist parties are determined more by their various political environments than by the fact that they are all called "Communist."

We turn next to the countries with which most of this book has been concerned, those that have received the impulse to modernization from the outside rather than from within and that therefore either have or in the future may come under the control of modernizing intellectuals. Among these countries, the future of Communist parties seems most secure in those that are already ruled by Communist parties.

To say that Communist parties that have been in power in certain countries for years and decades will presumably remain in control of these countries for some decades yet is by no means tantamount to suggesting that there will be no change. Change can and does take place within Communist parties, particularly if they succeed in transforming their own societies and thereby the bases of their own power. This has been especially obvious in the Soviet Union, where the Party has been in power the longest. However, the process of managerial intellectuals replacing revolutionary ones in controlling positions, which was stressed in the case of the Soviet Union in some of my articles, has also made itself felt in the Eastern European Communist-ruled countries as their industrialization has advanced.

Being pragmatically interested in developing their economies rather than, like revolutionary intellectuals, in realizing a preconceived scheme of society, managerial intellectuals tend to adjust to the conditions that they face in their countries. Thus Soviet industrial managers, in their drive for autonomy, have to compromise with the powerful bureaucratic managers who became entrenched in the Stalinist period, while Yugoslav industrial managers have attained their autonomy more easily. On the other hand, Yugoslav and Polish intellectuals have had to compromise with their peasants and grant them more freedom from government controls than the Soviet peasantry enjoys. Similarly, the Polish regime has had to arrive at a *modus vivendi* with the Catholic Church, leaving a powerful non-Communist force active in politics, while in all other Communist-ruled countries politics takes place almost entirely within the arena of the Communist party. In short, confronting different situations, the managerial rulers of various Communist countries cannot adhere to a uniform political pattern, and different systems evolve under the single label of "Communism." Attached as they are to the old mythology, the Communist rulers perhaps still prefer to think that they will arrive at the same ultimate goal, that they are merely taking "different roads to socialism." But the common goal, "socialism" or "Communism," is, as we have seen, merely a myth that always lies in the future, and it is the roads, which *are* different, that matter in the present and in fact determine the future.

Managerial Communist regimes, to advance their economies, also find it useful to engage in foreign trade and other relations—and not only with Communist-ruled countries. They make varied arrangements with different governments and in time each evolves an independent foreign policy. Yugoslavia was the first of the East European countries to do so, but gradually the others, perhaps most notably Rumania, have followed suit. Again, the crumbling of the old Communist myths and, more specifically, the transformation in the minds and at the hands of managerial intellectuals of the internationalist myth of world revolution from a call to action into a symbol of reassurance, makes the development of "national Communism" possible in foreign as well as domestic affairs. On the other hand, the myths held in common by Communist regimes are not without significance as bonds uniting them. Once again we find myths serving to retard the political consequences of economic and social changes.

If there are elements of "polycentrism" even between Communist countries in which managerial intellectuals are predominant, this is even more true between them and those still ruled by revolutionary intellectuals. Indeed, to speak of polycentrism with regard to the Sino-Soviet conflict is to imply that there are several centers in a single movement when in fact there is no single movement. As we noted in some of the articles, the conflict between revolutionary and managerial intellectuals can be a very bitter one indeed, and the Sino-Soviet conflict is, among other things, such a conflict being fought out on an international scale. However, the same conflict is taking place within China, too, where Mao's revolutionary intellectuals seem to feel gravely threatened by the "revisionism" not only of the Soviet regime but also of the managerial intellectuals they themselves created.

Even though in the present turmoil in China the authority of the Communist party itself has come into question, one may still predict that China will remain under Communist party control. That, however, is a fairly hollow prediction, since it merely suggests that whichever faction of intellectuals emerges triumphant will refer to itself as Communist and to its organization as a Communist party. The more interesting question, then, is whose Communist party will control China. Our hypotheses in this book merely lead us to suggest that if industrialization advances much further in China and if it is to advance, managerial intellectuals should eventually replace revolutionary ones in power. But even though this process would roughly parallel an earlier one in the Soviet Union, it would not necessarily mean a healing of the Sino-Soviet split. As we just noted, there are many possibilities of conflict among managerial regimes, too, particularly if they face such different conditions, both internally and externally, as the future managerial Soviet and Chinese regimes would presumably face.

If the Chinese Communist regime is now torn by a struggle between the revolutionary and managerial intellectuals, the other five Communist regimes in underdeveloped countries—Albania, Mongolia, North Korea, North Vietnam, and Cuba—can probably be regarded as still under the rule of revolutionary intellectuals. This is perhaps least true in Mongolia and North Korea, and even in Castro's Cuba there is no longer room for that archetypical revolutionary intellectual Che Guevara. In North Vietnam, the war in the South and against the United States, is likely to sustain revolutionary intellectuals in power, both because it keeps the issue of revolution alive in the South and because it destroys the beginnings of industry in the North itself. In the case of each of these regimes (except the Albanian one), the sympathy they are likely to have for the revolutionary as against the managerial attitude, which might draw them to the Chinese rather than the Soviet side, is, in various ways, tempered by dependence on Soviet aid. The very fact that their countries are economically backward, which is related to government by revolutionary intellectuals, makes them dependent on such aid. On the other hand, the very industrial backwardness that still permits revolutionary intellectuals to occupy positions of power in China also prevents these intellectuals from giving effective aid to such intellectuals in other countries. The Communist regimes of Cuba, North Korea, and North Vietnam, as well as Albania, then, can and must each pursue its own foreign policies (this is less true of Mongolia), further complicating the reality of "the Communist world," which is certainly not "one world," much less one "bloc," as it is still often referred to. Looking further into the future, we need merely repeat that the complexity is not likely to decrease, even if and when managerial intellectuals succeed the Hoxhas, Tsedenbals, Kim Il-sungs, Ho Chi Minhs, and Castros in power.

In underdeveloped countries that are not under Communist party rule, Communist and non-Communist modernizing movements tend to converge in terms of policies, ideology, and even organization, as I have insisted throughout this book. To be sure, this generalization does not tell us much about the fate of individual Communist parties, for convergence may mean that the Communist party absorbs its non-Communist rivals, as happened in Cuba, or that it is absorbed by them, as was the case in Egypt. What appears at first as two antithetical alternatives, however, turns out on closer examination to be merely a difference of degree. In both cases, the old sharply distinct Communist party is dissolved and, on the other hand, in both cases individual Communist leaders can be influential in the larger modernizing movement. Generally, then, one can predict that Communist parties in underdeveloped countries will lose their distinctive character, whether they disappear organizationally or not, and that some of their leaders will play significant roles together with other revolutionary intellectuals. Where there are now no Communist parties, as in many African countries, none may ever develop, but it is also quite possible that some revolutionary intellectuals will assume the name of Communists at some point.

In the conflicts that, as was stated earlier, almost inevitably develop among revolutionary intellectuals following their successful revolution, all factions, some factions, or none may call themselves Communists. Where some do, those who think of themselves as Communists may win, as they did in Cuba to some extent, or lose, as they did in Indonesia, or the conflicts may long remain undecided. Similarly, where managerial intellectuals emerge, they may or may not refer to themselves as Communists.

My "convergence thesis," then, does not permit any prediction as to whether much or little of the underdeveloped world will "go Communist," even though I am inclined to predict that modernizing intellectuals will come to power in most of it. We can be fairly sure, however, that these modernizing intellectuals will pursue certain policies growing out of their antitraditional and anticolonial attitudes, regardless of whether they think of themselves and are thought of by others as Communists or not. Always allowing for the self-fulfilling element of myths which *can* make Communists behave differently because they think they are Communists, one may say that in policy terms it makes little difference whether the modernizers coming to power are Communists or not, simply because the policies pursued by Communist and non-Communist modernizers are not necessarily different.

Communist parties thus are now in the process of losing their distinctive character, a development that will undoubtedly continue, probably at an accelerated pace. This is due to the convergence of Communist and non-Communist modernizing movements in underdeveloped countries on which enough has been said all through this book. It is also due to the tendency, noted earlier in this concluding essay, of Communist labor parties in France and Italy to become like non-Communist labor parties in the rest of Western Europe.

However, Communist parties are not only becoming more and more like other movements operating in similar environments, they are also becoming less and less like one another if they operate in different environments. In the most advanced countries they are more or less insignificant groups that draw some support from intellectuals and sometimes from labor and operate on the fringes of the political system. In France and Italy, they are major labor parties, with considerable peasant and middle class support, representing the interests of these groups in an environment now becoming highly industrialized. In many underdeveloped countries, Communist parties represent factions of revolutionary intellectuals who sometimes manage to mobilize some labor and peasant support and in a few cases, as in China and Cuba, constitute the government. And in the Soviet Union and Eastern Europe, the Communist parties represent the ruling managerial bureaucracies.

How can such widely different strata and interests living in utterly different types of societies be represented by a single movement and ideology? The answer, of course, is that they cannot. They are represented by different movements and different ideologies which use the same symbols and the same name. The revolutionary intellectual in Egypt or India who yearns for rapid industrialization and the New Left intellectual in Britain or the United States who is appalled by some of the consequences of advanced industrialization, including bureaucratization; the bureaucratic-managerial intellectual in the Soviet Union or Yugoslavia, who seeks to maintain and expand his power, and the worker in France and Italy who still resents managers and bureaucrats— they can all unite in their acceptance of the myth of "revolution," they can all be "Communists."

But that their common myth means different things to them is made evident by the conflicts taking place within what is still called "the Communist world": various managerial Communist regimes are in conflict with each other, for example, those of the Soviet Union and of Yugoslavia. Various Communist factions of revolutionary intellectuals can be in conflict with each other, as are the two Communist parties in India. Communist managerial and revolutionary factions fight each other as is true within China and as between the Chinese and Soviet regimes. And the laborite Communist parties of France and Italy more and more come to ignore both revolutionary and managerial Communists, recognizing that the concerns of both are irrelevant to their own interests in modern industrialized countries.

If Communist parties are, on the one hand, no longer clearly distinguishable from non-Communist ones and if, on the other, they have come to differ so widely among themselves, what, then, is "Communism?" It might be tempting to reply that there is no such thing as Communism, but we cannot quite let it go at that. There was a time, in the years after the Russian Revolution, when there was only one Communist regime and when its ideology—one of revolutionary intellectuals claiming to represent a revolutionary working class—could appeal both to revolutionary intellectuals, as in China, and to alienated workers, as in France. The Soviet Union could then be regarded, as it was by Communists and anti-Communists, as the one functioning model of a Communist regime and Moscow as the one center of international Communism. Even then there were conflicts and factionalism among Communists, but the concepts of *an* international Communist movement, of *a* Communist ideology, in short, of Communism, were not without meaning.

In the meantime, Communist parties have come to represent different strata of different societies with ever more divergent interests. A number of these have come to power, thus providing different models to other Communist parties and rival centers of what was once a fairly unified movement. The central myth of Communism, that of revolution, changed and came to serve different functions. As I have shown at some length in much of this book, the proletarian, anticapitalist revolution turned, beginning in the late 1940s in the underdeveloped countries, into the modernizing, anti-imperialist revolution. And then, beginning in the 1950s, revolution became a symbol of reassurance to the managerial intellectuals (as it had, in a different way, long been for the laborite Communist parties of France and Italy), while it remained a call to action for the revolutionary intellectuals.

There is no need to spell out once again what this book is all about. Only the conclusion bears repetition: Communism is now no more than a myth—but also no less. For to call it a myth is not to suggest that it is not significant or even that it is not "real." It exists in the minds of people, hence it has behavioral, that is, real, consequences. But as a myth, it need not serve a single function. Communism has come to mean quite different things in different minds, and quite different policies can hence be pursued in its name. As a descriptive, analytical category, "Communism" has thus become useless, that is, it is no longer meaningful to describe a particular individual, movement, organization, system, or ideology as "Communist." But as a myth, "Communism" will be useful, both to those attached to it and those opposed to it, perhaps for generations to come.